Love to Hate

LOVE to HATE

America's Obsession with Hatred and Violence

Jody M. Roy

COLUMBIA UNIVERSITY PRESS NEW YORK

Columbia University Press

Publishers Since 1893

New York   Chichester, West Sussex

Copyright © 2002 Columbia University Press

All rights reserved

Library of Congress Cataloging-in-Publication Data

Roy, Jody M.

Love to hate : America's obsession with hatred and violence /

Jody M. Roy.

p. cm.

title: America's obsession with hatred and violence.

Includes bibliographical references and index.

ISBN 0–231–12568–2 (cloth : alk. paper)

ISBN 0–231–12569–0 (paper : alk. paper)

1. Violence—United States.

2. Hate—United States.

3. Prejudices—United States.

4. United States—Social conditions.

I. Title: America's obsession with hatred and violence. II. Title.

HN90. V5 R69   2002

303.6'0973—dc21   2002018894

Casebound editions of Columbia University Press books

are printed on permanent and durable acid-free paper.

Printed in the United States of America

Designed by Audrey Smith

c 10 9 8 7 6 5 4 3 2 1

p 10 9 8 7 6 5 4 3 2 1

For John R. Barfield Jr. (1963–1990)

CONTENTS

Before the arrival of the new millennium, I was fascinated by the notion that as we approached the year 2000 everyone seemed either to be scared or to be downright depressed. All we seemed to hear about on the news was Y2K bug, God's really mad, and the world will blow up at the stroke of midnight. In fact, as the likely end of the world neared, we were advised to start stockpiling food so that we could hide in the basement. This was supposed to be the new millennium. An event of a lifetime. Why were people so scared and depressed during a time that should be used as a stepping-stone to learn the lessons from the past millennium and incorporate them into the future?

It was during this time that I met Martin Bedogne and we decided to collaborate as filmmakers. We formed New Light Media to address what we felt were critical questions for all Americans: Why were people so negative when it came to the millennium? What had soured us about our present and our future? After a lot of thought and research, the answer became very clear: it is hate. Discovering that answer prompted new questions. Why is it that one group dislikes another group? Why do some people become so hostile toward others that they actually kill those who are different from them? And from exploring these questions we came to a startling realization. How one person or one group feels about another causes most of the social ills that plague our world. Unchecked, our willingness to hate will bring our world to its destruction.

We realized that we had discovered the secret, the reason so many of us felt hopeless as we approached the year 2000. In order to get along in this world in the new millennium, in order to restore not just our hope but also our compassion, we needed to begin a dialogue on why we hate. So we created the documentary, "Journey to a Hate Free Millennium," which depicts the stories of Matthew Shepard, James Byrd Jr., and the students at Columbine High School, all victims of tragedies inspired by hate. Throughout the documentary, we discover how the victims' families are handling the deaths of their loved ones and how hate has affected their lives. More important, we discover how each family has dealt with their own hate and turned it into something positive. Each offers a towering example of the power of compassion and hope to eradicate hatred and violence. Each of them also offers solutions we all can enact to end hate in the world.

Our documentary has been very successful. I personally have traveled to more than two hundred colleges and universities, one hundred middle and high schools, and various symposia addressing the issue of hate and how we can overcome it in our lives. I found myself shocked by how many people, especially young people, were starving for the opportunity to talk about this subject and how it affects their world, their lives.

It was during my travels with the documentary that I went to Ripon College, a small, private school in Wisconsin, where I met Jody Roy. Jody attended my presentation and soon e-mailed me saying that her life had been changed by the encounter. She explained that she was writing a book on the subject of hate and asked if I would be interested in reading it and possibly writing the preface. At first, I resisted the idea, for I was in the process of writing my own book, *My Journey with Judy*, which is based on my experiences with Judy Shepard and our efforts to make a difference in this world when it comes to the subject of hate.

As time went on, Jody and I began to correspond by e-mail more frequently and, as our relationship evolved, I began telling her of various projects under way at New Light Media. One of them was our educational guide for *Journey to a Hate Free Millennium*. Our goal was to be able to advance the educational mission of our documentary by marrying it to an accessible and compelling guide that would allow educators themselves to present our program to those people who would most benefit from it: the young people who soon will emerge as our leaders in the new millennium. In the final stages of developing our educational guide, I asked Jody to take a look at what we had produced so far.

Jody studied the draft and sent me back her ideas and notes on how we could expand what was, in my opinion, already an amazing educational guide. I was incredibly impressed with her contributions. She was able to take our material and add a component that transformed the guide into exactly what I had envisioned it to be in its finished state. She was able to add to our guide the necessary ingredients that would allow educators to understand how to use our materials so that they could tackle what can be both a very simple and a difficult subject to tackle— the subject of hate

So impressed was I with her contributions, that I was ashamed to admit I had not yet spent the necessary time to read her book, *Love to Hate*. I took the next week to spend time with her book and truly digest the concepts she was presenting in its pages. In doing so, I allowed myself, the supposed expert, to learn a great deal more about this subject called hate. Once finished, I realized why she and I had been brought together. Jody and I were meant to work together in some way. Whether it was to have her contribute to our guide or for me to write this preface, I came to a realization about what connects both of our works.

Both of our works had accomplished what it is that I think is most important when it comes to the daunting task of ending hate in this world. We had both created educational vehicles that had become part of the solution and not part of the problem. This is the very essence of New Light Media. Our overall goal is to become part of the solution. To create educational materials and to be so passionate about our goal to constantly and consistently be part of the solution that we inspire others to make the same commitment.

We all must understand that each of us has the ability throughout the day, every day, to become part of the solution when it comes to ending hate in our world. This can be represented in many ways, and my most favorite representation came during one of my lectures when a young mother stood up in the audience saying that choosing to be part of the solution or the problem had been a ongoing struggle for her. She explained that while driving to my seminar she had picked up her two kids from high school and as she was rushing them home so as not to be late for my presentation, she had passed two boys beating each other up on the sidewalk in front of the high school. She knew both of the boys and their parents. She realized as she was sitting in my audience that she had done nothing. She never stopped the car to try to talk to the boys. She chose not to call the school to report the incident to the principal, and she had yet to contact the parents to let them know that she had witnessed a problem with their children. She looked at me as she finished and, with tears in her eyes, she said, "I think I am part of the problem."

This story truly illustrates the degree to which each of us can be part of the problem. Choosing to ignore that hate exists and denying that it is around us each and every day is, I truly believe, being part of the problem. I know without a shadow of a doubt that each of us has the ability to be part of the solution when it comes to the subject of hate and overcoming it in both our personal lives and our world. This book, *Love to Hate*, is part of the solution. It will allow you to begin the process of understanding why it is that we Americans truly love to hate and what it is that we can do to become part of the solution rather than part of the problem.

Brent Scarpo
Producer/Executive Director
New Light Media
Denver, Colorado

ACKNOWLEDGMENTS

I wish to thank all the people whose encouragement and assistance enabled me to create *Love to Hate: America's Obsession with Hatred and Violence*. I owe much gratitude to the following people for the particular help and motivation they have given to me: John Michel and Susan Heath of Columbia University Press, for their wise counseling during the revision process; Donna Marquart and Deano Pape, for technical support above and beyond the call of duty; Maggie Dalton-Herzberger and Alan Herzberger, for offering me invaluable feedback early in the writing process; Brent Scarpo and the staff of New Light Media for inspiring me to broaden my vision of the purpose of my work and providing me with exciting opportunities to act on that new vision; the Ripon College speech majors, for constantly challenging me to think about old topics from new angles; the men of the Wisconsin Gamma chapter of Phi Delta Theta, for keeping me grounded; Jean Hooker, Jason Fischer, and, especially, Toby Olsen, for keeping me sane and the rest of the world safe throughout this entire process; Eric "Stugen" Vallafskey, for always having my back; Tony McClintock, for being my uncannily powerful "good luck charm"; Matt Belling, without whom none of what I now do would be possible; Jon Roy, for his constant support and for tolerating without complaint the sheer amount of time in our lives and space in our home *Love to Hate* consumed in recent years; Elizabeth Dalton Roy, for inspiring me in ways I never could have imagined a few years ago; and the late Donald D. Dalton, for everything.

A lone gunman rushes the door of a Jewish community center, opening fire on any person in his path. A group of kindergarten-aged students are the first to encounter him. He does not discriminate—his bullets rip through three of the children, a teenage helper, and an adult employee of the center. While fleeing, he shoots and kills a postal worker.

Two young men wearing long black trench coats enter a suburban high school. It is their high school, filled with their classmates and teachers. They take their time. More than two hours pass before they kill themselves. In those two hours, they kill thirteen others.

All across the nation, small-town residents lock their doors and windows tightly at night, many for the first time in decades. Those living near train tracks suffer a special fear as the so-called Railway Killer eludes police again and again. From Texas to Illinois, the tally of slain bodies continues to climb.

The first report is of a black man shot down in front of his children. Soon after, word crosses the airwaves that a group of Orthodox Jews has been targeted by a drive-by shooter. Almost immediately reporters announce that a car driven by Asian teens also has been hit. One day later a Korean student is killed outside his church. It is the Fourth of July—America is celebrating her national identity: the land of the free and the home of the brave.

Being American always has required bravery. The bravery to fight oppression, the bravery to forge a nation from a diverse mix of people, the bravery to embrace democracy not simply as a theory of government but as a way of living. It is only recently that being American has come to mean being brave enough to go to school, brave enough to walk down a public street, brave enough to close your eyes and drift to sleep in your own bed.

The four stories recounted above most probably sound familiar. Sadly, they are real cases of violence that occurred over the course of just four months in 1999. While they were among the most highly reported incidents of violence during that time, the victims constitute only a fraction of the total number of Americans violently attacked by other Americans in any given four-month period.

Although we have long conceived America as the land of the free and the home of the brave, these days we perhaps are reflected more accurately in the phrase used by Pope John Paul II to describe us: a culture of death.[1]

But are we really a culture of death? The phrase "culture of death" seems to imply that we somehow enjoy, even cherish the violence and those who commit it. Surely we do not. Don't we revile these terrible acts? Don't we label the perpetrators "monsters"? Of course we do. The four cases above are the cases of Buford Furrow, the white supremacist who attacked the children in the Jewish Community Center's day camp in California; Eric Harris and Dylan Klebold, the Columbine High School students from Littleton, Colorado, who committed the most lethal of the string of school shootings in the 1990s; Angel Maturino Resendez, among the most recent serial killers to terrorize Americans; and Benjamin Smith, the disenchanted university student who briefly affiliated himself with the World Church of the Creator and later rampaged through a two-day killing spree in Illinois and Indiana.

We recognize all these killers as bad people, even evil people. We don't live in a culture of death, we say, because we despise those who kill.

But it is unlikely that we can name even one of their victims. What do we know about the three children attending day camp? Their teenage helper? The employee of the center? The postal worker? Any of the twelve students who will never graduate from Columbine High School? The teacher who will never again teach? We are unlikely to remember the name of the woman killed by the tracks in a small Texas town or the names of any of the other seven people who lost their lives to the Railway Killer or the black man whose children watched him die or the Orthodox Jewish men or the Asian teens or the Korean student.

We reward the violent with one of our most valued commodities: celebrity. We do not celebrate the innocent. We usually don't even remember their names. When we remember them at all, we remember only that they were killed. But the killers we remember. And by remembering them, we write our own legacy. America at the turn of the millennium no doubt will be judged by future generations as we ourselves judge the past: by the records we leave of those who emerge from the masses to become *known*.

The question then becomes, how do we escape the culture of death? How do we rein in the violence that has become a defining characteristic of America? Individually and as a society, we finally have to admit that we are, as a country, obsessed with hatred. Although we like to romanticize it, our fascination with hatred is not romantic. It is a seedy flirtation, an illicit affair. We publicly profess our commitment to compassion and peace, yet we carry on with hatred and violence on the side. In recent decades, we've become ever more brazen, parading our liason out in public for all the world—including our children—to witness. Should it really surprise us, then, that some of our children, born as they were into the midst of our flirtation with hatred, lash out violently? Should we be shocked that our longtime obsession finally spawned a culture of death? Of course not. We should be surprised, shocked, and even appalled only at our own foolishness in believing we somehow could sustain a long-term fling with hatred and violence without compromising the integrity of our commitment to compassion and peace.

How then do we begin to change? We first must admit that we have been willing parties to this affair. No one forced it on us. While hatred and violence can be seductive, we ultimately chose and keep choosing to give in to their temptations. By finally, fully owning up to the fact that we have been willing parties in this obsessive relationship, we empower ourselves to end it. As we all know, it only takes one side leaving to end a love affair.

I began thinking of America's relationship with hatred and violence as an obsession several years ago. As a professor of communication, I have focused my scholarly research for more than a decade on the question, "How do people become persuaded to hate other people?" From my formal studies of organized hate groups to my informal discussions with students about their reactions to violence in the media, I've come to realize that we Americans like to accuse other people of hating and being violent, but nearly all of us, myself included, harbor a fascination with hatred and violence. We are quick to point the finger of blame at killers, hate group members, even rap artists for promoting violence, yet we have a voracious appetite for both real and fictional stories about the very people we say are dangerous.

My thoughts about our relationship with hatred and violence crystallized in 1999 when news broke of the Columbine massacre. I happened to be at home that afternoon and, like millions of others, watched the live coverage of a mass murder in progress. I couldn't take my eyes off the television. "How could this happen?" I asked myself. "What has our world come to?" The news reporters echoed my thoughts, asking "Why? Why?," as we all watched video of a bleeding teenage boy hanging out of a window as SWAT team members dared a rescue attempt.

Having spent more than ten years studying the most extreme incarnations of hatred and violence, I am more jaded than most people. Over the years, I have developed a necessary survival skill, the ability to distance myself from my research subject. My scholarly detachment enabled me to watch coverage of earlier school shootings—Jonesboro, Pearl, Paducah, among others—as little more than cases-in-point of established academic theories. So what was it that made Columbine unique for me? Was it the live coverage? No. Was it the sheer number of victims? No. Columbine was unique for me because as I sat on the edge of my seat watching live coverage of a mass murder, I cradled my infant daughter in my arms. Columbine was the first time I encountered my research area not just as an academic but as a parent.

I am a professor and a mother, a researcher and a consumer of popular culture. In writing Love to Hate, I have tried to balance those roles, drawing on scholarly approaches to the critical study of hatred and violence to create a book that is an engaging, accessible, and ultimately practical resource for anyone who is concerned about hatred and violence in our society. Thus my primary goal in Love to Hate is not to deepen academics' theoretical understanding of hatred but, rather, to invite a much wider audience to join in the conversation about how hatred and violence are affecting us all.

As a result of the events of September 11, 2001, many people are anxious to participate in such conversations. The terrorist attacks on the United States and the ensuing international "war on terrorism" have taken center stage in conversations, as well as in the American cultural consciousness. On some levels September 11, 2001 and its aftermath have changed most Americans profoundly.

Yet, as attention has narrowed onto threats from abroad, Americans have risked losing sight of the forms of home-grown hatred that so recently gave rise to the rash of school shootings, the Oklahoma City bombing, and other horrific acts of violence. The hatred that inspires such violence has not left America. If anything, the "war on terrorism" provides new impetus and outlets for hatred and violence here in the United States. For example, within less than a week of September 11, more than two hundred people perceived to be Middle Eastern or Moslem were the victims of hate crimes in the United States; two were killed.[2] Additionally, the fear and anger nearly all Americans have felt since September 11 make people, individually and collectively, more vulnerable than they have been in decades to the seductive powers of hatred.

While Love to Hate does not directly focus on the events of September 11, 2001, it is about the American attitudes toward hatred that gave rise to violence before those events and that have continued to inspire violence every day since. If we hope ever to live in an era free of hatred and violence, we must not allow our legitimate concerns about international terrorism to distract us from equally legitimate concerns about the persistent reality of hatred and violence within our own culture.

I wrote Love to Hate with two purposes in mind. First, I want to help my readers realize the subtle ways in which our fascination with hatred expresses itself in our popular culture and in our everyday lives. Instead of waiting for another outrageous act of violence like the Columbine shootings to force us to take notice, we need to become aware of the constant stream of messages in our culture telling us all that hatred is cool and that violence is a viable solution to life's problems. More important, we all need to consider how we react to those messages and the ways in which we too may be conveying those messages to others, in particular to children. Second, I hope Love to Hate will inspire my readers to take a stand against our society's casual tolerance of hatred and violence. As I've already stated, the most difficult but most critical task will be for each of us to admit the part we have played in carrying on America's love affair with hatred and violence. There are many steps we can take individually and must take as a society to secure a safer and more loving future. I will explore some of these solutions throughout the pages of this book.

Love to Hate is divided into three parts. The first, "Our Love-Hate

Relationship with Hatred," explores the very nature of hatred in our lives and how we send and receive mixed messages about hatred almost constantly. The second part, "Hate, American-Style," examines both obvious and subtle manifestations of hatred, from neo-Nazi supremacy groups and serial killers to the popular music, movies, and television shows we and our children enjoy. Finally, "Freeing Ourselves from Our Obsession with Hatred" offers practical solutions we can take—as parents, as consumers, and as voters—to move America away from the culture of death and toward a culture of life. In the appendices, I have provided some interactive tools that the reader can use to begin the process of changing their own attitudes toward hatred and violence.

I ask readers to understand that in order to disempower our obsession with hatred and violence we must first dissect it. At some points in *Love to Hate*, some readers may find the process of dissection itself to be extremely difficult. In particular, the consideration of how popular culture constructs stories of serial killers in chapter 5, and the exploration of a tragic hate crime in the conclusion, may be difficult for some readers to encounter. I have included these discussions not to sensationalize violence but, rather, to reveal how violence is sensationalized. I ask readers to remember that I am not telling "new" stories but simply retelling stories most Americans have heard before. In hindsight, the horror of the cases is almost overwhelming. However, it is important to remember that when these stories were told originally, most Americans did not recoil in horror; rather, they sat in rapt attention as various media spun out the most gruesome details of extraordinary acts of hatred and violence.

Of course, we cannot dive into a consideration of this subject without first pausing to define hatred itself. A dictionary offers synonyms for "hatred" such as "repugnance," "detestation," and "abhorrence." Those terms don't really help us grasp the scope of "hatred." Hatred is complex and dynamic. It is at once an emotion, a passion, a force, a cultural commodity, a motivation, a value, a status symbol, and a source of power. Hatred is not a static thing, an object we can bottle up and label. Rather, hatred exists between and among us. Hatred is not simply a term denoting a feeling humans sometimes experience but a filter through which we humans at times choose to see the world and be in the world. We give hatred life in our thoughts and words. And when we fail to realize the power of those thoughts and words to influence our behavior, we invite the kind of violence that led Pope John Paul II to label America at the dawn of the new millennium a "culture of death."

Love to Hate

PART 1

Our Love-Hate
Relationship with Hatred

CHAPTER 1

Us Versus Them

India versus Pakistan, Black versus White, Muslim versus Jew, the Allies versus the Axis, North versus South, America versus Britain, Men versus Women, Shirts versus Skins, Bears versus Packers, Pepsi versus Coke . . .

Comparing and contrasting is a normal, even a necessary, part of being human. It allows us to learn about everything and everyone in our world. Dividing the world into categories allows us to manage the vast amount of information we must process in order to survive. But we are not computers, sorting facts into categories with complete objectivity. Because we are human, our categories are heavily laden with biases and so we sometimes move beyond the normal and necessary use of comparative thought and into the dangerous arena of "us versus them" thinking. In this chapter we will examine when and how we cross that line and learn how such thought patterns can enable, even encourage, hatred.

OUR CONCEPTS OF SELF AND OTHER: US AND THEM

For most of my early years, I cherished my best friend, Brian. Then, suddenly, we despised each other. It turned out that my best friend in the whole world, my pal Brian, was . . . it's still hard to say . . . Brian was . . . one of them . . . you know what I mean . . . Brian was . . . well . . . a boy.

Until the summer we both turned seven, our co-ed friendship had never been a problem. He was Brian, I was Jody, and that really was all that mattered. We were not yet mature enough to know that little boys and little girls often do not get along with each other very well. But during our seventh summer, we stopped being Brian and Jody and started being "a boy—yuck!" and "a girl—gross!"

Tension between little boys and little girls is a normal, if sometimes painful, part of growing up. We come to understand the nature of who we are by comparing and contrasting ourselves to others. Very small children often play doctor as an innocent means through which to learn how girls' and boys' bodies differ. They approach the differences with a scientist's curious but matter-of-fact air: they note what makes each body unique without judging one to be somehow better than the other. By grade school, most children spend at least some time believing that the opposite sex has what we used to call "cooties," a second-grade term meaning repulsive. At this age, children swear they will never develop a romantic interest in "them" and threaten either to run from or punch in the arm any one of "them" who might ever proffer a kiss. To the chagrin of parents, of course, this stage is followed by puberty and adolescence.

What we must understand, though, is that the sexual attractions between adolescent boys and girls (and adult men and women, for that matter) could not occur if they were not preceded by the childhood battle of the sexes. During those years, boys and girls develop a sense of their own identity in comparison to those of the same sex and in contrast to those of the opposite sex. They begin to define the self in relation to others. As children, we use "them" to discover "us."

As adults, we continue to use ideas of "us" and "them" in a variety of useful ways. Perhaps most basically, concepts of "us" and "them" define families. For example, "we" are the Roy family. The members of my family, both immediate and extended, are united by various biological and legal ties. Those ties offer all of "us" a sense of security and comfort in a vast world of "thems." Literally, family provides the familiar. For as much as we all (and I do mean all) at times complain about our families, families offer something few other groups can offer: people who have known us and whom we have known for most, if not all, of our lives.

A powerful sense of belonging attends such familiarity. Recently one of my cousins paid me a visit. We had not seen each other in several years and, for at least ten years before that, had seen each other infrequently. Because of our age difference we had not even been especially close while growing up. Yet, from the moment he walked through the door, we were completely at ease with each other. Why? I think it has something to do with his loaning me his bib overalls after I fell (got pushed) into a mud puddle on Easter morning about thirty years ago. I think it has something to do with how much he used to like to eat pudding. I think it has something to do with the smell of our grandma's basement, the taste of her apple pies, the feel of the afghan that rested on the back of her couch. Although we hadn't seen each other in years, my cousin and I still share "us" today.

Of course, families do not hold exclusive rights to such connections. Friendships are born of two people choosing to unite as "us." On college campuses, some students opt to ensure that they will belong to an "us" by pledging a fraternity or sorority. Potential members, so-called rushees, are drawn to promises of lifelong friendships and immediate entry into a powerful network of alumni/ae. The pledging rituals of the Greek organizations stress the paramount importance of loyalty to the group and, while tensions and dissensions do occur, generally the members of the groups rally around each other in times of crisis and celebration. In this way, such formalized friendship associations are much like families—while not all the members necessarily always get along, they're all right by your side in bad times and always show up for the big events in your life, especially if you're serving food.

Corporate America also relies on the ideas of "us" and "them." Recruiting of new employees often focuses on appeals such as "join the winning team at Company X." Once hired, new employees undergo some type of training or orientation process that, if it is constructed wisely, attempts to develop loyalty to the company. And corporate loyalty is a priceless commodity: it reduces turnover and the attendant costs of retraining; it bolsters "free" public relations as happy employees discuss "our" company with outsiders; it even reduces the likelihood that an employee will hurt the company by revealing sensitive information. Perhaps most critically, though, employee loyalty boosts productivity. Loyal employees work for "us," not just for a paycheck.

Clearly, concepts of "us" and "them" play important and healthy roles in society. By helping us develop our understandings of our selves and of others, us/them thinking patterns allow us to grow up and, once there, to form relational bonds with others in our families, among our friends, and on the job. Yet, while such thinking is a necessary part of our lives, sometimes it can become twisted into a dangerous form of polarizing thought that lies at the very core of hatred.

THE SELF AGAINST THE OTHER: US VERSUS THEM

At what point does normal, healthy "us and them" thinking cross the line and become the potentially dangerous "us versus them" thinking? As a general rule, people cross the line into "us versus them" thinking when they use attacks on the other as a way to strengthen the self. In other words, this kind of thinking involves pushing down "them" in an attempt to raise up "us." We all are guilty of thinking in such patterns some of the time.

Let's return to the childhood battle of the sexes. As I have noted earlier, for at least some period of time we all go through a phase of distaste for the opposite sex as a normal part of our development. During this phase, girls and boys often move beyond the basic comparisons and contrasts needed for self-awareness and into playground variations on us versus them patterns. Suddenly games pit boys and girls against each other because neither will willingly be on the same team. All children understand that the winners of such contests are the superior sex, at least until the next ringing of the recess bell.

Of course, not all instances of us versus them thinking revolve around male-female feuding. Regardless of gender, bullies are veritable icons of the us versus them phenomenon. Children who fall victim to a bully are often told by parents and teachers that the bully simply is acting tough, that he actually is scared and insecure. For the bully's young victim such advice is of course totally useless. However, it really does seem to be true in most cases. Bullies normally *are* scared and insecure. They prey on other children as a means of bolstering their own sense of self. For the school yard tough, who he is, sadly *all* he is, is what he can take from another child for the moment: the bully's "me" is elevated only by hurting "them." Unfortunately for all of us, of course, the really dangerous bullies are not found on playgrounds but in boardrooms and in political office.

In order to fully understand the nature of the "us versus them" mindset, we need to consider several of the destructive thinking patterns that characterize it. Among the most important thinking patterns that play a part in this mentality are absolutism, stereotyping, scapegoating, and dehumanization.

ABSOLUTISM

Absolutism occurs when a person sees only two sides of an issue and then polarizes those sides. It lies at the very center of us versus them thinking. In fact, it would be fair to say that healthy "us and them" thinking begins to devolve into the potentially dangerous form "us versus them" when absolutism comes into play.

Absolutism is perhaps easiest to understand in terms of colors. A person in the grip of absolutist thinking sees only black and white. The person not only refuses to recognize red, green, and yellow but cannot even allow himself to appreciate the shades of gray in between black and white.

While few people are absolutist in all aspects of their lives, many of us approach certain issues about which we are particularly sensitive with absolutist thinking patterns. For example, many otherwise openminded people simply refuse to consider that there may be sides other than the "right" side and the "wrong" side of the hotly contested abortion debate in America. According to pro-life advocates, almost all of whom ground their position on abortion in their beliefs about religion, their side is the side of "right," the "moral" side, the side supported by God. Because they are convinced that their position is not simply *a* right position, but *the only* right position, they necessarily believe that all who disagree with them must be wrong. In this case, as with any case in which the position is rooted in religious claims, the belief that God is on "our" side entails the conclusion that the other side is evil.

In the case of the contemporary debate over abortion, this tendency toward absolutism has done much to cloud the issues. Most basically, when members of the pro-life movement apply absolutist thinking patterns to their opposition they sometimes falsely portray the existence of pro-abortion lobbyists instead of pro-choice representatives. Few Americans have actually heard of anyone who is pro-abortion. Why? Because no one is advocating that abortion is a great thing, something all women should want to experience. The assertion that a pro-abortion movement exists is, itself, what logicians call a straw-man argument, meaning it is an illusion of an opponent the arguer herself creates then, not surprisingly, is able to defeat. Because they are based on faulty reasoning, straw-man arguments are labeled fallacious.

I am not indicting all the arguments of the pro-life movement as fallacious. But I am saying that as a result of taking an absolutist stand on abortion, members of the pro-life movement sometimes fallaciously assert the existence of a pro-abortion countermovement. By doing so they create a world that is painted only in black and white. Lost are such complex shades of gray as we might find among people who believe women should have the right to choose but pray no woman ever finds herself in the position of needing to choose.

Members of the pro-life movement are certainly not the only people who tend toward absolutist thinking. In fairness, some members of the pro-choice movement can be equally absolutist. The more radical members of both the pro-life and pro-choice camps display classic absolutist thinking when they suggest that anyone who is not with them may as well be against them. This position rests on the notion that everything is either black or white. When someone says, "You're either with me or against me," they are denying the legitimacy of a third, fourth, or even millionth side of an issue. Most fundamentally, "You're either with me or against me" denies us the right simply not to have an opinion on a particular issue. Absolutists cannot accept the fact that others may be completely unconcerned with the issue to which they are devoting so much energy.

Absolutist thinking patterns carry heavy risks—and not only for those who use them. When a person polarizes an issue, he or she makes compromise an impossibility.[1] If they conceive their position to be wholly "good" and the opposition to be wholly "evil," then they simply cannot allow themselves to come to the bargaining table. Those who embrace absolutist thinking, of course, see no problem with the inability to compromise; for them, compromise with the opposition, regardless of the issue at hand, is a form of compromising with the devil. As such, stalwart unwillingness to negotiate is seen as a virtue. But with compromise no longer a viable option, only two courses of action remain: giving up the cause or escalating attacks on the opposition.

While those who espouse an absolute mindset see the issues at hand as perfectly clear-cut, to those looking in from the outside, complicating exceptions quickly emerge to even the most absolute of arguments.

Let's return to the abortion debate for a moment. Even among the most adamant pro-lifers, it is possible to find those who believe abortion to be morally acceptable if the life of the mother is at stake. Clearly, if this exception can be made, then "abortion is wrong" is not a *wholly right* position. Here we find one of those troublesome shades of gray.

But I do not want to give the impression that any of these problems are the private property of the pro-lifers. Pro-choice advocates face the same tensions within their arguments when they assume an absolutist stance. For instance, within the ranks of pro-choice advocates are some who believe that teenage girls should have to provide proof of parental notification and consent before being allowed to have an abortion. Yet another shade of gray.

Clearly, absolutist thinking patterns can be problematic. Absolutism polarizes sides artificially and thus enables us versus them thinking. By disallowing compromise, absolutism also encourages radical action in response to the opposition. There is perhaps no better example of this than the killing of doctors who perform abortions by members of radical factions of the pro-life movement. How ironic. How gray.

STEREOTYPING

Stereotyping is categorizing gone bad. As I have already described, sorting things, and people, into groups based on common characteristics is not only a normal but a necessary mental faculty that allows us to manage the immense amounts of information to which we are exposed over the course of a lifetime. Obviously, while the items we sort into various categories share many things in common, sometimes we must oversimplify their commonalities in order to make our own mental filing system useful. For example, if we sort automobiles into the categories of car, truck, and van, we create a workable basic sorting system. But into which category do we place a Jeep Grand Cherokee? By oversimplifying its characteristics, we can label it a car, a truck, or even a van. Or, if we encounter lots of vehicles similar to the Jeep, we could create a fourth category: sports utility vehicle.

While categorizing is both a normal and necessary human mental function, some categorizing simplifies too much and becomes stereotyping. Generally, we can say that a person is stereotyping if he or she forms an oversimplified category based on ignorance about the items or people in the category. Stereotyping actually occurs as a result of the logical fallacy known as hasty generalization, in which a person makes conclusions about all members of a group based on too limited information about a particular member of the group. For example, I would commit a hasty generalization if I decided that all members of the college graduating class of 2003 were worse than average writers because a particular member of that class wrote an extraordinarily bad paper for a course I teach. By extending that single, unique example into a standing belief about all the members of the class of 2003, I would be guilty of stereotyping.

Stereotypes represent a dangerous form of thinking in our society. When a person stereotypes a group of people, he or she reduces those in the group to only one or a few characteristics based either on very limited experience with the group members or based simply on prejudices learned from others. Let's return to the example of the class of 2003. When I stereotype the group based on the actions of only one member and conclude that the members of the class of 2003 are all bad writers, I reduce the class members to that one skill. Regardless of whether or not they are in fact bad writers, by defining them only in terms of that characteristic, I overlook their other qualities—in this case, relevant academic skills involving mathematics, speaking, and critical thinking. So when I stereotype the class, I hurt them in two ways: first, I unfairly conclude that what is true for one member of the group must be true for all; and, second, I focus all attention on one characteristic and thus tend to ignore other qualities that define the group members.

Stereotyping is an all too common thinking pattern in our society and, sadly, rarely deals with characteristics so benign as writing skills. Rather, stereotyping can be found at the core of almost all forms of active prejudice against groups of people, whether those prejudices center on race, ethnicity, religion, gender, socioeconomic class, or sexual orientation.

Throughout American history, whites have held stereotypical views of people of color. The earliest European explorers to find land met and immediately stereotyped native peoples in America and Africa as animalistic, savage. Such stereotypes about people of color allowed the institution of slavery to develop. While socioeconomic classism raged within white communities, even the most elitist of whites did not consider the enslavement of poor whites to be a viable option in a *healthy* society. Why? Because they perceived even the poorest of whites still to be fundamentally like themselves. In contrast, because stereotypes of people of color involved accusations of savagery and exaggerated animal-like qualities, whites could rationalize slavery on the grounds that the slaves were fundamentally "other" than themselves. In other words, the stereotypes whites had created about people of other races allowed whites to divide the world neatly, absolutely into "us"—whites/humans —and "them"—non-whites/somehow not fully human.

Although the institution of slavery was destroyed in America more than a century ago, some people continue to believe racial stereotypes even today. Young black men, in particular, are feared by many whites. Are most young black men people to fear? Hardly. Most young black men, like most young white men, busy themselves with school, work, and family obligations. Yet, sadly, many whites really are afraid if they encounter a young black male or, especially, a group of young black males.

Such fears, most often groundless in reality, can be traced to the legacy of stereotypical thinking. Because of the de facto segregation that persists in many areas of the country, many white people have had little actual contact with black people. For these whites, then, the bulk of their knowledge of young black males comes either from the media or from what they have heard from other members of their segregated community, a community that is, by definition, ignorant of the realities of young black men simply because it includes no such men. Such stereotypical thinking about people of other races will continue in our culture until information from actual encounters replaces assumptions derived from stereotypes.

Of course, we must realize that people of all races can fall into the pattern of stereotyping and can fall victim to the stereotypical thinking of others. Too often we fail to consider the stereotyping of whites by blacks, for example. Clearly, because whites traditionally have held the reins of power in society, their stereotyping and attendant prejudices have had more potential to do harm. Those who study race relations often note the critical distinction between "prejudice" and "racism."[2] Prejudice means simply to prejudge—it is often based on inaccurate stereotypes and is often unfair because it occurs *before* real experience. However, prejudice is not necessarily harmful because the person who holds the prejudice may not have the power to act on his or her biases. For example, a poor white woman may have prejudices against black men that center on her belief in the stereotype that black men are "lazy." She boasts to her friends, "I'd never hire one of them." Of course, because she herself is poor, she is not in a position to hire or fire anyone. Her prejudice has no more force than the breath behind her idle words to her friends.

On the other hand, racism is prejudice backed with power. In the era of slavery, both whites and blacks in the South held prejudices about each other. But because whites had all the power in that society, only whites were capable of being racist. Today, although whites still hold power in disproportionate numbers, people of diverse racial and ethnic backgrounds have gained power in a variety of areas of society. As a result, it is now possible for the color lines of racism to shift. A poor white woman could be the victim of the racism of a wealthy Latino man, for instance, if his prejudice against whites kept him from employing her in his factory. Ironically, as a perk of overcoming the obstacles of racism, many people of color now find themselves moving into positions of power from which racism is possible.

Not all stereotyping occurs at the larger societal level we think of when we think of issues such as racism. For many people, stereotyping and its consequences are encountered first, and quite profoundly, at school. Schools are veritable gold mines for those who want to study stereotypes because the social structure of cliques is a manifestation of stereotypical thought patterns. No person is simply a "jock," "nerd," "society girl," "hood," etc. Yet, within American schools, especially at the high-school level, students are defined by each other and, in some cases, by teachers and administrators based on the stereotypes associated with their clique.

The classic 1980s teen film, *The Breakfast Club*, is a testament to this phenomenon.[3] In the film, five students, each representing a different social set, spend a Saturday together in detention. Over the course of the day they unite in opposition to the school administrator who himself stereotypes them completely. As the students interact, they begin to break down the artificial walls that divide them and learn of the reality of each person. Yet their individual realities include the very real constraints they face as a result of the power of cliques in the school. For example, the society girl at one point admits that while she has developed relationships with the other four, she probably will not speak to some of them in the hall the following Monday because she fears the ramifications: namely, she knows that if she were to speak to a nerd she would be ostracized by the members of the society clique.

Until recently, I believe most of us believed that school cliques were simply an unavoidable part of growing up. Although we perhaps wished they would go away, we never really thought, after we ourselves reached age twenty or so, that they were cause for substantial concern. Then we all heard the news reports about the school shooting in Littleton, Colorado. In the 1950s, stereotyping kids into categories such as "jock" and "nerd" was not right, but it was not deadly. Today, the stereotyping that defines school cliques seems to have become every bit as dangerous as the stereotyping that underlies racism or any other form of *adult* hatred of "them."

SCAPEGOATING

Scapegoating occurs when we unfairly place blame for a problem onto another person or group. Because that person or group is in fact not at fault, or at least not solely responsible for causing the problem, scapegoating is a fallacy of causal argument.

Small children are notorious for scapegoating. Children often redirect blame toward another child, most often a child who is younger and innocent. How often have you heard, "I didn't do it, Billy did!" from the mouth of a child standing all alone at the scene of a household crime, often covered in such evidence as mud or grease? By pushing the blame for the problem onto another child, the scapegoater tries to escape responsibility. With small children, the motivation for scapegoating normally involves avoiding punishment. When the child claims, "I didn't do it, Billy did!" she is essentially saying, "Please don't punish me."

Many times when adults use scapegoating tactics they too hope to avoid punishment. For example, adult criminals sometimes offer up someone else's name under interrogation, claiming that the other person actually was responsible for the crime. "I may have been there, but I didn't pull the trigger—Bill did!" Like a child, the adult criminal attempts to push the blame for his or her crime off onto another person in order to escape punishment or at least to reduce culpability and, with it, the degree of punishment.

It would be unfair to suggest that children and criminals hold exclusive rights to scapegoating. In fact, we are all susceptible to the thought pattern of scapegoating when we face difficult situations. As a college professor, I sometimes see otherwise intelligent and ethical students fall into scapegoating patterns when they fall behind in their studies. "The professor in my math class gives too much homework. It's not fair. He doesn't understand that I have other classes. That's why I need to ask for an extension on my deadline in your class, Professor Roy." "I broke up with my girlfriend last week. Now she keeps calling me every night wanting to talk about it. So I haven't been able to do my reading when I normally try to do it." "My car wouldn't start again. That car is no good. I keep telling my dad I need a new car, but he just says 'I'm not getting you another car, you don't take care of the one you have.' I don't know what he's talking about. It's just not fair. I mean, doesn't he realize that I am too busy to be walking to and from classes all day. I have things to do, you know. My dad just doesn't understand. So, that's why I didn't get my paper in on time." Competing priorities, the demands of romantic relationships, and cars and fathers are all real issues in the lives of most college students. Of course, they are not the *causes* of a student's failure to complete assigned work on time. That failure is the result of the student's decision not to do the work in a timely fashion.

We all tend toward scapegoating, at least for a moment, when under extreme pressure. When faced with an irate boss or spouse, or a police officer who says we were doing thirty-five m.p.h. in a twenty-five m.p.h. zone, almost all of us revert back to our younger days and rehearse in our minds all the things other people have done/are doing that *caused* us to miss the meeting, forget to pay the utility bill, or need to drive too quickly. In other words, for a split second we try on, "I didn't do it, Billy did!" just to see if it stills fits. Most of the time we are grown up enough to admit that it does not. In fact, a large part of laying claim to being an adult is taking responsibility for problems when we truly are the one at fault.

Yet, throughout history, Americans faced with what they have perceived to be crises have fallaciously placed blame onto "them" and elevated scapegoating to a mass, or public, phenomenon. The McCarthy era of the 1950s serves as an excellent case in point. For several years, under the leadership of Joe McCarthy, a United States senator from Wisconsin, many Americans came not only to believe that communists had infiltrated the government and several other sectors of society but also that these alleged infiltrators were responsible for almost all the problems then facing middle-class Americans. "Reds" were blamed for everything from destabilizing national security by stealing nuclear secrets to crippling America's moral fiber by playing rock-'n-roll on the radio.

While such claims seem clearly erroneous today, at the time they were very appealing to many otherwise rational, middle-aged, middle-class Americans. The 1950s were an era of great change and, therefore, great challenge to the traditional values and lifestyle of those same middle-aged, middle-class Americans. Advances in technology resulted in dramatic changes in awareness of the wider world and, with it, its threats. The proliferation of affordable air travel, automobiles, and televisions, just to name a few innovations, brought new influences into middle-American living rooms. A farmer in central Iowa watched his daughters swoon to the sights and sounds of Elvis Presley on *The Ed Sullivan Show* playing a kind of music traditionally associated with black rhythm and blues nightclubs. He also watched news reports of New York City beatniks, Little Rock segregation protesters, and Russian advances in space technology. The whole world opened up, and it opened up right in the middle of the farmer's central Iowa living room. It was a time of dramatic change, dramatically played out right in front of the farmer's eyes. Even though precious little actually changed immediately on his farm or in his community, he perceived the greatness of the changes in the world because with advances in technology he now was party to the changes. And some of them scared him because they seemed to threaten to chip away at the value of the kind of life he always had lived. "Who is responsible for this?" "Who is trying to take away my way of life, the American way of life?" Senator Joe McCarthy offered a neat and convenient answer: "The Communists, of course."

Very real threats to safety, both physical and emotional, exist when large sectors of the public fall into the thought pattern of scapegoating. In the McCarthy era, for instance, many people lost their jobs as a result of the public madness that led to the scapegoating of social ills onto alleged Communist spies. A century earlier, when American Protestants blamed the social and economic upheavals of the times on newly arrived Catholic immigrants, many people lost their lives in the violent riots that plagued most eastern cities.

Of course, history's most outrageous and deadly example of the dangers of scapegoating occurred in Germany in the first half of the twentieth century. Adolf Hitler centered the Third Reich around the belief that the Jewish people were to blame for literally all of the problems then facing Aryan Germans. In *Mein Kampf* he portrayed Jews as a parasitic infestation of German culture, destroying Aryan ideals and promise from within.[4] Onto the Jews Hitler heaped blame for everything from the economic collapse following the German loss in World War I to the spiritual malaise of the German people following decades of war and economic depression. Hitler's arguments in *Mein Kampf*, as well as in his many rallying speeches during his reign, made the Jewish people the scapegoats for German problems. While Jews long had been held as "other" by virtue of their ethnicity and faith, Hitler further encouraged the German people to view the Jews as a *threatening* other by making them the scapegoats for substantial social and economic woes. The Jewish people thus were turned from a relatively benign "them" defined by ethnic/religious differences into an allegedly sinister "them" defined by evil motives to hurt "us," the *innocent* and *superior* German people led by Hitler.[5]

Ironically, when we offer up another as a scapegoat as a way to absolve ourselves of blame, we actually endow "them" with greater power. If the scapegoat is alleged to have caused the problem, then the scapegoat is bestowed with the power to have caused the problem. We tend to make scapegoats of those who are less powerful than we are simply because we *can* do so; those with more power would be able to stop our unfair blaming. Thus the child blames a spill on her younger sibling, not on her mother, because she knows that mother has the power to disprove the claim. Yet by placing blame for our problems onto another we elevate their claim to power. If I blame my baby sister for spilling the milk, I suggest to others that she has the power—in this case the agility and strength—to have lifted the milk carton in the first place. In order to be blamed for causing a problem, one must be described to, at least, have the capability to cause the problem.

Scapegoating, then, involves placing blame on someone with less power and, in the process, making it appear as if they have more power. Before Joe McCarthy terrified Americans about the so-called Red Scare, the Communist Party in America was, at most, a consortium of urban intellectuals that carried little or no significant political weight. However, after McCarthy blamed them for causing the breakdown of America's moral core and national security, they suddenly were a force to be reckoned with in American society—a force that would preoccupy Congressional debate, media coverage, and the public's fears for quite some time. Likewise, it was Hitler's diatribes blaming the Jews for the collapse of Germany's strength that elevated the Jewish community to the level of perceived power that made them a *threat* to the German people. Because the Jewish community had little power, Hitler could make Jews his scapegoat; yet, in doing so, he himself endowed them with power—specifically, with the power to be credible as a force that could destroy Germany from within.

Clearly, when we fall prey to the thought patterns of scapegoating, we lose sight of normal standards for what is reasonable. Although scapegoating can provide us with some temporary relief from culpability—and guilt—about the situations we face, it also puts those we falsely blame at risk of repercussions. In an odd twist, scapegoating also necessarily forces us to vest power in the scapegoat even though the scapegoat originally had less power than we did. While scapegoating seems illogical and even counterproductive when we calmly examine it, the sheer frequency with which it is used—by individuals and by whole societies—provides proof that it is, unfortunately, a common thought pattern in the world of "us versus them."

DEHUMANIZATION

When we dehumanize another person, we strip "them" of any connection they might possibly have to "us." Dehumanization is a prerequisite to acts of extreme violence because it allows us to deny that our actions actually are hurting, even killing, another human, another one of "us." Although we most comfortably associate the use of dehumanizing thought patterns with serial killers and other social outcasts, dehumanization patterns also characterize the rhetoric we ourselves produce or, at least, accept during times of war and of significant domestic turmoil.

American leaders make use of techniques of dehumanization in order to rally the public against an enemy during times of war. For example, since September 11, 2001, President George W. Bush has characterized Osama Bin Laden and the Taliban regime of Afghanistan as "evil-doers," suggesting at times that their motivations and actions are nothing short of demonic. President Bush's use of dehumanization tactics is not without precedent. A decade earlier his father, President George H. W. Bush, described Iraqi leader Saddam Hussein as murderous, inhumane, and savage. President Reagan had used similar tactics to cast Manuel Noriega as a monster during America's brief military engagement in Panama. And during the Vietnam War both President Johnson and President Nixon portrayed the North Vietnamese leaders as vicious and inhumane.

Of course, for a war effort to succeed, dehumanization tactics must be applied to the opposition troops as well as to opposition leaders. American GIs do not normally face off with the leadership during combat. Rather, they must be prepared to face and kill other soldiers. When troops meet in combat, especially in the kind of close combat waged most recently in Vietnam, soldiers must encounter another person, another human, another one of "us" in the field and then be able to turn off the recognition of "us" (humans) and focus narrowly in on the idea of "them" (the enemy fully dehumanized) if they are to kill. Soldiers are not essentially killers: they are *people* serving in a position that sometimes requires killing. As such, they must be trained not simply to commit the acts that result in killing but, more critically, to undergo the thought processes of dehumanization that allow them to kill. Only if such training is successful can the soldier, who until being called to service had been, for example, a grocery store clerk, look into the eyes of the enemy and *not* wonder what that man or woman does for a living when not at war, whether they have children, if they too are scared. The soldier who looks into the eyes of the enemy and sees "us" instead of "them" is not only an ineffective link in the military chain but very likely to become a casualty of war.

While dehumanization tactics are necessary in times of war, they are simply dangerous when they infiltrate human thought in other contexts. Serial killers and rapists dehumanize their victims because they only can be so cruel if they lose sight of the person they are hurting. Knowing this, law enforcement agencies make every effort to rehumanize victims who are believed to be hostages of such criminals. By repeating such a victim's name, showing photos of the victim engaged in various activities, and allowing the victim's family to plead for their loved one's safe return, the authorities hope to force the killer or rapist to see the victim as a person, for once the victim again is perceived as human, it becomes much more difficult for the criminal to hurt them.

Sadly, tactics of dehumanization can be found in a variety of forms in media to which most of us are exposed on a daily basis. In the powerful video series entitled *Dreamworlds*, Sut Jhally, a professor of communication at the University of Massachusetts, presents a startling perspective on the dehumanization of women in many music videos made since the debut of MTV in 1981.[6] Jhally forces viewers to see images embedded in the videos—images we take for granted as "normal" during casual viewing—by showing strings of repetitive images without their accompanying soundtracks. Images of female body parts and of women performing overtly sexual behaviors seem to jump off the screen at the viewer when seen in silence or in the company only of monotonous tones. *Dreamworlds* has inspired some controversy because Jhally also intercuts images of sexual violence from music videos into the gang rape scene from the movie *The Accused*. When viewers watch the images from the music videos while hearing the soundtrack of the rape, many find it difficult to keep track: which image is the rape and which is the "harmless" music video?

Although difficult to watch at some points for virtually all audiences, *Dreamworlds* raises important points about the ways in which women are portrayed in the "dream world" of music videos. Many videos contribute to the dehumanization of women by showing only a few body parts (legs, buttocks, and breasts in particular) instead of whole women, thus encouraging viewers to objectify women by losing the person in the part. "She" becomes merely "that piece of ass." Further, even when women are shown "whole," they tend to be shown in roles that place them in inferior positions to the men in the videos. Men are rock stars while women are back-up singers or dancers; or, men are rock stars while women are strippers or prostitutes hired by the band. In some cases, women actually are portrayed as animalistic, shown chained or caged, prowling on all fours, even bending to lap up a drink with their tongues. By reducing a whole woman only to certain body parts, by placing women in inferior roles, and by infusing women with animal-like traits, some music videos dehumanize women and thus enable plot lines in which women are made the passive sexual objects and targets of violence for the men in the videos.

Perhaps the most important point made in *Dreamworlds*, though, is the implicit one that all these images parade before us on a daily basis, but we do not *see* them until they are wrenched from their normal context. I have used the *Dreamworlds* videos in courses with college students for five years now. Each semester I watch my students watching *Dreamworlds*. Inevitably, their faces first register looks of disbelief. Subsequent writing assignments bear out this observation. Several students in each class will admit that, for as much as the first half-hour of the documentary, they felt Jhally was simply sensationalizing. Significantly, those students who initially most resist the documentary tend to be those who self-report the heaviest viewing of MTV and other video networks in their leisure time. The real power of *Dreamworlds* comes in the second half hour when Jhally's editing refuses to give viewers a break from the painful monotony of these dehumanizing images of women. At this point in the documentary, my students become very quiet. The shuffling of papers and clearing of throats that characterize even a normally attentive audience give way to dead silence in the classroom. In their writings, students frequently recall wanting the video to be over and feeling as if they themselves were trapped (though, as an important side note, viewing of this video is completely voluntary for my students). *Dreamworlds* is too compelling to walk away from, yet too disturbing to embrace.

Dreamworlds feels confrontational. *Dreamworlds* feels like an assault. Yet it is assaulting us with the same images we readily consume not only in music videos but in all forms of media, including advertisements, countless times each day. The genius of Jhally's *Dreamworlds* is that it forces, or perhaps invites, us to look at the images surrounding us as if we were seeing them for the first time without hundreds of thousands of other similar images jading our view. *Dreamworlds* thus makes us feel like video virgins. And from that perspective images of women we have come to take for granted as "normal" suddenly appear demeaning and terribly, terribly sad. The line between attraction and repulsion dissolves as we encounter women being thrown around rooms, women being locked in cages, women being dragged across floors, women being pushed into walls, women being shoved onto beds, women being fondled, women being licked, women being bitten, women being stripped, women being taunted, women being written on, women being chained, women being whatever the males in the video desire them to be. As we endure these images, over and over and over, absent their catchy lyrics and familiar tunes, we begin to really see the images. As I have said, watching *Dreamworlds* is painful, because at some point almost everyone who watches it realizes that they are finally *seeing* what they have been watching every day for years: a dream world in which women are fully dehumanized and, therefore, "legitimate" targets of sexual aggression and even violence.

Thinking patterns that involve notions of "us" and "them" are normal and allow us to compare and contrast, sort and categorize, and perform other critical mental functions. However, sometimes we cross the line from "us and them" thinking and enter the realm of "us versus them." Absolutism, stereotyping, scapegoating, and dehumanization tactics characterize the "us versus them" mentality. As I have demonstrated, while such fallacious thinking patterns can be found in relatively benign forms in everyday life, they also can become horribly dangerous in some circumstances.

In this chapter, I have offered only a few briefly considered examples of what can happen when the thought patterns that characterize us versus them thinking are not kept closely in check. In the chapters that follow I will explore in great detail some of the most dangerous instances of the uses of these thinking patterns in recent years, including the rise of substantial white supremacist activity in America and the seemingly endless stream of mass murderers and serial killers who terrify us. But before we launch into the analysis of such extreme cases, we need to consider carefully the subtle ways in which hatred is manifested throughout our culture and how we have come not only to tolerate but even to encourage hatred.

CHAPTER 2

Hate Talk:
The Mind/Language Connection

"I hate you!" We've all heard it. We've all said it. As small children we spat "I hate you" at those we most loved—our parents—before we really even understood what the words meant. But while we may not have understood the meaning of "I hate you," we already understood at a very early age the power of the word "hate." As adolescents, we blazed through our first romances, often falling into "I love you" only to crash down into "I hate you" within a matter of days. As adults, most of us reserve "I hate you" for the most extreme situations. We now understand not only the power, but also the tragically terminal meaning of saying these words to another human. Yet circumstances do arise that inspire us to utter "I hate you." And more often than we say the words aloud, we think them about another person in the privacy of our own minds.

"I hate you" has meaning in the English language and power within our culture. We can look "hate" up in the dictionary. If we speak the word "hate" to other English speakers, they will identify rather precisely the emotional state to which we are referring. But what if "hate" had no meaning? What if the word "hate" never had been in dictionaries of the English language? What if you screamed "I hate you" at an enemy and they looked quizzically into your eyes and said, "What does that mean?"

What if we lived in a culture where the language system did not include the word "hate"? Would we still be able to hate if we were raised not knowing hatred even existed?

Our obsession with hatred is embedded in our language. We socialize our children—as we ourselves were socialized—to tolerate hatred and violence. In this chapter of *Love to Hate*, I explore how profoundly language structures influence how we think about ourselves and others. First, I consider the very nature of the mind/language connection. I then look at particular language structures we all commonly use that can embody our obsession with hatred and thus carry it forth into each new generation. While many elemental language structures and communication patterns have an impact on our thinking, I focus on only four in great detail: naming, diminutives, reduction, and metaphors. Throughout the study of these four language structures, I pay particular attention to the ways in which our use of language intersects with, reinforces, and even enables the elemental thought patterns of hatred I introduced in chapter 1: absolutism, stereotyping, scapegoating, and dehumanization.

THE MIND/LANGUAGE CONNECTION

A relative of mine teaches in a remote village high in the mountains of Papua New Guinea. According to the correspondence I receive from her and her husband, one of the greatest challenges they face is getting their students to turn in homework on time. Such a challenge is, of course, far from unique: teachers all across America face the same challenge every day. My relative explained, however, why teaching timeliness is a particular obstacle in that region of Papua New Guinea. At the end of the day when she reminds her students, "Don't forget, your report is due tomorrow," the students sincerely reply, "Which tomorrow?" Many of the indigenous peoples of Papua New Guinea do not share the Western concept of time as a linear progression from the past through the present and toward the future. Nor do they share the Western understanding of time as something that can be parceled out in allotments— days, this day, the next day—as if humans controlled time itself. Words such as "tomorrow" have no real meaning for people who do not conceive time in the same way as it is conceived in the West.

Cross-cultural barriers to communication force us to see the infinitely complex relationship between culturally dependent understandings of the world and how those understandings are expressed in language. What we normally fail to appreciate until confronted with such an example is that every aspect of our experience as humans is shaped by the culture in which we live and the language we speak. In order really to comprehend how deeply our fascination with hatred is embedded in our lives, we need to consider some basic elements of the relationship between culture and language—between how we talk and how we think and what we value. Becoming consciously aware, at least for a few moments, of the mind/language connection allows us to examine our own ways of talking in a new light and helps us identify how language structures we use nearly every day keep us entangled in our obsession with hatred and violence.

Language theorists disagree about the direction of causality in the relationship between culture and language: some argue culture shapes language while some argue language shapes culture. As with so many debates, the truth probably lies somewhere in the middle: language and culture shape each other and thus develop and change over time together. However, regardless of the direction of cause and effect, as members of a particular culture raised within its unique cultural/language system, each of us reflects the attitudes, beliefs, and values inherent in the system itself.

Inextricably intertwined with each other, culture and language exert enormous force on us throughout our lives. Think of culture and language as a pair of contact lenses through which we view the world. Once the lenses are in place, they shape how we see the world around us. If we wear a pair of contact lenses designed to make everything appear taller and thinner than it really is, we perceive everything we see to be taller and thinner than it really is. Of course, if we actually wore a pair of contact lenses that distorted reality, as soon as we realized the problem we would return to the eye doctor and demand a new pair and, likely, a refund.

But when the contact lenses are cultural and linguistic, instead of optical, we have little to no ability to determine the ways in which they may distort our view of reality because we have no way to experience reality directly. From the moment we are born, our interactions with others begin to slide cultural/linguistic lenses onto our eyes. By the time we are adults, it is as if the contact lenses of culture and language are actually fused to our eyes: not only are we incapable of noticing the ways

in which they may distort our view of reality but we also lose the awareness that we even are looking through lenses. In the following sections
of this chapter, I attempt to show how these lenses perpetuate our obsession with hatred and violence.

WHAT'S IN A NAME?

Negative labels litter our language. Such pejorative references evidence
our deep-seated obsession with hatred. Negative labels have the power
to ostracize and stigmatize groups in our society. As with any element of
the mind/language connection, negative labels are most powerful when
we lose sight of the fact that the labels are creations of our hatred. Even
though we now toss around some pejoratives, such as "bitch," in casual
conversations, the terms retain their ability to hurt because, when
uttered in the right tone, under the right circumstances, the full and
painful weight of the terms comes crashing down.

Over the past three decades, progress made by the gay rights movement has truly opened the closet door on the gay-lesbian-bisexual-trans-
gendered (GLBT) community. In the process, the term "gay," in particular, has entered common usage of the English language as a descriptor
of a group of people. Yet, even in an era when gay characters can be
found on popular primetime television shows, "gay" can still function
as an attack when spat out in hatred. The history of labels applied to
members of the GLBT community provides an excellent case in point
of the complex relationship between what we call each other and how
we think about each other.

Even as I write this in the year 2001, after having taught several classes
about this particular case study, I find myself perplexed by what name
to use. Although no longer carrying the intense social stigmas of the
recent past, "gay" is simply inaccurate because it does not necessarily
include lesbians, bisexuals, or transgendered persons. The most accu-
rate designation—gay/lesbian/bisexual/transgendered community—is
so awkward as to be nearly unmanageable. So, for the sake of compromise, I will rely on the acronym GLBT in this section when referring to
the entire population of people who do not identify themselves as
strictly heterosexual.

The care it was necessary for me to take in thinking through and writing that previous paragraph is central to the issue we need to consider:

how a name, a lack of a name, a name enforced by opponents, and a name embraced by insiders can have an impact on our perceptions of each other and whether we tolerate, or hate, each other.

The twentieth century has witnessed many changes in the labels attached to the GLBT community. But we must remember that the labels themselves are more than *just* names. Name changes reflect changes in thinking and, in turn, change thinking; the very process of naming is an element of our language system that shapes, and is shaped by, our thoughts.[1] A closer look at the history of labels applied to the GLBT community in the twentieth century will demonstrate how some kinds of names, by their nature, encourage hatred among us, while others at least have the potential to encourage an atmosphere of mutual recognition and respect.

Sexual desires and activities outside the boundaries of institutionalized heterosexual marriage are not a twentieth-century anomaly. Ancient Greek literature acknowledges the existence of sexuality other than heterosexuality within the culture of the time. And, as any antihomosexual religious activist will tell you, the Bible contains several references to homosexual activity. As Christianity became entrenched in Europe, codes formalized against any sexuality outside traditional marriage. Heavily influenced by early Puritan settlers, most American colonies adopted strict laws governing sexual behavior and thus planted the seeds of sexual bigotry in the American system.

Because most Western societies so wholly deplored same-sex relations, most people were raised to assume that such an outrageous "atrocity" simply could not occur among their friends, family, or neighbors. Ironically, this "assumption of heterosexuality," as it is called in academic circles, for centuries allowed many people to maintain same-sex relationships relatively safely: because the notion of homosexuality was unthinkable, no one really thought to suspect or accuse. For example, during the nineteenth century unmarried women sometimes lived together throughout their adult lives, sharing finances and responsibilities, as well as a particularly close friendship. Termed "Boston marriages," many of these arrangements were likely nothing more than matters of convenience between friends; but many, we now realize, were long-term lesbian commitments.[2] The assumption of heterosexuality prevented even the most rabid homophobes of the nineteenth century from *seeing* the reality of some Boston marriages.

Because society deemed same-sex relationships unthinkable, it assigned no name—positive or negative—to those occasionally caught in compromising sexual positions. Although the term "homosexual" appeared in dictionaries of the English language in the early nineteenth century, common references still centered on the notion of sodomy. Instead of labeling the people, our ancestors simply labeled the deed. Thus a person may have committed the act of sodomy, but the person himself did not warrant an all-encompassing label based solely on the act. People attracted to members of the same sex existed as a nameless entity. The absence of a popularly accepted label such as "homosexual" or "gay" facilitated the assumption of heterosexuality because it allowed, even encouraged, society to deny the existence of GLBT *people*.

As such, the namelessness itself of the GLBT community evidenced the absolutist thinking in society at the time. As I have discussed in chapter 1, absolutism, or presuming everything either to be wholly good or wholly bad, characterizes hatred; in order to hate, a person must conceive others, and by implication also themselves, in absolute terms.

For many years Americans condemned members of what we now call the GLBT community to the ultimate fate of absolutism: namelessness. To be nameless is to not exist in the cultural-linguistic cauldron that is society. To be nameless is to be completely disenfranchised. The nameless cannot organize to demand rights. The nameless cannot call out to each other for help. The nameless cannot even identify themselves with clarity in the privacy of their own thoughts, for even in that haven they, as products of society, still do not have a richly textured term of self-identity. Thus, namelessness truly is the absolute form of the absolutist thought pattern of hatred. Whereas today's racial bigots say, "I am good because I am white. You are bad because you are black," for centuries society sent the then-nameless GLBT community the even more profoundly damning message: "We are. You are not."

In 1895 a scandal surrounding Oscar Wilde shattered the Western world's comfortable assumption of heterosexuality.[3] The author of such critically acclaimed works as *The Picture of Dorian Gray* and *The Importance of Being Earnest*, Wilde's often flamboyant, always egotistical behavior drew attention on both sides of the Atlantic. Yet, even though Wilde lived his life in the spotlight, the assumption of heterosexuality insulated him from attacks for many years during which he routinely engaged in same-sex romances.

Ultimately, Wilde's greatest passion brought about his downfall. In the early 1890s, Wilde fell madly in love with a dashing young man named Lord Alfred Douglas. The two remained nearly constant companions even after their affair ended. Douglas, whose penchant for the outrageous surpassed even Wilde's, flaunted his sexuality. As both became increasingly less discreet, Douglas's father, the legendary boxing enthusiast the Marquess of Queensberry, demanded that Douglas stop associating with Wilde. When Douglas refused to comply, his father took public aim at Wilde who, in turn, filed a libel complaint against the aristocrat.

Wilde's suit against the Marquess of Queensberry backfired. Queensberry's lawyers marched forth a parade of young men who testified that Wilde had had sex with them. The judge threw out the libel suit and charged Wilde with sodomy and indecent behavior. World media attention now focused not on Oscar Wilde the author, nor even on Oscar Wilde the socialite, but on Oscar Wilde the predatory sexual pervert who had corrupted young men. When the criminal trial ensued several weeks later, the prosecutor turned Wilde's own literary words against him, asking, "What is the 'Love that dare not speak its name'?"[4] Never one to back down from a challenge, Wilde described for the court the intense love sometimes shared between two men. Wilde then spent the next two years in prison.

Because the world press covered the scandal in such detail, the impact of Wilde's trial carried forth even as he himself languished in jail. For many years the word "Oscar" entered British and American slang as a term of contempt. Black-market pornographers amassed small fortunes selling depictions of same-sex intimacies under titles such as "The Sins of Oscar Wilde." Most profoundly, though, the man who coined the phrase "the love that dare not speak its name" had begun the naming process. As the lead character explains in the novel *Maurice*, by E. M. Forster, "I'm an unspeakable of the Oscar Wilde sort."[5]

Although the controversy surrounding Oscar Wilde immediately saved the GLBT community from the hell of namelessness, it also helped usher in the pseudoscientific purgatory of labels such as "invert" and "homosexual." Before medical researchers put GLBT persons under the microscope at the turn of the twentieth century, sodomy was an act not a defining quality of a person. With the advent of biological and psychological studies of sexuality, a person who committed the act of sodomy became an invert or a homosexual.[6] An invert was nothing more than an invert—it was all that the person was.

Such all-encompassing labels also carried implications of defectiveness. An invert's psychosexual development had stalled out. The homosexual was emotionally immature. Sexual inversion resulted from severe childhood trauma that the person was not strong enough to overcome. While the researchers did suggest that homosexuals did not choose their sexuality—in other words, they were not just flagrantly stamping on social customs—the researchers nevertheless concluded that homosexuals were defective people. Thus, by creating labels for GLBT persons, instead of for their behaviors, the turn-of-the-century researchers defined the people themselves as defective creatures.

As such, the first scientists to study homosexuals inadvertently dehumanized them. Another of the characteristic thought patterns of hatred, dehumanization enables extreme acts of violence because it encourages people not to recognize their shared humanity, the most fundamental building block of tolerant relationships. Significantly, many of the most influential sexuality researchers in the early twentieth century were German. Scientific "evidence" that homosexuals were defective members of the human species was well publicized by the time Adolf Hilter rose to power. During the reign of the Third Reich, Hitler insisted that all known and suspected homosexuals be tagged with a pink triangle and removed to concentration camps for extermination to ensure that their defective traits would not weaken the "pure" Aryan bloodline.[7]

While the threat of persecution in Germany was unparalleled anywhere else, inverts and homosexuals throughout Europe and America still had to be very careful about revealing their sexuality. The use of insider code words such as "gay" and "queer" allowed members of the GLBT community to arrange meetings and pass along information without raising too much suspicion. "Gay" allowed people to self-define. "Gay" allowed members of the GLBT community to assign their own connotations to their identity.[8] However, because "gay" functioned as an insider code word—and *had to* for the safety of gay people—the GLBT community simply could not use the term openly to combat popular negative labels such as "Oscar" and "invert."

By the 1950s, the once-secret code words used only by members of the GLBT community had become derogatory slang hurled at the community by outsiders. Police in urban areas wised up to the meaning of "gay" and used their new understanding to root out and raid underground meeting places. The obsessive middle-Americanism of 1950s culture rejected anyone who violated middle-class WASP norms. Gays and queers did not meet society's gender role standards. Gay men were "sissies," "pansies," and "fairies" who lacked the strength of "real" men. Lesbians, though still rather rarely acknowledged at all, were written off as "mannish" and incapable of attracting men.

The popularizing of such negative labels in the 1950s encouraged stereotyping, yet another thought pattern characteristic of hatred. A pansy could not fight in a war, protect innocent women and children, or probably even support them financially. As a result of such stereotypes about gay men, society effectively emasculated a man it labeled a fairy.

As I discussed in chapter 1, stereotyping and scapegoating often go hand in hand. Scapegoating, or placing blame onto others, defined much of the 1950s as Joe McCarthy blamed all of America's problems on communist infiltrators. But we must not forget that McCarthy also identified gay government employees as a particular risk.[9] Why? Because, he charged, they would be particularly susceptible to blackmail plots by the Soviets. At the most basic level this notion relied on society's biases: because gays were not accepted by society, the prospect of being revealed as gay was a sizable threat—careers, friendships, and families all could be destroyed by the allegation of homosexuality. But at an even more fundamental level, this McCarthy era theory of gays as a national security risk also relied on the stereotypes about gays. A pansy no doubt would be too weak to stand up in the face of a threat of blackmail. A fairy would not have the courage to say "no" to the communists. Clearly, then, the stereotypes attached to labels such as "gay," "queer," "pansy," and "fairy" in the 1950s enabled scapegoating of many of society's problems onto the GLBT community. That, of course, provided further grounds for hatred.

When civil rights movements exploded onto the American scene in the 1960s, the GLBT community began to organize as well. The young movement demanded an end to persecution. As the movement became fully established in the late 1960s and early 1970s, leaders began to use the terms "gay" and "queer" as rallying cries. Protests featured slogans such as "Gay and Proud" and "I'm Here, I'm Queer." In the process of demanding an end to homophobic laws, the GLBT community took ownership of its own identity. What had been negative labels imposed by outsiders now became symbols of empowerment as the GLBT community determined to assign its own, positive connotations to the terms.[10]

In the four decades since the GLBT community organized publicly, it has continued to co-opt negative labels once hurled by opponents. The Nazis' lethal pink triangle now symbolizes unity and identifies safe zones in schools, such as faculty offices where students may feel free to discuss GLBT issues. Some leading groups within the GLBT community actually have incorporated the old pejoratives into their names. For example, one of the more radical GLBT rights groups goes by the name Queer Nation. By adopting and ever so gradually redefining the labels once used to ostracize GLBT persons, the GLBT community has undercut the power of such terms to propagate the process of hatred.

The progress of the GLBT rights movement in the late twentieth century has been nothing short of astounding. Many states have abolished antisodomy laws. Hawaii recognizes same-sex marriages; Vermont grants full legal benefits to domestic partners. Amid a storm of opposition, Ellen Degeneres "came out" in the mid-1990s, both in real life and on her television sitcom, *Ellen*. Within only a couple of years of *Ellen's* controversial breakthrough, a comedy called *Will and Grace*, featuring openly gay men, entered the primetime line-up with virtually no outcry. Gay people still are a small minority in our society, but openly gay people now exert a significant influence on American popular culture. A bit more each year, "gay" is becoming a demographic descriptor and losing its power as a negative label.

Of course, the increasing tolerance of openly gay people does not mean all gay people are safe from hatred and violence. The brutal 1998 slaying of Matthew Shepard reminded all of us that some of our fellow Americans still perceive members of the GLBT community to be perverts of "the Oscar Wilde sort," defective "inverts," and even "queer" threats to the American way of life. As members of Fred Phelps's antigay lobby protested Shepard's funeral, they carried signs proclaiming "God Hates Fags." It is, sadly, clear that people like Fred Phelps still cannot see past the dehumanizing hatred of terms such as "fag" to the humanity of a person like Matthew Shepard.

IT'S THE LITTLE THINGS

I love Travis, my sweet, cuddly, little puppy. To me Travis's soft black nose—tinged with one tiny spot of pink—is just about the cutest thing on this planet. Only his downy ears, which flop slightly toward the edges, rival his nose for my most tender affections. Travis is my dog-baby, my sweetest little friend, my puppy. To the rest of the world, of course, Travis is an eighty-pound German Shepherd/Husky mix with a decidedly bad temper. He flails himself at the windows, sliming drool at everything in his path, every time a bicycle passes in front of our house. He barks viciously at anyone who dares pull into our driveway. Travis is a seriously territorial guard dog with the size and temper to back up a standoff with any intruder. But, to me, Travis is my precious puppy and always will be.

I like to try to convince myself that I conceive Travis, now six years old, still to be a puppy simply because I am one of those annoying dog owners who views her pet as a child. Travis truly is my baby, albeit a very large and noisy one. Yet, if I am honest with myself, I must admit that, in part, I think of Travis as a "puppy" because it is convenient for me. If Travis is a "puppy" instead of a six-year-old dog, I can blame his frequent misbehavior on his youth instead of on my failure to train him appropriately. If Travis is a "puppy," I can allow myself the fantasy that he someday will grow out of his mischief. If Travis is a "puppy," I can blind myself to how scary he actually is to outsiders—my "puppy" is not really a terrifying territorial beast, he's just misunderstood.

When I think of Travis as a puppy, I am relying on a powerful element of the mind-language connection called a diminutive. Diminutives allow us to make another person, thing, or in my case dog, smaller and younger than it actually is. As a result, diminutives also strip power from the person, thing (or dog) to whom they are applied. Put simply, "dogs" can be scary. My dog, Travis, really is scary. But puppies are not scary. My eighty-pound "puppy" is, as I have said, just misunderstood.

Unfortunately, I am not the only person who uses diminutives. Nor are most diminutives as innocuous as my insistent notion that Travis will forever be a pup. Many of the diminutives that have entered common usage in our language have contributed to the oppression of whole classes of people for centuries. While we can cull any number of examples from our history, perhaps none has had a more profound impact than "boy," a diminutive long assigned to black males of all ages in this country.

"Boy" originated as a reference during the era of slavery. Slave traders, slave owners, and plantation overseers reduced adult black males to boys and thus compounded their bondage by also denying their adulthood. Even in the Northern states, free blacks faced substantial and pervasive racial prejudice; there too whites commonly referred to fully grown black men as boys. Following the Civil War and passage of the Thirteenth, Fourteenth, and Fifteenth Amendments to the Constitution—which, in combination, legally enfranchised blacks as full American citizens—bigotry against blacks remained the norm; black men, in particular, felt the wrath of racists. In reaction to blacks' new legal status, groups such as the Ku Klux Klan emerged. The Klan helped pass the so-called Jim Crow laws that kept blacks from using their newly secured rights. The Klan also used violent scare tactics, like lynchings. Yet, whether legal or lethal, the Klan's activities sent one clear message: no "boy" would be allowed to freely exercise the rights held sacred by white *men*.

As the twentieth century dawned, prejudicial treatment of blacks persisted. When the Great Depression took hold in the 1930s, black men suffered more than most. Because blacks already were clinging to the bottom-most rungs of the economic ladder, they were displaced by the crash in disproportionate numbers. White men desperate to feed their families now took over jobs previously deemed fit only for "boys." Only tip-driven service positions—valeting, bell-hopping, shoe-shining—remained fully open to black males. Because the positions themselves relied on subservient attitudes, the diminutive "boy" seemed to acquire an appropriateness it had not so fully enjoyed since the days of slavery.

World War II marshaled in the first outcries of resistance to the demeaning of adult black males. Although blacks had served in the military since aiding in the Union cause during the Civil War, the white military establishment rarely allowed blacks to serve as full combat troops in critical positions. The sheer size of the Allied effort in World War II opened new opportunities for black men, opportunities that challenged the assumptions underlying the term "boy."[11] Black soldiers made even greater strides during the Korean War in the late 1940s.

But, ultimately, it was the onset of the large-scale Civil Rights movement in the 1950s that marked the beginning of the end for the diminutive. From the Little Rock, Arkansas, school desegregation protests of the mid-1950s to Martin Luther King, Jr.'s March on Washington nearly ten years later, black Americans demanded equal treatment under the law. Although not a legal issue itself, a critical component of the struggle for civil rights involved combating the attitudinal effects of several centuries of adult black men being referred to as "boys."

I want to consider here some of the profound effects "boy" has had on both blacks and whites in America. Specifically, I examine how the diminutive itself facilitated white hatred of blacks by perpetuating dangerous stereotypes. The word "boy" is another example of the power of the mind-language connection, for it has encouraged hundreds of years of hatred and violence.

The thinnest of lines divides hatred from fear. Even a cursory examination of white racists' hatred of blacks reveals an underlying fear of blacks. Throughout most of American history, white fears have emanated from stereotypes about blacks in general and adult black males in particular. Significantly, of course, whites themselves created and entrenched the stereotypes. As I demonstrated in chapter1, stereotypes are a flawed form of thinking because they are based on limited and/or biased information. Nevertheless, once a stereotype is accepted by a group of people, the stereotype itself functions as their reality. A closer look at the diminutive "boy" suggests that the term helped whites manage the fears they felt in the face of dominant stereotypes about blacks. Thus, the diminutive—an element of the mind-language connection—helped people cope with the effects of stereotyping, a flawed thought pattern of hatred. In what follows, I examine a few examples of the stereotypes about black men in order to understand how "boy" served as a coping mechanism for many white Americans.

The stereotype that blacks were childlike justified the institution of slavery in America for about two centuries. Largely Christian, white Americans simply could not have reconciled their religious beliefs with slavery unless they could rationalize slavery itself as a moral good. The stereotype that blacks were childlike allowed this rationalization. White slave traders and owners felt that they were saving a people too mentally and spiritually immature to save themselves. The term "boy" directly reflects this stereotypical assumption about blacks.

But the diminutive exerted power far beyond the stereotype of blacks as childlike: "boy" also undercut other stereotypes, those that made many whites afraid of blacks. Perhaps most profoundly, "boy" helped verbally emasculate adult black males. White thinking assumed blacks to be savage and animalistic. As such, adult black males were believed to be wildly sexual; their sexuality knew no limits—white women, in particular, were at risk in the presence of adult black males. By restricting all black men, regardless of age, to a perpetual childhood, "boy" helped whites suppress their fears of black male sexuality by encouraging whites to perceive black *men* as nothing more than over-grown children.

Finally, the diminutive helped whites dismiss black men as a potential political or economic threat. Put simply, men challenge each others' dominance: boys do not scare men. By conceiving adult black males as boys, whites denied (at least in their own minds) the legitimacy of black men as a political voting bloc or consumer or labor sector. Thus, in the years following the Civil War and well into the twentieth century, white politicians rarely spoke to the interests of black men, just as advertisers and investors rarely approached black men as a viable economic force. "Boys," it was presumed, had neither the intellectual horsepower nor the material resources to be significant players in the political and economic worlds of men.

Clearly then, the word "boy" functioned as a diminutive in that it made adult black men seem smaller, younger, and, as a result, less threatening, to many white Americans. "Boy" grew out of early justifications for slavery and, over the years, helped protect the institution of slavery. After emancipation, "boy" contributed to the legitimacy of Jim Crow laws and encouraged social and economic discrimination against adult black males in particular. "Boy" eased whites' fears about black men and thus played directly into the stereotypes at the root of racial hatred. "Boy" also insinuated itself into the consciousness of American blacks, eating away at adult males' self-identity and pride and adding a painful internal obstacle to the struggle for equality: namely, the need to accept one's self as truly equal, fully enfranchised, adult.

Today, only the very, very old and the most virulent of bigots publicly use the term "boy" in its diminutive sense. Yet the legacy of the diminutive still persists in the mind-language connection. When white women clutch their purses as an adult black male passes near them in an airport, "boy" echoes out from the past. When a white father chills as he notices a black man noticing his teen-aged daughter, "boy" cries out. "Boy" harnessed the stereotypes that drove fear and hatred like a well-trained team. "Boy" is nearly dead now. And the stereotypes too are showing their age. But when they do rally in moments of tension, "boy" still haunts us.

YOU ARE SUCH AN ARM!

Imagine yourself in the midst of a heated argument with one of your friends. A point of minor disagreement happens to converge with the bad moods both of you have been coddling all day long. Suddenly, you're both ready to duke it out over a relatively insignificant issue. Because you are friends, you would never dream of escalating to violence. But you will allow yourselves to vent your accumulated rage at each other, knowing that a perk of friendship is inevitable forgiveness. The barbs start flying back and forth between you. Because you've known each other so well for so long, you can track each others' hot points with a finely tuned radar. You coldly suggest your friend's penchant for over-dramatizing is causing the fight. He rallies (with an exaggerated amount of flare, typically), blaming your tendency to overanalyze. Unbeknownst to your friend, your boss also criticized you today for this trait: the tension is more than you can take. Well . . . "over-analyze this, buddy!" you shout in frustration (and with an accompanying gesture you remember from high school). Shocked at your aggression, your friend looks you square in the eyes and declares, "You are such an arm!"

How would you react to such an assault on your character? I know how I would react: I'd laugh like a crazy person. And, why not? Obviously my friend must be a crazy person to say something so crazy, so why not join in?

In fact, the seemingly inane retort, "you are such an arm," is a language structure called reduction in which a whole person is reduced simply to one part. Americans frequently use reduction. The reduction "you are such an arm" sounds silly only because it violates the normal pattern we use for reducing: namely, when we want to hurt someone by reducing them, we reduce them to a body part about which our society has some level of discomfort. This silly example makes it easier for us to see the actual process of reduction simply because it is so absurd.

But although this example is absurd intentionally to make a point, reduction itself is very powerful. By definition, when we reduce another person to one of their parts, we make them an object—they become nothing more than the one part. As such, reduction necessarily dehumanizes because it keeps us from seeing whole people and thus prevents us from empathizing with them and caring about them. A closer look at some of the popular ways reduction plays out in our society will help illuminate further how the use of this language structure contributes in its own unique way to our obsession with hatred.

Perhaps because of our Puritan heritage, we Americans long have preferred to reduce our enemies to the nether regions of the human body. In moments of conflict, we do not refer to each others' arms and legs or fingers and toes. No, we Americans aim our verbal punches below the belt—directly below the belt. We reduce our opponents to penises, vaginas, and anuses, though we usually do so via the most colorfully graphic slang terminology we can muster. By reducing people to parts of the body our society deems "dirty," we label the people themselves as dirty. Our preferred pattern of reduction suggests not only that our enemies are not whole but also that they are unclean, impure. On both levels, reduction encourages us to believe that those people we reduce are inferior to us.

Although we tend to reserve verbal reductions for fights wherein both parties clearly recognize the hateful intent of the terms, American culture long has tolerated visual reduction. Because visual reductions normally are not connected to an obviously confrontational situation, we easily forget that they too promote the sort of objectification and dehumanization that lie at the very heart of hatred. I want to discuss here two avenues in which visual reduction reigns supreme—the world of pornography and the world of advertising.

American courts and legislatures have tried in vain for decades to define obscenity. Hundreds of definitions have been offered, but all seem somehow to include too much or too little to function as the bases for viable laws. While apparently none of us Americans are able to define obscenity adequately, we all seem to recognize the obscene when we see it. Consider for a moment how to differentiate between an "artistic" nude and a "pornographic" nude. What leads a person or a society to declare one piece "art" and another "pornography"? No doubt there are many factors, among them the context in which the work is displayed (for example, City Museum of Art versus Bobby Jack's House of XXX All-Nude All The Time). But even if we remove contextual factors about location, marketing, and medium, the works themselves often give clear evidence of their own nature.

Visual reduction characterizes pornography; our subconscious recognition of this trait helps us to identify pornography even when we cannot define it. Many pornographic images focus on body parts not whole people. The pornographer's camera often literally reduces. Yet even when whole bodies are shown, they are displayed in such a way as to guide the viewer's focus to a particular area of the body. A picture of a whole woman, displayed spread-eagle on a motorcycle with her naked crotch front and center of the photo, directs the eye to her genitals. *All* of her may be in the picture, but only one *part* of her is the subject of the photographer's gaze and, in turn, the viewer's gaze.

Although such techniques of visual reduction are most obvious in the world of pornography, the world of advertising also makes use of reduction to associate products with particular body parts. Advertisements sometimes rely on lighting to direct the audience's attention. For example, an advertisement might use backlighting subtly to enhance the triangular area between a standing woman's legs. The woman herself recedes into the shadows of the background, while the product—front/middle of the shot—is framed by her legs. Some advertisements are far more overt.

Because advertising images bombard us constantly (estimates are that we encounter about twenty thousand ads every year of our lives[12]), we sometimes lose sight of the techniques commonly used in the advertisements themselves. As products of our own culture, we have been raised to accept the technique of reduction as a primary visual tool of advertisers. We rarely stop to notice how pervasive reduction is in the thousands of images we encounter each day. Of course, as I have already demonstrated, we are at our most vulnerable when we have our defenses all the way down.

While the level of reduction in advertisements is usually far less severe than in pornography, reduction in advertising probably affects us all the more because we do not stop often enough to question it. When we encounter a pornographic magazine, we are naturally on the lookout for techniques such as reduction that turn women and men into objects. Yet those same techniques can and do sell perfumes, cars, and vacation packages in magazines anyone can buy in the check-out line of their local grocery store.

Perhaps because reduction now is so common in the world we *see* around us, we also willingly tolerate reduction in our language. Humans have been calling each other "asses" and the like for centuries. It does seem, though, that in recent years we have become far more accepting of the public use of such terms. Words once reserved for moments of heated conflict now flit casually about in conversations taking place in shopping malls and restaurants. A couple of years ago, a man was actually taken to court for yelling some choice words at the top of his lungs in a canoeing area where young children were present.[13] The story made national news not because the public use of such language was unique but because someone finally had been taken to task for using such language in public.

Whether visual or verbal, reduction discourages us from seeing whole people. By reducing others to parts, reduction makes it difficult for us to empathize with them and care about them. As such, reduction helps us think of other people as objects, as somehow less human than we are. The language and even visual structures of reduction thus enable dehumanization, one of the key thought patterns of hatred.

LOVE IS A BATTLEFIELD

I cannot remember, let alone count, the number of times I have been called a "bitch." I have a relatively bad temper that I did not learn to harness at all until I was well into my thirties. I am what you might call short on patience and long on mouth. And, of course, there's my job and my attitude toward it. I am a professor. To the chagrin of some students, I am a professor of the old-school variety, meaning I believe tough assignments, strict deadlines, and "counting off for grammar errors" build character. Under the circumstances, I'm quite sure I'm being conservative when I say I have been called a "bitch" several hundred times in my life.

Yet for all the times I have overheard mumblings in the hallway after I have handed back exams and all the times I have heard grumblings by waitstaff as I strode toward a restaurant manager's office waving a complaint card, I only really remember one time someone called me a bitch. And, although it has been nearly ten years, the memory of the sound of that word spat out in judgment by a friend stings as much today as it did so very long ago.

In recent years, our society seems to have taken some of the taboo status off the term "bitch." For more than a decade now television network censors have allowed prime time sitcom characters to call each other bitches. "Bitch" also appears rather frequently in the lyrics of popular songs. Many of us now use "bitch" as a humorous reference in casual conversations.

Yet for all its common acceptance, "bitch" still retains its power to sting. Buried beneath the popular, light-hearted usage of the term is the original seed of its meaning. "Bitch" is a metaphor and, as such, its meaning derives by comparing the person to whom the term is applied to the actual meaning of the word. Although "bitch" is now used to refer to aggressive women, "bitch" technically refers to a female dog. The popular meaning of the term—the notion of the aggressive woman—

builds from the image of a wild, snarling, protective, potentially lethal mother dog. We may not consciously think of that true meaning of the term when we teasingly tell a friend she's being bitchy, but we all understand that image: it is what gives "bitch" meaning not only as a popular, humorous term but also as a powerful pejorative. The metaphor "bitch" inherently dehumanizes the woman at whom it is aimed. The day one of my dearest friend called me a bitch at the scene of a car accident, he made me feel the *true* meaning of that term. At that moment, I felt stripped of who and what I was not by the accident but by his words.

Metaphors function as one of the most common language structures that, when used carelessly, perpetuate our attraction to hatred. So many of the hateful names we call each other are metaphoric: dog, pig, chicken, slug to name but a few. "Bitch" no doubt is one of the most commonly used metaphors in our slang today. And, because it still does have the power to hit its victims like a slap in the face, "bitch" is a very obvious example of the power of metaphors to shape how we feel about each other and how we make each other feel.

While "bitch" may be one of the most obvious examples of the power of metaphors to carry hateful thought patterns like dehumanization, I want to consider for a moment another example that is much harder to see and, because of that, probably effects us all the more. As I warned at the beginning of this chapter, looking inside our own mind-language connection poses a significant challenge. Few aspects of our language so test our analytical abilities as the language surrounding language itself, specifically the language we use when talking about arguing. It is important to understand the ways in which we have been socialized to think about arguments themselves, not just the hateful words such as "bitch" that we sometimes use when arguing.

Our society overtly deplores violence. From an early age we tell our children not to fight with their fists but, rather, to learn to resolve their conflicts peacefully, with words. Many schools and even preschools now teach children rudimentary tools of verbal conflict resolution. In other words, we teach our children that physical fighting is bad but that arguing is okay and, if handled fairly, even healthy. I agree with this sentiment wholeheartedly *on the surface level*. Unfortunately, if we stop to consider how we actually conceive argument in our society, we quickly find that the way we talk about arguing actually glorifies hatred and, in the extreme, physical violence.

Our entire understanding of argument rests on the metaphor of argumentation as a war. The two parties in an argument are opponents. They line up their positions. They attack. They defend. They marshal facts. They win or lose. When in the heat of emotion, they may even refer to killing each other's arguments. These are but a few of the war-like terms that shape our understanding of verbal conflict. The argument-as-war metaphor is deeply engrained in our mind-language connection. I devote a class period in one of my courses to this concept. I challenge my students to talk to each other about an argument we have studied without using any terms that derive from the war metaphor. In more than a decade of teaching, I have yet to have a student meet the challenge. I've never met it either. The metaphor of argument as war is so fundamental to our way of thinking about argument that we simply do not have terms outside the metaphor with which to discuss the process of verbal conflict (which, of course, is an instance of the war metaphor, too!).

Our preoccupation with hatred resides in the argument-as-war metaphor. Over the centuries Western culture has come to think of argument as a battlefield and thus subtly to train each new generation to enter verbal disputes with a warlike mentality. By doing so, we teach our children, as we ourselves were taught, that argument is not a true alternative to violence but, rather, a different form of violence: in argument, the wounds are mental and emotional but nevertheless wounds intentionally, hatefully inflicted on the enemy.

Because this metaphor resides so deeply in the core of our mind-language connection, it may be easier for us to understand the way it effects us if we consider a true alternative. In the early 1970s, a communication scholar named Wayne Brockriede suggested that we should reconceive argument in line with a metaphor of love in which arguers are lovers.[14] In this view, the parties to an argument are not enemies waging battle each with the intent to claim victory; rather, they are partners engaged in a mutually reaffirming and productive intercourse that results in the betterment of both parties. Instead of one side "winning," both sides cooperate to produce a compromise that benefits everyone involved. It is strange to imagine a world in which arguers are thought of as lovers. We can barely wrap our brains around the concept because the metaphor of argument as war is fundamental to our culture and to the obsession with hatred our culture embraces.

I doubt our society ever will abandon its commitment to the argument as war metaphor; it is too much a part of who we are and how we interact with each other. But we need at least to recognize the metaphor for what it is: a powerful element of the mind-language connection that shapes how we think and behave. The argument as war metaphor encourages a conflict mentality. Argument as war pits us against each other and reinforces the most fundamental aspect of our fascination with hatred, the "us versus them" mindset. Argument as war is a metaphor, just like "bitch." And just like "bitch," these days it normally eases its way in and out of our lives barely even drawing our notice. But no matter how innocuous it may seem, this metaphor too still has power. It too can come crashing down on any of us at any time. Just ask any "bitch" in a parking lot: trust me, she'll tell you how much pain one little metaphor can cause.

When the subject of hatred comes up, we all are tempted to point the finger at those who hate obviously—hate group members, killers, and other people whose extreme hatred expels them to the very fringes of our society. But as I have shown in this chapter of *Love to Hate*, we all perpetuate our attraction to hatred when we allow ourselves thoughtlessly to use certain elemental language structures in our everyday conversations. We can use the processes of naming, diminutives, reduction, and metaphor in a variety of positive ways. However, we also can warp these language structures to facilitate our fascination with hatred. When we use such structures without thought to their impact, we deepen their influence in our own lives. We also send our children another wave of mixed messages about hatred and violence.

Several years ago, a movement called "political correctness" swept across America. So-called PC advocates insisted that we all reform our speech and writing to eradicate negative references to others. Some PC advocates managed to enact speech codes on some college campuses and in some businesses that made the utterance of certain racist and sexist terms grounds for disciplinary action. Critics charged that speech codes violated First Amendment guarantees of freedom of expression.

I myself do not advocate speech codes: I fear the compromising of the First Amendment far more than I fear being the target of even the most hate-filled words in our language. But what I fear most is our tendency to ignore the power of the language we use to hurt others and, ultimately, to hurt ourselves. I do not so much hate those who stupidly spew out ugly words; rather, I *fear* living in a world with people who do not fully comprehend the meaning and the power of "I hate you."

CHAPTER 3

Hate Is Cool

Like most American children, I learned early to identify which kids in my neighborhood were considered "cool." Those deemed "cool" ruled the loosely defined territory of our neighborhood—a sprawling trailer court and the adjacent lower-middle-class housing development in a small Midwestern city. If a regular kid did not like me, then, well, some regular kid did not like me, so what? But if one of the cool kids did not like me, then I had a problem. Why? Because being rejected by the cool kids meant the very great likelihood that all the kids in the neighborhood would follow suit. So, like most American kids, I learned to know who was cool and to play my cards accordingly. Fortunately for me, one of the true kings of coolness in my part of town was my oldest cousin, thus providing me with a certain degree of social insurance just by association.

Researchers from a variety of fields have studied the complex dynamics of human social hierarchies. From governmental and corporate organizational structures to the social ladder of kids in any given neighborhood, when humans meet up in groups they tend to arrange themselves in relation to a single leader or a small group of leaders. Within social structures those in leadership roles center the group and function as a base of authority. One way in which leaders enact their authority is by serving, albeit sometimes unconsciously, as role models for the behaviors and attitudes of others in the group.[1] The notion of leading by example comes alive in most groups when lower-ranking members emulate their leader(s) as a way of fitting into the group itself.

Significantly, though, in a society as large and complicated as America we sometimes turn to role models who are not actual members of our particular social structures. Over the course of the twentieth century, as the mass media rose to prominence, popular cultural icons have emerged. For better or worse, in a large and complex society where that which is seen and heard via mass media is one of the few remaining shared experiences of the people, these cultural icons sometimes replace real leaders as role models for behavior and attitudes.

If cultural icons can serve as role models for behavior and attitudes, what messages are our icons sending? In other words, when American kids look around to find out what is cool in their efforts to find their place in society, what cultural icons embody coolness? Unfortunately, some of our most compelling icons—both past and present—suggest that hate is cool. And in a society in which "cool" marks status in many sectors, most significantly those involving adolescents, we must be troubled when the notion of being cool really means being cold to the needs, rights, and feelings of others.

Of course, not all popular icons are icons of "cool" and thus not all popular icons send that message. If any good has come about as a result of the events of September 11, 2001, it surely is the emergence of everyday heroes and heroines such as firefighters and police as cultural icons. The mass media's focus on the bravery of emergency service personnel and other real-life heroes and heroines during and after the terrorist attacks has provided American children—and adults—with a new assortment of role models. I saw the impact of this during Halloween 2001 when, amidst the normal population of tiny ghosts, goblins, witches, and cartoon characters, my daughter and I encountered a surprising number of junior firefighters. But while the rise of real-life role models of compassion and courage is heartening, it does not mean that the icons of cool that have dominated the landscape of popular culture for so many years have been replaced.

In order to get a clear understanding of icons of cool in our society and how those icons send both subtle and overt signals about hatred, in this chapter I discuss "cool" on a variety of levels. First, I consider a couple of the traditional icons of cool—cowboys and bikers—and examine not only their place in American popular culture but also the ways subtle and overt cues about hatred infuse each. Second, I consider a contemporary arena for icons of cool—the music industry—and analyze the ways in which rock and rap stars sometimes convey hateful themes. Finally, I explore reactions to today's icons and uncover what I believe are some of the most alarming messages about hatred American children now encounter.

Before jumping into the analysis of cultural icons of cool, I want to offer one note of caution. While it is tempting simply to blame those who create or enact the icons (movie producers, rock stars, etc.) for the presence of hatred in our society, we must remember that they create the icons for a willing, even eager audience—us. Pushing the blame onto those who help shape our icons of cool while we continue to consume their messages is just another expression of our obsession with hatred.

TRADITIONAL ICONS OF "COOL": THE CASE OF THE COWBOY

The image appears slowly over the horizon. With the sun blazing in the background, we see him only in silhouette. The Stetson-style hat, cocked to the side. The broad shoulders and lean waist. The holster and guns draping loosely over sauntering hips that seem to keep time to some inaudible tune. And, finally, as he emerges fully, the trademark boots, the subtle clinking of the spurs.

There he is. Wyatt Earp, Doc Holiday, Clint Eastwood, and John Wayne rolled into one. One tiny six-year-old hero of the backyard frontier, that is. For much of the twentieth century, American boys have preoccupied themselves with dreams and games involving cowboys. Pint-sized "pardners" have roamed summertime streets and ruled recess for decades. Late October normally brings a small herd of would-be cowboys to the costume shops. Those same tykes inundate Santa with requests for child-size chaps, hats, holsters, and guns.

Young boys' quests for cowboy paraphernalia are themselves part of our popular culture. For example, the very funny movie, A Christmas Story, revolves around one boy's yuletide campaign for a particular type of pellet gun endorsed by his favorite movie-star cowboy.[2] He leaves notes and clippings about the gun around the house, mentions it often in conversations with his parents, even features it in an essay for school.

Yet every time he raises the subject, some adult warns he'll put his eye out and dashes his dreams of being fully outfitted like his hero.

While we adults have an almost automatic response to a pellet gun — "you'll put your eye out" — we rarely if ever offer children cautions about the larger issue: the very nature of the cowboy icon. It is after all the adoration of such icons in movies, books, and television that fosters in children the desire for toy guns. As such, we need to consider the messages behind the symbol or, in this case, the cowboy behind the gun, in order to understand both the positive and the potentially negative sides of this enduring icon of American popular culture.

First, and perhaps most fundamentally, the cowboy icon has two basic incarnations: the cowboy hero and the cowboy villain. Cowboy heroes often appear in roles such as sheriff, leader of a cattle drive, or what I'll call a "wandering hero," such as the Lone Ranger, who appears much like a frontier Superman wherever and whenever help is needed. Writers and producers most commonly place cowboy heroes in conflict either with "Indians" or with the cowboy villain. In contrast to the other classic bad guys of the Western genre, cowboy villains pose a special challenge because they are essentially the alter ego of the cowboy hero; the cowboy villain shares the hero's skill with a gun, his horse-riding maneuvers, and his knowledge of the land. What distinguishes the two, of course, is character: the cowboy hero is essentially good, while the cowboy villain is essentially evil.

Even if we assume that our cultural icon of the cowboy only involves the cowboy hero — an assumption I suspect may not be as safe today as it was in the 1950s — we still find ourselves with a complex icon capable of sending mixed messages about hatred and violence. Among the issues surrounding the cowboy that merit some consideration are: the actual profile of the cowboy and thus the connotation of "us" offered to those who identify with the character; the absolutism that seems a central feature of almost all stories starring the cowboy; the tendency of the cowboy to dehumanize his enemies; and, ultimately, what such features of the icon say about the cowboy's fitness as a traditional role model for "cool."

I would like to begin with a basic consideration of the profile of the cowboy icon. What does he look like? How does he react in various situations? Who are his friends, his enemies, his family? How does he accomplish his goals?

Although I have never in fact tried the following experiment, I'm quite sure I know what results it would produce. Enter any classroom, office, factory lunchroom, shopping mall, or bar in America and ask every person you meet to describe a cowboy. I can almost guarantee that the first word out of each person's mouth would be "He . . ." Now, I admit it seems rather obvious that a cowBOY would normally be considered a male. But let's stop and consider the issue a bit more carefully. While males surely were responsible for most of the sheriffing, cattle driving, Indian skirmish-waging, and wild-horse corraling on the American frontier in the nineteenth century, they were not there alone. Hidden in the annals of history are the women—the settlers, farmers, teachers, nurses, business speculators, missionaries, and, in a few cases, gunslinging Annie Oakley types. Also buried in the past are the other men of the American West—the doctors, lawyers, farmers, ranchers, preachers, investors, and carpenters to name just a few. The American frontier was a complex social environment in which the cowboy was but one character type.

Yet only the cowboy has been elevated to the status of cultural icon. Several features of his profile lend him a compelling air. First, and perhaps most basically, the cowboy's physique and physical prowess are at the very pinnacle of American ideals for men. While the typical working cowboy in 1875 may have had a potbelly overhanging his gunbelt and, after a few weeks on the hot and dusty trail, a scent worse than that of a skunk, the cowboy *icon* has been portrayed almost universally in literature and movies as a ruggedly handsome, physically appealing character. Classic twentieth-century leading men such as John Wayne and Clint Eastwood have shaped our notions of how cowboys looked in the past.

The uniformity of advertising appeals based on the cowboy suggests how very clear the image of the cowboy is in our minds. For example, several popular brands of men's cologne center their advertising campaigns around the cowboy and the implicit argument that men who wear the colognes will be appealing in the same way that the cowboy is appealing. But let's stop and think about that for a moment. Realistically, what would an actual cowboy have smelled like—on the trail, in temperatures hovering over ninety degrees, for weeks on end, with a bunch of cattle and a horse, and his last bath—taken in community bath water at Miss Beverly's Saloon—a distant memory? Is this a scent one would really want to pay money for? I doubt it. But we don't see the model dressed like a cowboy holding a lasso in one hand and the cologne bottle in the other and think of an actual cowboy; rather, we think of the cowboy icon who, apparently, smells like pine trees, citrus, and a tiny bit of synthetic musk.

The cowboy icon, then, is a sanitized version of reality, an image born of early "cowboys" such as Roy Rogers, then reborn in all the other ruggedly handsome men who have enacted the icon, from the Duke to the Marlboro Man. From the amalgam of their physiques and manner-ism emerges the profile of the cowboy icon: tall, lean, and muscular, with a strong jaw and piercing eyes. His age varies, but he is never so young as to be naïve nor so old that we even for a second would ques-tion his virility. He is male, always and absolutely, rigidly upholding social conventions about masculinity in all his actions and, in turn, rein-forcing those conventions for those who watch him.

Ironically, the cowboy's traditional masculinity, though perhaps the critical centering element of his character, almost never leads him into the most traditional male social roles of husband and father. Rather, the cowboy usually is depicted alone, though not obviously lonely. We rarely see the cowboy with close friends. We rarely see his family of ori-gin. We rarely see him take a wife and start a family of his own. To the extent that the cowboy involves himself with women, he most often car-ries on some sort of informal dalliance with a woman who, in the era of actual cowboys, would have been socially taboo. But the cowboy does not care: he loves the prostitute with the "heart of gold," just not enough to make an "honest woman" out of her in most stories. The cowboy is not the marrying kind. He is unsettled and unsettling. No woman can tame him. He is like the wild stallion—untamed, free, strong, proud.

And here we find the essential "coolness" of the cowboy icon. He is cool in the way the stallion is cool—he is a force of nature society may sometimes think it has tamed but, in fact, never will. His innate wild-ness and the fact that he alone controls the wildness inside himself are the grounds of his claim to "cool." His knowledge of these traits allows him to slowly, confidently walk down the dusty street, knowing he could be shot at any moment, because he trusts that he will somehow sense an opponent's movement in time to spin, draw, and shoot to kill in the knick of time. His self-knowledge guides his hand to his hat as he cock-ily tips it to a local lady, making her blush because they both know she will think of him that night as she lies in bed with her portly, timid hus-band. Thus it is the coolness of the cowboy that raises him to the status of icon, for without his cool he would be just another smelly guy on a horse, riding quickly toward home so his wife does not get angry that he is late for dinner.

With this general profile of the cowboy icon in mind, I want to investigate what this "cool" character tells us about hatred. First, in the literature and movies where we find him, the cowboy icon lives in a world of absolutes. The cowboy hero, though sometimes shown to have a dark side in his own personality, ultimately makes the commitment to fight for the side of "good." The cowboy hero literally dons his white hat as a symbol of his status as our hero. As such, he plays the sympathetic character in narratives; when we cheer him on we are cheering for all of "us" and reinforcing our shared value commitments. In consequence, those the cowboy battles are not simply "other" or "them" but necessarily become a "bad" other because they are pitted in conflict with *our* hero. In the basic plot lines of cowboy narratives characterization is overt, even stereotypical; there is little room for complex and ambiguous morality.

Yet, within the seemingly crystal-clear morality tales pitting good against evil, a truly ambiguous message is often to be found: in a society that claims it believes hatred is bad, one of our foremost popular culture icons, the cowboy hero, is quite often saying that hate is cool. As I discussed in the first chapter, absolutist thinking patterns themselves can easily be warped into the dangerous form of "us versus them" thinking that lies at the very heart of most hatred. In stories involving the cowboy icon some elements of "us" and "them" are required simply to allow the plotlines to advance because stories need some form of tension to develop. However, normal conceptions of us and them cross into the potentially dangerous arena of us versus them when the cowboy's enemies are defined solely by their other-ness and not by any clearly explained evil motivations. For example, stories of the cowboy icon convey us versus them patterns when the "Indian" is delivered up as the enemy simply because he is Indian. When the cowboy opposes others simply because they are not "us," with no reason or motivation given, the cowboy icon is sending audiences a message: that cool guys hate people who are not part of their group.

In addition to being defined as bad because they are not part of the cowboy's group, the enemies of the cowboy in literature and the movies are very often victims of various dehumanization strategies. Perhaps no bad guy in American popular culture has been dehumanized quite so fully or so frequently as the "Indian." No doubt racist in origin, portrayals of Native American characters as savage, animalistic, and thus essentially subhuman typify most stories involving the cowboy hero. The dehumanization of the Indian is, of course, a critical mechanism in the stories involving cowboys: for if the cowboy is good and he kills the Indian, then the Indian must be very bad. Dehumanization strategies encourage us to view the Indian as negative and thus enable us to view his death at the hands of the cowboy as justified. In this way, then, cowboy stories employ dehumanization strategies in the same ways governments do in times of war: as a means to rally us so solidly against an enemy that we do not question killing the enemy as a moral good.

Even when the Indian is moved out of the role of bad guy and into the role of sidekick, he is often still shown in negative ways. Take, for instance, Tonto, the sidekick of the Lone Ranger and perhaps the most well-known Native American character in American popular culture. While a good guy shown to be both compassionate to those in need and loyal to the cowboy hero, Tonto nevertheless always is displayed as somewhat uncivilized (by the Lone Ranger's standards) because he resists the white man's style of dress and norms of behavior. His character never fully develops: he is only the sum of his interactions with the Lone Ranger and other whites. We never really learn about Tonto's family, his tribe, his ideas and values. Tonto inhabits what is called a satellite role: he revolves around the lead character and has no real existence outside of that character's perspective.

This could of course simply be written off by saying that Tonto is treated rather poorly in the Lone Ranger tales because they are the Lone Ranger tales, not the Tonto tales. While that is true—stories by their very nature must focus in on a lead in order to develop—it nevertheless misses the more fundamental point: there never have been lead roles for the Tontos in the stories that comprise American popular culture because the us associated with the cowboy icon does not include Indians, or women, or dentists, or any of the other roles people fill in order to keep our society functioning. Only cowboys refuse such roles and stay truly "free." As such, by the logic of the cowboy stories themselves, only cowboys are fully human in our popular tales of the Old West.

What then do we learn from our hero, the cowboy icon, about what it means to be "cool"? First, we learn that coolness involves an aura of wildness, a sense of independence in the extreme that elevates him above others but also isolates him and detaches him from others. Second, we learn that it is cool to see the world in absolute terms and, as a result, participate in us versus them thinking patterns. Finally, we learn that it is cool to dehumanize those who are different not only when "they" are the enemy, but even when "they" approach "us" in such tangential roles as sidekicks.

The question then becomes, is the cowboy icon evil? I don't think so. But is the cowboy icon as good a social role model as we were raised to believe? I don't think that either. Rather, my examination of the cowboy icon suggests that the icon itself and the stories involving the icon that have featured so prominently in American popular culture for decades send mixed, even contradictory messages about hatred. On the one hand, our frontier hero defends us, leads us, and embodies such central American values as independence and self-reliance. On the other hand, however, the cowboy also tends to partake in absolutist and dehumanizing thinking patterns and to exist in a state of at least partial detachment from society. The cowboy icon, then, symbolizes not just independence but indifference, not just toughness but in some cases intolerance. He straddles the line between coolness of self and coldness to others and thus embodies the flirtation with hatred that runs parallel to our culture's commitment to compassion.

TRADITIONAL ICONS OF "COOL": THE CASE OF THE BIKER

In recent years it appears as if Harley Davidson has taken the lead from the Marlboro Man in the race for coolest honors in American popular culture. Due no doubt to such factors as urbanization and the simple passage of time, the reality of the cowboy falls farther into the past each year. At the same time, however, increases in both leisure time and disposable income have allowed thousands of Americans to act out their fantasy of the biker's rebellious life on the open road. The only catch, of course, is that such weekend warriors are not Hell's Angels, but firefighters, business owners, contractors, and accountants.

Whereas the cowboy icon appeals to Americans of all ages and, in fact, traditionally holds great sway among very young children, the biker icon tends not to find an audience below the age of adolescence. However, while few adults actually devote time and money to living out their cowboy dreams, a large and growing segment of the American adult population now dons black leather and mounts a "Hog" as often as they possibly can. That being the case, I want to consider more carefully the nature of the icon of the biker, the subtle ways in which hatred plays into stories surrounding the icon, and how the icon seems to be moving into an increasingly important position as a role model for adult Americans seeking to be cool.

Images of the biker have appeared in American movies, music, and television shows for about half a century. In the 1950s and 1960s, motorcycle gangs often thrilled audiences as they roared through low-budget films. These B-movie bikers preoccupied themselves with alcohol, violence, and the corruption of "good" young women. The image of the biker created in such films is one of complete, or at least very nearly complete, debauchery and detachment from the society at large. In fact, the bikers appear to be attached only to each other through their mysterious gang bonds that have apparently been forged over years of violent, depraved hell-raising. In 1969, the film *Easy Rider* began its ascent to cult status and, with it, raised the image of the biker even higher on America's cultural awareness chart.[3] More recently, the biker gang has been presented as a futuristic nightmare in movies such as the *Mad Max* series.[4] Yet whether it is the old-fashioned biker B movie or the fantasy bikers of science fiction, what emerges is a picture of the biker and his gang as a barbarian horde on choppers.

While stories involving whole gangs of bikers were originally the most common venues for the icon, another variation emerged in time that cast the biker in the even more sinister role of demon. The 1980s cult classic, *Raising Arizona*, provides a good example.[5] Throughout the movie, a grizzled, filthy, leather-encased man-beast tears across the desert highways on a monstrosity of a motorcycle. He is a ghost, a vision of hell, a demon, in this case comically encircling the main plot. Yet while the comedic nature of the film tames the character somewhat, an essential fact remains: when the icon of the biker fills the role of demon, the icon loses its connection to us humans even though it retains a powerful mystique for viewers.

Perhaps the most significant incarnation of the biker icon is that of the biker with the heart of gold, the biker hero. Unlike the more generic members of the biker gang, this biker always plays the lead role—he is the biker who drives the plot and with whom we might be able to sympathize. Unlike the demonic biker, this biker is not really evil, he is just misunderstood. To the chagrin of some middle-class father in every movie, it is always some semi-innocent young woman who believes she alone understands the biker and that her love has the power to transform him into the kind of man her daddy too could love. What she usually realizes in the final scenes of the movie, of course, is that if she changes him he loses that which drew her to him in the first place. He loses that indefinable quality that makes sweet young things offer themselves up to him. He loses that charismatic presence that makes other men intuitively know he is a force to be reckoned with, that it is his birthright to be leader of the pack. Put simply, if he changes, he loses his cool.

While present in many tales, the central image of the biker icon as the biker hero was undoubtedly defined by Marlon Brando's performance in the 1954 film *The Wild One*.[6] Brando's character is defiant, rebellious, and in large measure detached from mainstream society. He rebels for the sheer sake of rebelling. Yet for all his antisocial posturing, the plot reveals that beneath the bravado lies the proverbial heart of gold.

Perhaps the most well-known biker hero in American popular culture is the character Fonzie from the long-running television program *Happy Days*. Fonzie too is a "wild one" whose innate goodness makes him the show's hero. However, a key theme of the show is Fonzie's struggle to reconcile his biker sensibilities and urges with his emotional connections to the patently middle-class Cunningham family and their values.

From the generic bad boys of the 1950s and 1960s biker B movies to the futuristic biker gangs of today's science fiction, from the demonic incarnation of the biker to the unlikely hero of the biker with a heart of gold, the biker icon has clearly made its mark in American popular culture. Yet within the variations on the biker theme, what characteristics are central to this icon?

First, there is the actual physical appearance of the biker icon in the mass media. Scattered throughout film and television portrayals of bikers are obese, long-haired, heavily bearded, filthy members of biker gangs, demonic or otherwise. Normally, though, this image of the biker is reserved for satellite characters: unimportant gang members in the B movies, extras in larger crowd scenes, or generic biker bad guys in stories in which biker culture itself is not central to the plot. But when we are dealing with the biker hero, he, like the cowboy, is normally shown to have a ruggedly handsome face and lean, strong physique. He is physically attractive even though some of his actions are socially repulsive. Of course, no discussion of the physical appearance of the biker would be complete without mention of *the* outfit: dark pants (either jeans or leathers), T-shirt, black leather jacket, black boots, and sunglasses.

Beyond his general appearance and attire, the biker icon can be identified by his attitudes. At heart, the biker is defined by his position in opposition to the establishment. Specifically, the biker is shown setting himself against traditional middle-class American social structures and values. Every aspect of his lifestyle expresses his hatred of the mainstream. The thunderous roars of his engine and the ear-shattering cracks of his pipes disturb the peace. The seemingly endless parties and barhopping display his lack of regard for the mundane responsibilities of family and job. He reduces women to ornaments to be possessed then discarded. He threatens and may even harm the average man who crosses his path. The drinking, the fighting, and, of course, the sheer speed at which he drives mock the very notion of public safety. Even the black clothes he wears warn all he encounters that he is something dark, something outside the red-white-and-blue norm.

The icon's cool arises from the tension between the biker and the society. Like the cowboy, the biker is cool because he is detached from the rest of us. He too rarely is shown with family or close friends; at most, he associates with the members of his gang, all rebels themselves, of course. The women in his life, though ever-present, are merely conquests and not people with whom he forms deep emotional connections. He is alone, then, but not lonely. He is free, independent, untamed as he cruises down the highway on his chrome stallion. And we admire him as he speeds by because we declare that kind of free, independent, and untamed man to be the very pinnacle of cool in our society. There's just one catch, of course: it is *our* society he has rejected in order to be free.

And here we find the place at which our convoluted relationship with hatred again becomes an issue. While the biker icon often commits hateful and violent acts in the mass media, the icon also conveys mixed messages about hatred at a much more fundamental level. Because the biker is defined by his rebellion against society, the icon necessarily stands in an us versus them relationship with mainstream American values. Yet it is with precisely the people who hold dear those mainstream American values that the biker has been elevated to the status of pop culture icon. For example, it wasn't Fonzie's old gang mates who made him the king of Milwaukee; rather, it was the Cunninghams and all the families of all the other kids who hung out at Arnold's Drive-In, families who would be the butt of jokes in a biker-gang hangout.

Due to a variety of changes at the Harley Davidson corporation, not

least of which was the institution of an absolutely brilliant new marketing concept, hundreds of thousands of mostly middle-aged, middle-class
Americans have moved from watching the biker icon in the media to
enacting the biker lifestyle for themselves in recent years. These so-
called weekend warriors spend tens of thousands of dollars equipping
themselves not only with top of the line bikes but with additional
chrome, custom paint jobs, full-leather bags, and, of course, as many
variations on *the* outfit as they can fit into their closets. Like the little
boys who fill their holiday wish lists with chaps, holsters, and cap guns,
these bigger boys and girls desire more and more genuine Harley Davidson products so that they can continue to enact their fantasy of the life
of the biker learned from popular stories about the lifestyle of the icon.

There is just one horribly ironic catch to it all: living the lifestyle
made cool by the biker icon part-time is like being a little pregnant; it
just does not work that way. Ultimately, there is no such thing as rebellion with a warranty. When members of the American middle-class—
those with enough disposable income actually able to afford to live out
the biker lifestyle on the weekends—roar off down the highway on their
bikes, they are participating in the fantasy of coolness that surrounds the
biker icon in popular culture; like kids playing cowboys, they literally
are playing biker. I know all the weekend warriors out there who see this
will immediately respond, "No, that's not it. You just don't get it. We
ride for the love of riding. We're not 'playing' biker." I happily accept
that argument from anyone and everyone who owns a motorcycle and
the gear needed to ride it safely and comfortably (i.e., leather jackets
and chaps). To those riders, I say, "More horsepower to you! Have a safe
and fun ride!" However, I'm skeptical of that argument made by anyone
who spends more money on T-shirts and chrome after-market decora-
tions than they spend on gasoline in any given year. Such purchases are
physical evidence of the desire to enact the fantasy life of the biker icon;
they don't have one thing to do with cruising down the highway. In fact,
if the true sense of freedom were the actual goal, then lusting after such
items—and having to stay tied to a job in order to afford them—would
be counterproductive.

I am not suggesting that people should not be able to outfit themselves and their motorcycles the way they see fit. What I am saying is
simply that the recent craze for the biker lifestyle has as much if not
more to do with advertising and media-created images of the lifestyle of
a popular cultural icon of coolness than it has to do with actually riding

motorcycles, free and unencumbered by social pressures. On a Saturday night at a biker rally, the weekend warrior may appear poised to rebel against any social norm he encounters. But, realistically speaking, he is not going to rebel Monday morning, no matter how much he may want to, when his alarm goes off. Why? Because the weekend warrior has to go to work and earn a living so he can make the mortgage-sized monthly payment on his new scooter and, maybe, even have enough money left over for yet another T-shirt. Because what real honest-to-God hard-core biker rebel wouldn't pay $22.95 to wear a corporate logo on his chest?

The biker icon differs dramatically from the cowboy icon in the age of American it seems to entice and in the sheer amounts of money it seems to encourage them to spend. However, beyond those distinctions, both the cowboy and the biker play similar roles in our culture. Both icons, at least in their heroic forms, are portrayed to be physically attractive and are thus presented as appealing to the audience; the cowboy and the biker are the characters we are encouraged to be like because they are presented as not just atop but actually above the social ladder. By virtue of their appearance, actions, and attitudes, the cowboy and the biker have earned the label "cool" and the status that label carries with it.

As the analysis offered above indicates, both the cowboy and the biker have earned their cool in large part by detaching themselves from society, by participating in violent actions, and by displaying hateful attitudes that our society claims it tries to discourage. Yet we have elevated both characters to the status of icons in our popular culture. As I mentioned at the very outset of this chapter, it would be one thing if we simply have icons who seem to celebrate our flirtation with hatred by sending mixed messages about hating. However, it is something entirely different—and more serious—when we realize that we have such icons in an era in which many people of all ages lack actual role models in their daily lives. If the Lone Ranger and Fonzie were simply mass media characters with little impact on us, then we need have little concern over them. But when such characters become important, even primary, role models for how to earn the social cash we call "cool," then we can only expect that children and the adults they grow up to be may very well come to believe that developing the social coldness that comes along with being that cool is the best way to become the leader of the pack we call "society."

COOL (OR FLY, OR PHAT, . . .) TODAY

Whereas images of cowboys and bikers have paraded in and out of our mass consciousness for decades, new breeds of mass-mediated heroes have arrived on the scene in more recent years. While it remains to be seen if these new images will be raised by society to the status of lasting popular culture icons, they already serve as important role models of cool for America's youth. I suggest that anyone doubting this claim spends some time at a local mall where I can guarantee wannabe versions of at least two or three rock or rap stars can be found cruising up and down the aisles on any given Friday night. Of course, not all adolescents fully mimic the behavior of celebrities. However, most teens can still be influenced by the general attitudes and values put forth by cool music stars. Because they are at a stage of development inherently filled with confusion, teenagers are particularly vulnerable when faced with ambiguous messages about the appropriateness of hatred in our society. In this section, I introduce just a few of the cool characters who rule the mass-mediated school at which our young people now do much of their learning and consider what kinds of messages they are sending about the subject of hatred. Additionally, I consider how our reactions, as a society, to these icons may be sending messages about hatred and violence far more confusing and dangerous than anything rockers and rappers themselves are saying.

THE RAP MURDERS

Rap music exploded in popularity during the 1990s. Although rap as a musical genre was several decades old, the 1990s witnessed the rise of hip hop culture to prominence not just among young urban blacks but across America's youth culture. Sometimes funny, sometimes ominous, rap lyrics and the sampled tracks that accompanied them could be heard on the streets of Harlem and in the fraternity houses of Harvard. Rap tracks consistently climbed to the highest levels of the charts. MTV, accused by some in the 1980s of discriminating against black artists, placed hip hop videos in heavy rotation by the mid-1990s.[7]

As rap continued to make inroads into the mainstream market, tragedy struck at the very core of the hip hop community. In six months' time, two of the most popular and important rappers of the decade were shot to death. Significantly, although both murders remain unsolved, allegations continue to implicate the associates of each slain man in the death of the other.

Tupac Shakur burst onto the hip hop scene in 1992 with his first solo album, *2Pacalypse Now*.[8] In the four years that followed, Tupac scored hits with several more albums including 1995's *Me Against the World*, which debuted at number one on the charts. Tupac also explored his acting talents, costarring in 1993 in the film *Poetic Justice* and later in *Bullet* and *Gridlock'd*. In the early and mid-1990s, Tupac Shakur's name became synonymous with hip hop success: his brand of so-called gangsta rap helped define the era.

But Tupac's name also became synonymous with trouble as his exploits offstage drew police and, of course, the media. Although Tupac had no criminal record before his rise to stardom, he often ran afoul of the law after achieving fame. As a result of a variety of charges, he spent much of 1993 and 1994 in jail. Between stints behind bars, Tupac was wounded in a shooting. He claimed his assailant had attempted to rob him, but some speculated that the pioneer of gangsta rap may have been the victim of gang violence.

Following his parole in 1995, Tupac signed with Death Row Records, one of the largest rap labels, which based much of its marketing on the notion that its artists were authentic, that they lived the lives they rapped. Around this time, the West-Coast-based Death Row in general and Tupac in particular engaged in a verbal battle with various East-Coast rappers. At the outset, it appeared as if the jibes were nothing more than public tauntings, perhaps for the sheer amusement of the audiences or perhaps part of a marketing scheme to draw media coverage to a brewing feud in the industry. Tupac contributed to the verbal battle as much as any of the Death Row artists by claiming in one of his songs to have had an affair with Faith Evans, wife of East-Coast rap phenomenon, The Notorious B.I.G.

Yet nothing in the war of words prepared the hip hop community for the news on September 13, 1996, that Tupac Shakur had been shot. Although he survived for six days, Tupac never regained consciousness. The assailants, who remain unknown, attacked Tupac as he rode in a car through the streets of Las Vegas. Most commentators have argued that Tupac's murder was not a random act of violence but, in fact, bore many of the characteristics of a gang-ordered hit.

Unlike Tupac Shakur, The Notorious B.I.G., a.k.a. Chris Wallace, was well known to police before his rise to fame.[9] As a young man growing up in a rough section of Brooklyn, New York, Wallace was imprisoned for selling crack cocaine shortly after dropping out of high school. After reexamining his life, Wallace determined to turn his life in a new and more positive direction and devoted himself to music.

Wallace's major break came when legendary hip hop producer Sean "Puffy" Combs heard one of his demos. Combs quickly signed Wallace to his Bad Boy Records label where Wallace followed up successful guest appearances on other performers' albums with his own independent debut, 1994's *Ready to Die*. *Ready to Die* earned The Notorious B.I.G. *Billboard's* Rapper of the Year award.

Biggie stayed in heavy demand. During 1995 and 1996, he appeared on a variety of albums, including a guest spot on a Michael Jackson track. B.I.G. even experimented with acting, playing himself on the TV show *New York Undercover*. Meanwhile, because of the success of his first solo album, the hip hop community anxiously awaited a new solo release by The Notorious B.I.G.

Life After Death . . . 'Til Death Do Us Part hit music store shelves in 1997. Ironically, while promoting the album in March of that year, Chris Wallace was gunned down in Los Angeles. Immediately, rumors spread that the murder of The Notorious B.I.G. was an act of vengeance for the death of Tupac Shakur. To the extent that the proverbial silver lining can be found in the very dark cloud that hung over the hip hop community in the 1990s, that silver lining appears to be the 1999 posthumous release of The Notorious B.I.G.'s *Born Again*. Produced by Biggie's long-time friend and collaborator, Bad Boy Records' Sean "Puffy" Combs, *Born Again* features vocal contributions from Tupac's Death Row brothers Snoop Dogg and Ice Cube.

The murders of Tupac Shakur and The Notorious B.I.G. obviously mark an important episode in contemporary youth culture. Of course, the murders themselves were merely the final twist in an already complex and hateful plot. Regardless of whether the supporters of either man had any involvement in the death of the other, the so-called East versus West feud in the hip hop community sent powerful messages about hatred and violence to America's youth. We simply cannot overlook the significance of role models who *may* have committed murder. Whether Tupac, Biggie, or their associates actually harmed each other or not, it seems to have been accepted by most of the MTV generation that they certainly could have done it, that they had the potential to have done it, that they even may likely have done it. Fans did not rise up outraged to deny the allegations that the murders were prompted by the East-West feud and were tied to gang activities. Neither did adults, parents in particular, express outrage that such real-world violence seemed to be becoming a hallmark of the youth-market music and video industries. Rather, while the rap murders earned lots of press coverage, almost no notice was given to the underlying fact that these days role models for a good portion of America's youth are men whose reputations for violence and gang involvement are serious enough that allegations of murder against them carry plausibility and, in turn, secure their credibility as popular icons.

THE DEVIL HIMSELF

Ironically, while Americans seem to have had little reaction to the real violence that invaded the hip hop community in the mid-1990s, they have launched a full frontal assault on the theatrical aggression and anti-social posturing of Marilyn Manson. A writer for *Rolling Stone* says, "imagine Alice Cooper times 10. Picture KISS on an acid and whiskey bender. Marry the gross-out hilarity of G. G. Allin with the ubiquity of Howard Stern. Combine the 'search and destroy' frenzy of Iggy Pop with the godless zeal of Ozzy Osbourne. Take two cups of the devil and throw in a pinch of P. T. Barnum and you still can't fathom all that is . . . Marilyn Manson."[10]

Marilyn Manson, which is the name of the band as well as the stage name of the group's lead singer, Brian Warner, first rose to national prominence in the mid-1990s when taken under the wing of Trent Reznor, an avant-garde producer and performer well established in the music world.[11] Under Reznor's tutelage, Manson produced *AntiChrist Superstar*, which debuted at number three on the charts in 1996. Manson's follow-up effort, *Mechanical Animals*, earned great success in 1998.

But it is not Marilyn Manson music per se for which the group is famous. Marilyn Manson is the music and at the same time more than the music. Marilyn Manson is throngs of fans in ghoulish attire, stage sets born of Satanic symbolism and Nazi nightmare, and, at the core of it all, lead singer "Marilyn Manson's" consistently outrageous performances and sometimes creepy responses in interviews.

The whole package that is Marilyn Manson has inspired significant public backlash. Around the United States, Manson concerts have been canceled (or simply not booked in the first place) even though Manson tickets are among the top sellers of the past decade. When concerts have been allowed, fundamentalist religious groups have protested on site. In some cases municipalities have acted to keep Marilyn Manson out, citing fears for public safety as their motivation.[12]

Yet for all the brouhaha over the Marilyn Manson phenomenon and that phenomenon's supposed threat to our society's moral standing, the members of Marilyn Manson apparently never have been implicated in serious criminal violence. Nor, quite frankly, would such an allegation seem particularly credible because it seems quite obvious, at least to the group's youthful fans, that Marilyn Manson is an act and nothing more. Middle-class, middle-aged fundamentalists don't seem to get that about Marilyn Manson. It certainly seems odd, however, that these same people who literally take to the streets to protest Manson said not a word in response to the rap murders. Here again is evidence of our tendency to send mixed messages about hatred and violence to our children: Manson's overtly theatrical performances of antisocial behavior draw public outrage from adults, but very real bloodshed within the rap community goes largely unnoticed. Is it really any wonder that today's youth sometimes seem confused about the values of the adults who surround them?

THE DEVIL'S KID BROTHER

While Marilyn Manson's neosatanic ghoul routine has been haunting fundamentalist Christians since the mid-1990s, the late 1990s witnessed the rise of an impish-looking boy-next-door whose complex raps seem to have offended nearly every adult constituency in America at some time or another. Described by one of his former producers as "the Marilyn Manson of rap," Eminem's pared-down stage persona makes him seem, simultaneously, less and more threatening than shock-rockers such as Manson.[13]

Born Marshall Mathers, Eminem exploded onto the national music charts in 1999 with the multiplatinum *The Slim Shady LP*. He cemented his dominance of the rap and pop charts a year later when *The Marshall Mathers LP* sold five million copies within a month of its release. In 2001, the rapper racked up three Grammies for the intensely cutting rhymes that have catapulted him to the very center of America's most recent controversy about popular music. When the accused homophobe took the stage to perform a duet with Elton John for the Grammy show finale, a small cadre of protesters marched in front of the auditorium. Advocates for tolerance—including Judy Shepard, mother of murdered gay college student, Matthew Shepard—spoke poignantly in public service announcements asking everyone to consider the consequences of words such as "faggot," a favorite of Eminem.[14] And, of course, tens of millions of Americans glued themselves to their televisions to see what all the fuss was about.

So who is Eminem? Here is the root of the controversy surrounding him and also the grounds on which some supporters base their defense of him. Eminem is, at any given moment, the characters "Eminem," "Slim Shady," and "Marshall Mathers," as well as a real guy from Detroit named Marshall Mathers. He is also the voice of "Stan," a deranged fan who kills his girlfriend, and a host of other first-person narrators who spew the hatred and violence that have made Eminem not just famous but infamous. Whereas Brian Warner consistently dons the stage persona of "Marilyn Manson," Eminem changes characters almost constantly without ever changing costumes to help his audience follow along. Thus even close observers are confounded when asked to draw the line between Eminem and Slim Shady, between "Marshall Mathers" and Marshall Mathers.

But most observers, whether close or casual, have been quick to draw a line in the sand about Eminem: people either love him or they hate him. Apathy is not a reaction Eminem inspires. Writer Eric Boehlert describes Eminem as "blatantly hateful, vengeful, and violent," known for "rapid-fire tales about rape, faggots, bitches, drug overdoses, and throat cuttings."[15] The Gay and Lesbian Alliance Against Defamation (GLAAD) contends that *The Marshall Mathers LP* "contains the most blatantly offensive homophobic lyrics we have ever heard. Ever."[16] Yet, music critics, in particular, applaud Eminem as the first genius of the new millennium. *VH-1.com* declares *The Marshall Mathers LP* to be "a bona fide masterpiece."[17] The *London Guardian* argues the song "Stan" has "all the depth and texture of the greatest examples of English verse."[18] Clearly, the Grammy voters agreed.

Although Eminem slips in and out of ostensibly fictional characters in his songs, his consistently violent lyrical themes seem to parallel his real life. Press coverage of allegations of criminal physical assaults and gun brandishing by the real Marshall Mathers encourage deeper reading of lyrics in which one of his personae fantasizes about killing his then real-life wife, Kim Scott.[19] Eminem, in all his incarnations, blurs the line between fiction and reality so deftly that even the most astute critics of music and popular culture seem unsure of what to make of him.

In his music, Eminem relies heavily on absolutism, stereotyping, scapegoating, and dehumanization, the very thought patterns that underlie both fictional and real hatred and violence in our society. In fact, he elevates the thought patterns of hatred to outrageously obvious levels rarely seen anywhere else in popular culture. Often comic and ironic in his approach, though, Eminem leaves listeners guessing about his real meanings: is he advocating violence or is he its most sarcastic critic? As such, the very ambiguity of his intentions embodies our fascination with hatred. Just like the potentially lethal influence of gangsta rappers who celebrate violence in their lyrics whether or not they actually embrace the harsh reality of gang violence in their private lives, the irony of Eminem's infinitely complicated, character-driven raps may well be lost on young people eager to emulate the latest icon of cool to dominate the youth music scene.

IT'S NOT JUST "THEM," IT'S US

It is time to consider our reactions, as a society, to icons of cool such as Tupac Shakur, The Notorious B.I.G., Marilyn Manson, and Eminem. Ruben Navarette Jr. maintains that children are not nearly as likely to be influenced by pop culture role models as most of us fear they are. He states, "If your kids are raised properly, they are no more likely to bash gays or assault women after listening to Eminem than they would be to engage in cannibalism after seeing *Hannibal*."[20] I agree, *if* children have been raised not only just to deplore violence and embrace diversity but also to recognize the inherent fallacies behind hatred and to be active, critical consumers of popular culture instead of passive receptacles willing to accept any message that flashes across the screen. Unfortunately, I do not think that is true of most kids today and thus I question the wisdom of dismissing the power of popular culture icons to influence behavior.

However, there is a second issue implied by Navarette's commentary, an issue most of us would prefer to sidestep. Namely, Navarette suggests that *we*, the real, adult, day-in-day-out role models for our children, have greater sway over them than rock and rap stars. I wholly agree with this claim. And *this* is what terrifies me about the cases of Tupac, Biggie, Manson, and Eminem. For if we take a moment to examine the messages that we are sending to children through our reactions to these controversial icons, we will find that we are glorifying our obsession with hatred and violence far more insidiously—and more profoundly—than the icons themselves are. I want to approach this from several different angles.

First, when we directly blame these icons for our children's attitudes toward hatred and violence, we ourselves are role-modeling for children one of the fundamental thought processes of hatred—that of scapegoating. I am not suggesting these icons are blameless. Rather, I am suggesting that we are at least equally culpable for reinforcing America's fascination with hatred when we casually toss all blame onto popular culture and thus reentrench by our example that scapegoating is acceptable. Tupac Shakur and The Notorious B.I.G. did not perpetuate gang violence in America alone. Marilyn Manson did not cause the Columbine massacre. And, Eminem has not been behind every instance of gay-bashing since he started topping the charts. To lay all blame on popular culture icons is not just irresponsible, it is dangerous. As I pointed out in chapter 1, scapegoating prevents us from seeing the real, complex lines of causality that actually shape our world. We cannot change our own attitudes toward hatred and violence until we finally, fully admit that *we* are as responsible for their existence as "they" are.

Second, we can find another great example of our tendency to reinforce our obsession with hatred in the words we use, or passively tolerate, when talking about controversial icons. By scanning editorials and even critical reviews of recent stars or simply recalling conversations about them, it is easy to find that people often label gangsta rappers "thugs." The members of Marilyn Manson—not their stage persona—are written off as "freaks." Eminem seems to be referred to as "trailer trash" at least as often as he is referred to as a rapper. But I have yet to find an article condemning the stereotyping, dehumanizing, classist attacks on Eminem intrinsic to phrases such as "trailer trash." Those who casually call him "trailer trash" usually denounce him for his use of pejoratives such as "faggot" and "bitch." As I discussed in chapter 2, "faggot" and "bitch" can be dangerous words when they are used without thought to their implications. "Thug," "freak," and "trailer trash" are equally dangerous, but we seem content to accept them if they are aimed at people we do not like.

Third, if we actually hope to make our children's future more compassionate than our own past, we ultimately have to be willing to face the most subtle and, in my opinion, ugliest truth about our society's reactions to icons such as Tupac Shakur, The Notorious B.I.G., Marilyn Manson, and Eminem. Specifically, if we recall the various scandals surrounding each of these icons, we have to admit that press coverage and, for most of us, our attention focused longer and more closely on Manson and Eminem than on Tupac and Biggie. Tupac and Biggie were actually murdered. Their stories ultimately unfolded in real criminal violence. They both took center stage in the kind of violent narrative we tend to relish. Yet their stories barely crossed most adult Americans' radar screens. No doubt there are many reasons for this, but one seems both too painful to mention and too painfully obvious to continue to ignore. Tupac and Biggie were black; Manson and Eminem are white. Just as the death of a suburban white teenager typically draws more media attention than the death of an inner-city minority teenager, so too does the potential influence of white icons draw more attention in America than the potential influence of black icons. When adult Americans, regardless of their own racial or ethnic heritage, pay only scant attention to icons who happen to be minorities, we tell our children more about hatred in our silence than we ever could with our words.

Finally, when we allow ourselves to stall out in dehumanizing our children's icons and scapegoating violence onto influences from popular culture, we risk overlooking a truly critical fact: these "dangerous" icons are not part of some foreign invasion of our culture—they are products of our culture. Tupac, Biggie, Manson, and Eminem were born and raised in America within the confusing cauldron of messages that long has resulted from our obsession with hatred and violence. Thus, while we must concern ourselves with the messages they now send to youth, if we really find those messages disturbing we also must remember that they did not arise out of a vacuum: today's icons of cool are simply singing new versions of the songs our generations sang to them when they were children.

ANOTHER KIND OF GLASS CEILING

For years feminists have argued that American women struggle to break through a glass ceiling, a nearly invisible layer of chauvinism that persists in preventing talented women from achieving the highest levels of leadership in business, academia, and politics. While some debate the reality of the glass ceiling in career contexts these days, a glass ceiling for women does seem to exist in the arena of violence, both real and iconic. In an editorial published shortly after the Columbine shootings, Jackson Katz and Sut Jhally pointed out an obvious fact that we all seem rather content to overlook: "This is not a case of kids killing kids. This is boys killing boys and boys killing girls."[21]

Virtually all acts of extreme violence in America are perpetrated by males. Although girls have shot and killed individual girls—and boys— all the mass murders that have occurred in American schools since the late 1990s have been committed by boys. Likewise, the overwhelming majority of serial killers are male, as are the hate group members who attack minorities.

While some innate factors may lie at the root of this striking difference between the sexes, cultural differences are also at play. Katz and Jhally are among a growing group of scholars who contend that American culture constructs the very notion of masculinity in terms of violence.[22] We tell boys not simply that hate is cool but that violent behavior is a requisite component of manhood. Although this particular argument remains outside the scope of *Love to Hate*, I agree with Katz and Jhally that future research into extreme crimes such as shooting sprees must consider specifically the relationship between gender and violent behavior.

I have already pointed out in this chapter, though, that traditional American icons of cool such as the biker and the cowboy intertwine masculinity with hatred and violence. At both subtle and obvious levels, some of today's male pop culture icons send the same message. But what messages are today's female icons sending, in particular to young women?

I follow popular culture and especially youth culture very closely. When I began the process of laying out *Love to Hate*, I rapidly checked through a long list in my mind of accessible examples I could use for each chapter. The biggest challenge I faced for most chapters was deciding which of too many good examples to eliminate. But in preparing this chapter, specifically a section addressing female icons, I struggled for months to come up with even a short list of possible case studies. Identifying female icons of cool from today's popular music scene is easy: Gwen Stefani, Alanis Morissette, Eve, Janet Jackson, and Madonna are just a few of many obvious choices. However, these women do not wallow in our obsession with hatred and violence in their lyrics or, from what we know from the press, in their private lives. In fact, they sometimes take powerful, public stands against hatred and violence. It would therefore appear that the pop music scene is in line with today's youth culture, wherein both the overt glorification and actual commission of extreme acts of violence are overwhelmingly perpetrated by males.

Clearly many Americans of all ages still are blessed with strong, real role models. Mothers, fathers, teachers, and local community leaders continue to provide examples for children as well as for other adults. Yet for virtually all children today, figures from the media also serve as models for behavior, in particular as guides to what is cool. For those children who encounter few real role models in their daily lives, such media models no doubt play an even more prominent role. As the media becomes more central to all our lives and we become more and more detached from our communities, we can expect that cultural icons will exert even greater influence over all of us in the future.

Some of our icons of cool from popular culture are rather complex characters. The enduring icon of the cowboy hero, for example, has long been regarded as one of the more purely good characters in American lore. And while the cowboy in many ways is a very positive character with traits worthy of emulation, the cowboy nevertheless also conveys such messages as "cool guys are detached from society" and "cool guys don't treat people who are different equally." In the same way, the biker icon embodies the notion that detachment from society is cool and overtly rejects values such as cooperation and consideration that are intrinsic to life within a community. Today, our preoccupation with hatred expresses itself not just in the real and theatrical violence played out in popular culture by cool celebrities but also in our sometimes contradictory reactions to those celebrities.

As we enter the next millennium we do so without two talented young men who chose to make their fame in the world of gangsta rap music. Tupac Shakur and The Notorious B.I.G. now lie in cold graves after too short lives lived in a world where hate is cool.

Thousands of other young men and women, many of whom modelled their lives on icons of cool from popular culture, have lost their lives to street violence in recent years. Their names, however, never made the national news.

PART 2

Hate, American Style

CHAPTER 4

Youthful Hatred:
Are We Tough Enough?

He called himself Super Steven. The rest of us just called him Stevie.[1] Stevie was about four years old when he moved in across the street from my family. Even though I myself was only seven at the time, I understood that Stevie's life and my life were separated by much more than just a road. Stevie's mother ran through men almost as quickly as she ran through cases of beer. Some of the men ignored Stevie, some tolerated him, some even treated him nicely. Some did not. When his life became intolerable, Stevie disappeared under a beach towel and, in his place, Super Steven appeared looking quite dashing in his beach-towel cape. Super Steven felt no pain, at least that's what Stevie told me once.

At any age, when we face problems we feel we cannot bear, we often seek a way to escape. Efforts to escape from the struggles of life sometimes result in drug and alcohol abuse and even in severe emotional and mental breakdowns. Yet while extreme urges to escape can result in such debilitating conditions, more mundane desires for a moment or two away from the stresses and boredoms of our daily routines often lead us to popular forms of entertainment as means of escape. Our minds wander freely as our favorite songs form the soundtrack for our day dreams. Or, we vacation for half an hour inside the comfortable world inhabited by our favorite television characters.

Occasionally the line blurs between the reality of daily life and the "reality" of the mass-mediated world. For most of us, such blurring is itself a rather mundane occurrence as we literally get lost inside the plotline of a good movie and temporarily give ourselves over to the story on the screen. Yet, for a very few of us, the blurring of the line between reality and the artificial world of the mass media carries great consequences. If such confusion involved only positive messages such as "sharing is good" or "eat your vegetables," we could safely leave concerns about the blurring of reality to academic researchers. However, when complex images of violence are pervasive in contemporary media, we all must become concerned.

Amidst the mixed messages we send and receive about hatred, some people cross the line that separates the tough posturing of coolness I discussed in the previous chapter from the dangerous reality of violence. In this chapter, I demonstrate when simply acting tough seems no longer to be enough by looking at two disturbing trends in American culture at the end of the twentieth century. First, I examine the rise of violent street gangs. I explore the irony of our society's condemnation of such gangs when popular music styles celebrate the so-called gangsta lifestyle. Second, I look at the disturbing phenomenon of school shootings and evaluate not only some of the media images alleged to have provoked the attacks but also the ambiguous messages sent about the attacks themselves in the news media's subsequent coverage of the stories.

GANGS, GANGBANGERS, AND THE GANGSTA MYSTIQUE

Gangs are nothing new in American society. As far back as the 1830s, groups we would label gangs by today's standards roamed the streets of most cities on the East Coast. Inspired by the general social movement against Catholic immigrants, some Protestant young men organized themselves into gangs with names such as the Blood Tubs and the Wide Awakes. The anti-Catholic gangs terrorized newly immigrated Irish who, in turn, formed their own gangs for both protection and retaliation. Anti-Catholic and Irish Catholic street gangs battled each other locally for dominance of neighborhoods and even participated in some of the legendary election day rioting of the early 1840s.[2] For more than 170 years, gangs have existed in America.

Yet while today's gangs may resemble the gangs of a bygone era in structure, they differ dramatically when we consider their propensity for violence. Gangs of the nineteenth century, even gangs of the first half of the twentieth century, did engage in violence; however, their violence most often involved only fists and was very rarely fatal. Today, disputes between rival gangs and even between members of the same gang are too often resolved with automatic weapons.

If gang membership today carries such high risks, we must ask ourselves what it is that continues to entice young people to join gangs. Clearly, some youth join because they feel they have no choice: in some inner-city neighborhoods gang membership is felt to be safer than walking the streets alone, thus being a potential target for *all* gangs. For others, gang membership is a must because older family members belong to the same gang and have created an expectation that the next generation will join too. Other young people join gangs to find a sense of belonging in a time and, in some cases, a place where community and family ties have raveled away. Still others join gangs as a "career" move, for gangs that traffic in drugs can offer an impoverished teenager a far more lucrative source of immediate income than any job in fast food or retail sales. Finally, some teens join gangs as an expression of their political opinions or as a statement of their racial identification.

But how do young people learn that gangs can serve these needs? Obviously, those children who grow up in gang-infested neighborhoods learn about gangs in the same way that other children learn about dairy cows or playgrounds: they simply absorb their surroundings. It is more complex to explain the rise of a gang in an area that previously had no gangs. Suddenly two or three teens simply seem to gather and begin behaving in ways that characterize gang activity. That we all can look in from the outside and warn "gang!" suggests the coherence of their behaviors. And, of course, the three kids who are worrying a small town learned the gang behaviors from exactly the same source that taught us how to distinguish a "gang" of three kids from three kids hanging around together. That source is the media.

As I have shown earlier in *Love to Hate*, today's complex media unite all of us by allowing us to share in the experience not only of the make-believe world of sitcoms and music videos but also the edited views of reality we see on the nightly news and in documentaries. The media allows the young boy in a small Arkansas town to study behaviors alleged to typify gang members' actions and then adopt those behaviors in his own life. As he modifies his style of dress, mannerisms, and use of slang, his parents worry that their son has joined a gang because they also recognize his behaviors from the media. Images of gang members and gangs in popular culture thus become something of a textbook for youth seeking actually to join a gang or for youth simply seeking to gain attention—from parents or from peers—by donning the image of a gang member made cool in some avenues of the media. Even those youth who have been raised around active gangs can find in the media reinforcement of the image of gang members as cool and tough.

As we begin the twenty-first century, America is still sending and receiving extremely mixed messages about gangs. On the one hand, we claim we detest gangs. We do not want our children involved or our neighborhoods infested. On the other hand, we turn a blind eye to the countless glorifying images of the so-called gangsta lifestyle on television programs and networks that target our children as audience members. I want to explore this rather ironic situation in more detail.

First, we must take into account the reality of gangs and youth violence in America today. In 1995, 809 people lost their lives to gang-related violence in Los Angeles alone. Gang membership in Los Angeles is believed to be in the range of 200,000. Some progress is being made though. Drive-by shootings in Los Angeles are down from a high of 3,400 in 1992; in 1995 fewer than 2,000 drive-bys threatened lives. In the past five years, between 36,000 and 39,000 crimes committed in Los Angeles have been attributed to gangs.[3] While Los Angeles may be the most notorious city for gangs and gang violence, it is not the only city to be plagued by gangs. Ninety-five percent of large cities and eighty-eight percent of small cities suffer from gang-related violence.[4] Across the United States, gang membership is believed to exceed 800,000.[5]

Of course, gangs inherently promote the types of thought patterns that characterize hatred. By defining the world in terms of such concepts as turf, colors, and alliances, gangs embody us versus them thinking in an overt form rarely seen elsewhere in our society. Gang members operate largely on stereotypes when they define rival gang members, and even members of their own gang, solely and superficially by their gang membership and rank. Such stereotypes, of course, promote absolutist thinking: for a "Blood," for instance, a "Crip" is completely evil by virtue of his gang membership. By dividing the world so sharply based on stereotypes, gangs also enable scapegoating because their stereotyped notion of their rivals provides a ready source of blame when things go wrong. Drive-by shootings and other instances of anonymous violence are automatically attributed to rival gang members, regardless of evidence. As a result of such scapegoating, the gang promises vengeance upon the rival gang. In order to carry out acts of directed violence, the gang ultimately utilizes techniques of dehumanization so that the gang members entrench a concept of themselves as good by violently attacking the rivals.

With this understanding of some of the realities of gang activity clearly in mind, I want to reconsider some of the images of gangsta lifestyle embedded in popular culture in recent years. Gangsta rap music, of course, provides the most logical starting place. In addition to Tupac Shakur and The Notorious B.I.G., some of the most famous rap stars seem to celebrate gang life in their music and videos. Take for an example Dr. Dre, the West Coast producer of rap legends Tupac, Eminem, and Snoop Dogg, and a renowned rapper in his own right. On Dr. Dre's 1999 album, *Dr. Dre 2001*, the artist reconfirms his allegiance to the street life he lived before earning fame and wealth.[6] In the video for "Still DRE," he and Snoop Dogg drive around what appears to be an inner-city scene slapping hands with young men on the streets and, in some cases, directing hand signals toward them. Normally, MTV blurs hand signals that are gang affiliated. That the signals in the Dr. Dre video are not blurred suggests that they are not of known significance to any particular gang. However, the use of hand signaling is a well-established means of intra- and intergang communication. While Dr. Dre and the cast of the video are probably not sending actual gang signals, the hand signals seem, at the least, to be a tribute to gang lifestyle in general.

Snoop himself bears discussion as I consider how media images may be glorifying behaviors associated with gangs. Born Calvin Broadus in Long Beach, California, the boy nicknamed "Snoop" by his mother learned early the realities of life on gang-ridden streets.[7] In and out of trouble as a teen, Snoop was arrested shortly after graduating high school and imprisoned for three years for selling cocaine. After his release from prison, Snoop began collaborating with rapper Warren G., who in time brought Snoop together with Dr. Dre. Snoop's frequent vocals on Dre's critically acclaimed album, *The Chronic*, earned Snoop a following before he had released music under his own name. When he did, his success was immediate: *Doggystyle* debuted at number one on the *Billboard* charts in 1993, no small feat for a solo debut album.

Yet beneath all Snoop's musical success in the 1990s was a consistent undercurrent of criminal allegations and gangsta posturing. In 1993 Snoop was arrested for murder. Although he was later acquitted, the shadow of criminal violence cast a pall over his public appearances. Snoop became perhaps the first person awaiting trial for murder to appear on a nationally televised award show. In fact, police attempted to apprehend Snoop at the function. Snoop managed to evade them during the show but later turned himself in at the police station. As a side note, Snoop was the first but not the only gangsta rapper to be sought by police during a nationally televised program. A member of the gangsta rap ensemble Bone Thugs-N-Harmony suffered a similar fate.[8]

Whether or not Snoop has actually ever been involved with a gang, his stage persona is based on the gangsta lifestyle.[9] In the 1990s Snoop normally arrived at public appearances wearing the extremely baggy pants, athletic team sweaters, and bandanas that typify the gangsta sect within the more general hip hop music scene. In his videos Snoop often flashes cryptic hand signals toward other cast members or directly toward the camera. And, of course, the lyrics of his music cannot be overlooked; as a self-defined gangsta rapper, Snoop overtly discusses gang life in America in his songs.

Because of his level of fame, whether he intends it or not, Snoop's choices about clothing, symbols, slang, and attitude in general serve as a model for behavior for those youth who look up to him. By donning a generic gangsta uniform in public, Snoop in effect signals approval of the gangsta lifestyle. I am not suggesting that Snoop is intentionally cultivating styles or symbols associated with gangs in general, let alone with a particular gang. His primary purpose no doubt is to lyrically depict the reality of inner-city life, a reality that features gangs. Yet, unless we all desire this reality to continue to plague our nation, we must be wary of the unintentional effects of gangsta rap. As a by-product of their fame, gangsta rappers' gang-influenced stage personae do function as cues for fans about what those young fans "should" do: a rapper's ethos as a celebrity compels his audience, especially his young audience, to emulate his style and behaviors. Regardless of whether artists such as Snoop say directly that "gangs are good," their public posturing as gangsta rappers still sends that message to fans, including the many young fans who are simply not intellectually mature enough to understand that descriptions and enactments of reality are not necessarily intended to encourage the perpetuation of that reality.

Lest I give the impression that a connection between rap music and gangs is a phenomenon found only among African Americans, let me assure you it is not. There are also Hispanic and Asian rappers who are equally guilty of gang posturing; these artists, however, receive almost no air time on major music networks such as MTV or VH-1. Due to the heavy rotation of African American rap artists on MTV, in particular, gang posturing by African American rappers has no doubt had the widest impact. Yet perhaps the most dangerous connection between gangs and music is a brand of music known as "Oi!," which is the preferred musical style of racist skinhead gang members. Whereas some African American rappers are alleged to be members of gangs, virtually all hard-core Oi! band members publicly announce their affiliation with gangs such as Hammerskin Nation. Because these bands are part of the larger arena of organized hate group activity in America, I will discuss them in much greater detail in chapter 6 of *Love to Hate*.

Clearly, a wide variety of musical performers now appear to be celebrating gang culture in their lyrics, their videos, and their public appearances. From sources as polarized as major African American rap artists such as Dr. Dre and Snoop Dogg to underground label skinhead Oi! bands, audiences of contemporary music are being told that the gangsta attitude and, in some cases, the lifestyle of actual gang members, is appropriate in our society. When we juxtapose such messages with the tragic reality of gang violence, we reveal yet another layer of our complex relationship with hatred.

Even more telling of the complexity of our attitudes toward hatred and violence, of course, is our seeming nonchalance in response to gang posturing as a relatively common feature in the mainstream music media. As a poor ex-convict in his early twenties, Calvin Broadus was in no position to demand a mass audience for his rhymes about gang life in the inner city. Music industry executives gave him his voice. Television and radio executives gave him his forum. And we gave him our ears. Or perhaps more to the point, we allowed him to speak to our sons and daughters without question while we left them alone in our own homes with MTV.

READING, WRITING, AND RIFLES

That the phrase "school shooting" even has meaning to us as we begin the twenty-first century is a terribly sad commentary on life at the end of the twentieth century. "School shooting" now is a commonly recognized term. "School shooting" will produce immediate results in a variety of databases and can be used as the framework for a productive search of the World Wide Web. When I say "school shooting" to the college students in my classes, I am assured that they understand my meaning. School shootings have become a cultural phenomenon, a societal tornado that, with apparently no warning, rips through the heart of a community.

Although high profile school shooting cases in recent years would lead us to believe that school shootings are on the rise, in fact the numbers have been pretty consistent throughout the 1990s according to a study conducted by the Justice Policy Institute. What has changed is the frequency of multiple victim shootings. During the 1997–1998 school year, forty people were killed by gunfire in American schools. Of those forty, eleven died as a result of the well-publicized shooting cases in West Paducah, Kentucky, Pearl, Mississippi, Jonesboro, Arkansas, Edinboro, Pennsylvania, and Springfield, Oregon.[10]

Much attention has been given by the media itself, by scholars, and by teachers and parents across the nation to what is causing these mass killings in our schools. Reasons seem almost as numerous as those offering them. Blame is being placed on television, on inadequate school security systems, on the parents of the killers, on video games, on a general cultural tolerance for violence, on inherent flaws in the brains of the killers, on particular movies, on genres of music, on peer pressure, on bullies, and on the status of gun control to name only a few. Realistically, of course, there is no single cause of such incidents but, rather, complex chains of causal factors. I do not pretend to know what caused any particular shooter to attack his schoolmates. What I want to consider in this section, though, are the ways in which our culture's obsession with hatred, expressed in such areas as news coverage, movies, music, and video games, provides a fertile ground for the types of thought patterns that are precursors to extreme acts of violence.

Without any doubt, the case that has exerted the most profound impact on our national consciousness is the April 20, 1999, school shooting in Littleton, Colorado. When the terror finally ended, twelve students and one teacher lay dead inside Columbine High School. More than twenty other students were injured, several very seriously. The two shooters were also found dead, from self-inflicted gunshot wounds.[11] While the sheer volume of victims in the Columbine case helped drive the story to the center of national attention, it must be remembered that when the story broke we did not know the scope of the tragedy. What we knew about Columbine that made it drastically different from the other cases was that the shooting was in progress. The Columbine killers took their time. The media arrived swiftly. The result: while students, teachers, and staff members inside Columbine High School endured hours under siege, the rest of the world, thanks to live coverage, watched the outside of the building for any signs of life. Within moments of the camera crews' arrival, networks labelled their coverage with such titles as "Massacre in Littleton" and "Crisis at Columbine." Almost immediately, Columbine was not simply a tragedy but a spectacle. And while we all mourned the tragedy, almost all of us also took part in the spectacle by watching the coverage on the edge of our seats in the same way we might watch a thriller movie.

The way the media covers crises allows us to view the stories as we would view a movie. Titling the coverage and adding a powerful theme song and logolike graphics give the story the same feel we normally associate with movies or serial television fiction: quickly, we recognize the package; we hear the first chords of the theme song and await the graphics formally announcing that it is time for our favorite soap opera, the feature presentation, or the latest news about the crisis we have been following.

More recently, of course, Americans witnessed and participated in this phenomenon on September 11, 2001. Within less than three hours of the first hijacked plane crashing into the World Trade Center, NBC, for example, had titled their live coverage "Attack on America" and had added stylized graphics and music to their broadcast. Shortly after President Bush vowed to bring the terrorists to justice, the major networks shifted from "Attack on America" to variations on "America Strikes Back" as the title for and unifying theme of the surrealistic, unrelenting coverage of the onset of war. Clearly, the magnitude of the events of September 11, 2001, made the events themselves seem unreal, much like the horror of the Columbine shootings seemed unreal. Yet the inherent nature of such events is compounded by media coverage that mimics the look and sound of cinematic features.

Additionally, the ways in which some news media outlets edit footage and insert file footage and voice-overs artificially dramatize events. Intercutting rather uneventful live coverage of people waiting outside Columbine High School with file footage of bloody victims from earlier shootings or running audio of the president lamenting national violence over video of crying children adds a cinematic flair to an already emotional story. Thus the format and editing techniques surrounding the news media's coverage of crises such as school shootings tends to blur the line between fact and fiction. The horrible irony, of course, is that such a confusion between reality and fantasy is exactly what many people accuse the school shooters of enacting.

When school shootings occur, the media coverage itself tends to embody several of the thought patterns underlying hatred. First, the media normally portray the killer or killers as evil and other than "us." Especially in the early days of the story when little is known of the killer, the media reduce the person only to the act of the killing and to traits that seem to be related to the violence—a love of violent games or films, for example. Granted, the killing is the heart of the news event. But it must be remembered that the media ultimately have the power to shape the story. By relying on absolutism and techniques of dehumanization, the media very often paint the killer as somehow other than the rest of us, as a demon living amongst us.

Yet, in doing so, the media fail to encourage us to see how very human and like us the killer may have been. I would suggest that it is only in seeing how "of us" school shooters are that we ever will discover the secret of preventing troubled youth from acting out in such horrible bursts of violence. This is because years or months or even moments before turning violent and becoming a monster in our eyes, a window of opportunity for intervention in the life of a young *person* exists. When in our outrage we focus only on the act of a monster killing one of "us," we sacrifice the potential to understand better the warning signs the next time one of "us" is becoming a monster.

In the time that has passed since the Columbine massacre, we have learned that Eric Harris and Dylan Klebold fully understood that their crime would inspire a media frenzy. In mid-December 1999, several media outlets revealed details of videotapes Harris and Klebold made in the days, even moments, before attacking Columbine High School. Eight months after America saw yearbook photos of the killers and wondered who they were, the courts that released the tapes and the media that aired them provided a source for answers: Harris and Klebold in their own words on their own terms. Harris jokingly asks, "Isn't it fun to get the respect we deserve?" as national and even international audiences watch a troubled high-school boy speaking into a videocamcorder in his bedroom. Klebold portends, "Hollywood will want to do this story," as we all watch yet another scene in the media movie that now is *Columbine*.[12] None of the thirteen people Harris and Klebold slaughtered at Columbine High School had the opportunity to make a videotape before being murdered. Even if they had, they are not the stars of this particular show anyhow: Harris and Klebold are the lead characters in *Columbine*. And from the evidence on the tapes they themselves made, Harris and Klebold knew we all would watch them if they did something really horrific and, therefore, really newsworthy.

Finally, media coverage of acts of extreme violence does have the potential to make heroes of the killers in the eyes of some, it is to be hoped very small, audience sectors. Of course, this is not something over which the media can exert any control. Nevertheless, we should not ignore the real potential for copycat crimes and martyrdom as a result of media coverage. All across the United States in the days following the Columbine shootings, other students threatened their schools, donned black trench coats similar to those made notorious in Littleton and, in a few cases, actually attempted new acts of violence. If movies about school shootings are thought to be blueprints for disturbed youth, undoubtedly media coverage of actual school shootings can be blueprints for the next wave of child shooters.

In doing some of my research for this book, I was shocked by the number of sites on the Internet that can best be described as shrines to Colombine killers Eric Harris and Dylan Klebold. One young woman who calls herself a "Trenchcoatchic" writes on her personal Web page, "Right now, my biggest hero is Eric Harris. I love Eric Harris. I respect him. . . . As soon as the story came out, I fell deep into the dramatic story of Eric Harris and Dylan Klebold. Everyone thinks they were screwed up and twisted, I think they were only troubled. I really wish people would leave them the hell alone."[13] The teens who have erected such cyberspace monuments to Harris and Klebold seem to embrace the killers as soul mates because, as the Trenchcoatchic puts it, "I have seen the problems they had for 10 years." But how does she know what problems Harris and Klebold faced? From media coverage about them as the stars of *Columbine* of course.

Almost immediately as news of the Columbine shooting broke, allegations surfaced that the killers had been motivated by dark forces within popular culture. Teens who knew Harris and Klebold reported that both young men had been particularly interested in violent movies and video games. As details of the crime became known, the similarity of the killers' plan of attack with a scene from the movie *The Basketball Diaries* led some people to point the finger of blame at the film itself. As I have said before, crimes such as school shootings are far too complex to allow the neat identification of causes. Nevertheless, that Harris and Klebold were known to be fans of a film that contains a scene very similar to their crime does warrant some consideration of the film not as motivation for committing the crime but perhaps as a model for the nature of the crime.

Scott Kalvert directed the 1995 film *The Basketball Diaries*.[14] Although the film itself was written by Bryan Goluboff, it is based rather closely on the semi-autobiographical novel of the same name published by Jim Carroll in 1978. Carroll himself stars in the film, with critically acclaimed actor Leonardo DiCaprio playing the lead role of Carroll as a teen. The film traces Carroll's descent from high-school athletic stardom into heroin addiction, prostitution, and emotional despair.

The scene of the film that has been the target of great critique as a result of the Columbine shooting, however, is one in which DiCaprio's character fantasizes a violent assault of his schoolmates. In the scene, DiCaprio is seen entering a classroom. He is wearing a long, black coat that, we quickly learn, conceals a large gun. Standing before the class, a chalkboard his backdrop, DiCaprio raises the gun from the folds of the coat and opens fire on the students.

The similarity of this scene to eyewitness accounts of Harris and Klebold's assault on the students and staff of Columbine High School is striking. But what does the scene actually tell its audiences about hatred and violence? On some levels, the scene and the entire movie seem to legitimize hatred. In the fantasy scene, as the young Jim Carroll attacks the class, he is a mid-1990s version of the cowboy hero, committing violence for the larger good of ridding the world of undesirables. His actions may be despised, but his motives are moral: the ends justify the means.

More generally, director Scott Kalvert met with a fundamental problem of morality tales when creating *The Basketball Diaries*: how does one show the horrors of the life of a heroin addict without showing the life of a heroin addict; how does one show the horror of a sick mind without exposing the audience to that mind? *The Basketball Diaries* graphically portrays the street life Carroll fell into as his addiction took control of his life. That is the subject of the film. Significantly, the overall message of the film is that drugs, and the violence and degradation surrounding drug abuse, are bad. Nevertheless, to make this point Kalvert must showcase the very subjects the movie deplores. Of course, Kalvert is not alone in facing this dilemma. Directors, lyricists, gangsta rappers, and authors (myself included) face it daily. So do teachers and parents who wrestle with questions about how to talk to their children about such topics as drugs and sex so as to inform them about realities and risks without tempting them with taboos.

While some elements of *The Basketball Diaries* embody mixed messages about hatred and violence, a couple of features of this movie actually seem designed to dethrone as a hero a person who is in fact violent. First, the school shooting fantasy scene itself is filmed much of the time from the perspective of a person conceivably in the line of fire of DiCaprio's character. The audience thus does not always look through the killer's eyes but, rather, often *at* the killer. We see him. We see the gun emerge. We see him train it at his victims. We ask ourselves if we will be one of them? This choice of camera angle discourages the audience from sympathizing with the killer's actions. Second, the scene clearly is portrayed as a dream sequence—specifically as a drug-induced fantasy—within the movie. To the extent that the movie centers on the character of the young Jim Carroll as the sympathetic lead, *The Basketball Diaries* lets us share his fantasies *as fantasies*. We understand him better for having seen the fantasy sequence, but because we understand him and sympathize with him, we recognize that he is *not* a killer. *The Basketball Diaries* does show an act of extreme violence, but it does not overtly glorify the act as so many movies do these days. If anything, the tale of Jim Carroll, fantasies and all, is presented as a morality tale arguing against a life of drugs, violence, and sexual promiscuity.

By all accounts, Harris and Klebold were fascinated by *The Basketball Diaries*. The way they staged their attack on Columbine High School certainly does resemble the school shooting fantasized by the character of Jim Carroll in that movie. A closer look at the movie itself indicates that *The Basketball Diaries* seems to send two contradictory messages about hatred and violence. On the one hand, the movie sets Carroll up within the fantasy sequence in a role similar to that of the cowboy hero icon of old. In this role his use of any means necessary, including extreme violence, is justified because he is the hero of his own fantasies; if he kills someone, they "deserved" to be killed. On the other hand, the movie is constructed to discourage sympathy with someone who actually commits such violence. If Harris and Klebold did imitate the school shooting scene from *The Basketball Diaries*, they missed the larger point of the life of Jim Carroll told in the film. Of course, it is no solace to the victims of Columbine to know that Harris and Klebold apparently misunderstood the movie on which they seemingly based their attack.

Music is another area of popular culture identified by many as a likely inspiration for the Columbine massacre. Specific allegations have been leveled against Marilyn Manson, middle America's favorite source of "evil" in the late 1990s, and the German bands Rammstein and KMFDM, both of which appear to have been popular with Harris and Klebold. As I mentioned in the previous chapter, Marilyn Manson proves rather problematic for detractors because the band is so overtly theatrical; teenagers seem to understand that Manson is an *act* even if adults do not. Additionally, while the entire Gothic scene surrounding Manson surely is one of doom and gloom, it is such a self-consciously glamorized version of tragedy that it seems to reverse on itself and become fun, in some cases fully comedic, for teens who are into being goth. The images Manson attaches to their music in videos certainly are dismal and, perhaps most accurately, creepy, but they are not violent per se. The lead singer cavorts about in leather and rubber outfits that probably feel more tortuous even than they look. His painted face grimaces as he sings "shocking" lyrics that attack traditional American social structures and religious ideals. But he does not physically attack other people.

To be sure, the sight and sound of Marilyn Manson is something to behold. Frankly, even though I myself forayed into punkdom as a teen, if I ran into the Manson band members in a dark alley these days I would probably faint! But just for a second. Because I think I'd almost immediately notice that they are an act and a very obvious and self-aware act at that. Do Marilyn Manson music and videos contribute to our culture of death? Without a doubt, because the group revels in imagery derived from sadomasochism, vampirism, and Nazism, among other sources. But in sharp contrast to many other musical groups, as well as films and video games, Marilyn Manson invites teen fans to dress up and play at spooky for an evening or even for the duration of a rebellious phase, not necessarily to embrace hatred and violence as a normal part of everyday life.

In contrast to Manson, however, are the German industrial rock bands Harris and Klebold apparently favored. Unlike Manson's version of extreme shock-rock, both Rammstein and KMFDM present a more "normal" front. Thus while it is possible that they are every bit as much a piece of theater as Marilyn Manson, they are not so easily identified (by teens especially) as "just an act." Rammstein, in particular, portray themselves in their visual imagery with a gritty realism. The video for "Du Hast" ("You Hate"), which marked their breakthrough with American audiences, resembles a Quentin Tarantino movie.[15] The video follows a group of ordinary looking men and a rather typical looking female cohort through a variety of scenes. Staged in a relatively bleak semirural setting the characters ultimately converge in a horrific shoot-out. Yet while we see the shoot-out and falling victims, we are not really invited to witness the victims' pain. As in so many videos, television shows, and films these days, the video for "Du Hast" portrays the commission of violence as a typical part of life but does not honestly tell us the story of the victims.

There are two important differences between Rammstein and filmmakers such as Tarantino. First, Tarantino shows both sides of violence. One of the most striking qualities of his films is the focus on the aftermath of violence. Whereas other video and film directors show shooting, Tarantino also makes us see being shot. I suspect I am not alone in how vividly I can recall the image of the man who lay dying, completely soaked in his own blood, for virtually the entire duration of the film *Reservoir Dogs*.[16] Tarantino does not let us pretend that being shot does not hurt. He makes us see the pain of violence. Media images of violence too often do not follow the action-packed excitement of a gun battle through to the reality of physical agony for the victim and emotional heartache for the victim's family and friends. Stories that fail to tell us the results of violence can encourage us to forget the results of violence. For adults, this pattern can cause desensitization as we lose sight of the victims' suffering. For children, however, this pattern can actually promote a deadly flaw in their cause-effect thinking: if children rarely see a gun shot cause pain, suffering, death, grief, they begin to lose sight of the very real dangers of gun violence.[17] The second great difference between Tarantino's work and the gritty reality of the Rammstein video, of course, is that Tarantino's movies carry R ratings, while Rammstein's "Du Hast" ran in regular rotation on MTV.

In the wake of the Columbine High School shootings, much attention was paid by the media to violent video games as another possible causal factor in Eric Harris and Dylan Klebold's decision to kill. Specifically, games such as *Doom* and *Duke Nukem* were criticized for their extreme levels of graphic violence. In the videotapes made by the Columbine killers prior to the shootings, Harris predicts, "It'll be like fucking *Doom*."[18] Of course, graphic portrayals of violence have been a part of popular culture in varying degrees for centuries. The Roman's threw *real* Christians to the lions. The Puritans burned *real* women accused of witchcraft. Duke Nukem does not *kill* anyone—both he and his victims are nothing more than computer-generated images. So in some sense such games mark great progress for humanity in that most of us now perform our violence inside the safety of virtual reality instead of actually committing it upon others.[19]

However, even if we do not actually kill when engaging in such play, we are still engaging in some of the emotional processes of killing. Popular games such as *Doom* and *Duke Nukem* transport the player into a first-person perspective as the killer. Unlike old arcade favorites in which players watched all the characters, including the one they controlled with the joystick, most violent video games today require players to see through the killer's eyes. This new wave of first-person video games allows or, if you prefer, demands players to rehearse the emotional stages of killing. If not, if the games truly are not emotionally intense performances of violence, then why do players become angry and nervous when being pursued and experience feelings of power and pride when destroying the enemy? It is clear that violent video games are enjoyable because they allow their players to act out such emotions and, by acting them out, purge themselves of pent-up feelings of rage in a safe and socially accepted manner.

But the only way we can act out the emotional highs and lows of violence is also in some way to engage in the thought patterns of dehumanization. Video-game villains thus come in one of two general forms: they are either generic bad guys who have no humanity because they have no individual character traits or mythic opponents whose traits are so inflated as to be superhuman and therefore not really human. When we play video games, then, we are invited to *kill* bad guys, which is morally acceptable. The problem is that in such games everyone other than the player's character is a bad guy worthy of death. Unlike military uses of dehumanization tactics in which "us" and "them" are defined by the sides of war, today's violent video games tend to dehumanize *everyone* else—instead of us versus them, first-person video games transport players into the world of me versus them. In such a world only the player retains humanity.

The horror of Columbine was its reality—the way in which it appeared to take the images from a computer game and enact them in real life. We will never know exactly what went through the minds of Eric Harris and Dylan Klebold as they prowled the hallways of Columbine High School terrorizing students, teachers, and staff members. But I think we can safely make a couple of assumptions about their thoughts. They did not look into the eyes of those they killed and recognize "us." They did not identify with the humanity they shared with their victims.

So too we no longer can identify with the humanity we shared with them. Harris and Klebold now are monsters—evil, savage, inhuman. By virtue of their crimes, they are no longer of "us." We wish they were alive only so that we as a society could kill them for having killed so many of us.

Dehumanizing thought patterns aren't just something "they" do. They are deep inside all of "us."

As a society, we publicly attest that we deplore hatred and violence. Yet hatred and violence seem to be a central theme in virtually all avenues of American popular culture as we begin the twenty-first century. We tell our children that gangs are bad, but we pay no attention as they become fans of gangsta rap. We tell our children that killers such as Harris and Klebold are monsters, but we buy our children games like *Doom* for a birthday present. Is it really any wonder that some children become confused when all of us are receiving and sending such contradictory messages?

In the wake of horrible crimes such as the Columbine school shooting, we gather as a nation in front of our television screens and mourn not only the loss of more children but also the loss of our own comfortable faith that something like that can't happen to someone like us. Columbine and all the other school shootings have made most of us realize that it can happen to *us*.

And thus we mourn together through the media when tragedy strikes. We pray that there never will be another Columbine.

And I share in this prayer. Yet I wonder why it is that it takes thirteen victims at Columbine to make us outraged when *fifty-six children die from gunfire in this country every single week.*[20] I wonder why we mourn as a nation the eleven children who died in Pearl and West Paducah and Edinboro and Springfield and Jonesboro, when we do not mourn the *eleven children who die every forty-eight hours in America as a result of family violence.*[21]

What does it take to get our attention and hold it? How tough do we all have to become before we say, "Enough!"?

CHAPTER 5

Glamorized Hatred:
Our Obsession with Serial Killers

The atmosphere of old-fashioned serenity and security drew me to the small town in which I reside. Yet only a few weeks after I first moved here in the early 1990s, news spread that a young girl was missing. Ten year-old Ronnie Eichstedt disappeared while riding her bicycle on an autumn Sunday afternoon. Immediately police and hundreds of volunteers combed the countryside in search of the little girl. As the days wore on and we all resigned ourselves to the reality that Ronnie had been abducted, one of my teaching colleagues commented, "Sometimes I am embarrassed to be human." That line—"sometimes I am embarrassed to be human"—echoed through my mind months later when I heard the local radio announcer report that Ronnie's body had been found.

No crimes inspire our rage and our terror like the patterned murder sprees known as serial killings. Like animals in the wild, serial killers stalk their victims. Like demons, serial killers subject their victims to hellish ritual torments. Yet serial killers are neither animals nor demons: they are humans. Serial killers are of "us" no matter how rigorously we deny them. Serial killers are of "us" no matter if we lock them away for life or put them to death. Serial killers are of "us" and that intimate and undeniable fact is what lends such tragic profundity to the remark "sometimes I am embarrassed to be human."

Although we humans have killed each other since the dawn of our existence, the public apparently only became aware of serial killings quite recently. London's notorious Jack the Ripper case in the late nineteenth century marked the first serial killing spree to receive widespread notice. As mass media technologies advanced in the twentieth century, news of outrageous crimes spread quickly and often took on a sensationalistic air. Americans, in particular, developed a fascination with both real and imagined stories about serial killers.

Yet in some ways any form of media coverage of serial killers glorifies hatred and violence in their most extreme forms. In this chapter I explore America's fascination with serial killers and how that fascination is served by the media. First, I consider just how prominent the image of the serial killer has become in popular culture. I then consider the case of Ed Gein, one of the first American serial killers to be the focus of national media attention. Finally, I examine in detail the case of Jeffrey Dahmer, the Milwaukee killer who captivated America's attention in the early 1990s. Specifically, I hope to demonstrate how particular styles of media story-telling encourage us to perceive killers like Dahmer to be celebrities. To do this I need to walk readers through the gruesome details of these cases. I ask readers to understand that my purpose here is not to sensationalize violence but rather to unmask how violence is sensationalized in our popular culture.

SERIAL KILLERS IN POPULAR CULTURE

Perhaps it is no coincidence that the nation with the most elaborate mass media has also produced the most serial killers of any nation in the world. Images of serial killers are a mainstay of American popular culture. Beyond news coverage of actual serial killings, movies, books, television programs, songs, and video games feature serial killers as stock characters. What follows is a quick survey of some of the most well-known images of serial killers in American popular culture.

Since Charles Manson's followers committed the Tate/LaBianca murders in 1969, Manson himself has come to define our idea of the serial murderer.[1] The crimes themselves, of course, were heinous. Actress Sharon Tate was eight months pregnant when the Manson family stabbed her to death and left four other victims strewn haphazardly about the Tate residence. The next night, the Manson family attacked Leon and Rosemary LaBianca as they lay sleeping in their bed. At both scenes the murderers smeared bloody graffiti on the walls. One of the ghastly messages, "Helter Skelter," is now synonymous with acts of outrageous violence.

When Charles Manson stood trial for first-degree murder and conspiracy to commit murder in June 1970, media coverage of the high profile case introduced Manson to the world. Manson's courtroom antics confounded observers. He carved an X into his forehead. He taunted jurors, witnesses, even observers. He often disrupted the proceedings in what many felt were attempts to draw media attention away from evidence against him. At one point, an incensed Manson actually lunged for the judge screaming, "someone should cut your head off!"[2] Manson and the female members of the family standing trial with him shaved their heads for the reading of the verdict. More than nine and a half months after the trial started, the jury found all defendants guilty and sentenced them to death. Because the California Supreme Court abolished the death penalty in 1972, however, the Manson family defendants are now serving life sentences.

Although Manson has been behind bars since 1970, he remains a prominent figure in popular culture. The infotainment media continue to air interviews with Manson in which he continues to fascinate us with his bizarre mannerisms and theories and, of course, those haunting eyes. Today he sports a swastika on his forehead. Several fortunes no doubt have been made over the years from sales of books such as *Helter Skelter* and the many other accounts of life within the Manson family.[3] One of the most controversial rock acts of recent years, Marilyn Manson, created their ear-catching name by marrying two icons of the twentieth century, the glamorous Marilyn Monroe and the glamorized Charles Manson.

Yet aside from continued coverage of Charles Manson and allusions to "Manson" as a symbol, the enduring legacy of the Manson family is the central role images of serial murder now play in our mass consciousness. The sensationalized Manson trial proved to the media, and more critically to advertisers, that we will tune in to see real horror stories. The Manson family demonstrated the wide market for serial killing in America. Apparently Charles Manson is more intriguing to us than other "real" news characters such as presidents and members of Congress. And fictional stories about serial killers are more terrifying than old-style horror stories such as *The Blob* and *Godzilla*.

Since the days of helter skelter in 1969, Hollywood has served up a buffet of movies and television programs featuring serial killings. In the 1990s, two such films drew extensive public notice. The critical acclaim surrounding the 1991 release of *Silence of the Lambs* had all of America talking about Hannibal Lecter and all of Hollywood talking about Oscar potential.[4] Directed by Jonathan Demme, *Silence of the Lambs* traces agents of the FBI's Behavioral Science Unit as they attempt to locate a young woman being held prisoner by a serial killer code-named Buffalo Bill because he skins his victims. Agent Starling, played by Jodie Foster, seeks assistance on the case from incarcerated serial killer and psychiatrist Hannibal Lecter, played by Anthony Hopkins. Starling learns from Lecter that she will only be able to catch the killer by learning to think as he thinks. In the case of Buffalo Bill, not until Starling understands *why* he skins his victims is she able to save the woman held hostage in a pit in his basement.

Whereas *Silence of the Lambs* invites viewers into the mind of the serial killer as read by FBI agents, *Natural Born Killers* invites viewers to witness America's reaction to a killing spree.[5] In 1994 controversy swirled around director Oliver Stone's film, which some argued was too graphically violent for general release and others argued glamorized serial killing for young viewers. Significantly though, *Natural Born Killers* itself does not glamorize violence; rather, the film centers around how violence is already glamorized in our society. Stone forces us really to see our own obsession with criminal celebrity when he displays before our eyes a story of the media's pursuit of fictional serial killers Mickey and Mallory Knox. In *Natural Born Killers*, the media, and with it the public, stalk Mickey and Mallory just as serial killers stalk their victims.

Of course, no discussion of images of serial killers in American popular culture would be complete without *Psycho*.[6] Alfred Hitchcock's 1960 thriller remains the standard against which all films of the genre are judged. Unlike more recent fare such as *Silence of the Lambs* and *Natural Born Killers*, Hitchcock's movie did not need to find an angle on the serial killing phenomenon: simply telling the story of a serial killer was itself a revolutionary new twist in film-making that left an indelible mark on the American psyche. The infamous motel shower scene, in which the as yet unseen killer slays the female traveler portrayed by actress Janet Leigh, still inhabits the nightmares of millions of American moviegoers.

Psycho tells the story of Norman Bates, a lonely and apparently naïve young man who operates the Bates Motel, a roadside hostel in a rather deserted area. Products of Norman's hobby, taxidermy, decorate the motel lobby. Although we do not see her face, we learn that Norman's domineering mother seems to dictate nearly all of his actions. As secondary characters in the film are murdered, we become suspicious of Norman. Ultimately, Hitchcock reveals Norman's secret: he long ago killed his mother and now kills others as "directed" to him by her corpse, which he had stuffed as his ultimate taxidermy project.

For nearly half a century, images of serial killers have figured prominently in American popular culture. From the legendary *Psycho* in 1960 to contemporary classics such as *Silence of the Lambs* and *Natural Born Killers*, tales of serial killings have become an entertainment mainstay not just with B-caliber horror flick buffs but with the general audience. If *Psycho* remains the standard for films about serial killers, the sensationalism surrounding Charles Manson and the Manson family remains the standard for media coverage of serial killers. Whether fictional or real, these most extreme and grotesque acts of violence have been fascinating American audiences for years.

THE REAL THING: MEET EDDIE GEIN

It would be comforting to think that movie madmen like *Psycho*'s Norman Bates and *Silence of the Lambs*'s Buffalo Bill were born in the imaginations of Hollywood directors. Unfortunately, Hitchcock and Demme modeled both Norman Bates and Buffalo Bill on Eddie Gein, the first American serial killer to captivate the world audience.[7]

Until police approached the Gein farmstead on November 17, 1957, the people who lived in and around Plainfield, Wisconsin, knew Eddie Gein as a quiet and slightly peculiar neighbor. Born in the larger city of LaCrosse, Wisconsin, in 1906, Gein moved to Plainfield as a boy with his parents, George and Augusta, and his older brother, Henry. Augusta Gein ruled her family with an iron fist, tolerating no dissension from either of her sons or from her mealy-mouthed, alcoholic husband. Augusta practiced her own stark brand of religion and indoctrinated her sons early on with her puritanical views about sin.

Augusta Gein was determined that her sons would not condemn themselves to hell by falling prey to worldly temptations. In fact, it was Augusta's concern that her boys would be corrupted by influences in LaCrosse that led her to relocate the family to an isolated farm outside the small town of Plainfield. Augusta taught her boys that all sexual activity was sinful. She endeavored to shield them from contact with all women other than herself and forbade them ever to date or to marry. Henry and Eddie had almost no contact with neighbors as children, and because they worshipped at the altar of Augusta Gein did not even socialize with others at church.

School provided Henry and Eddie their only opportunity to interact with people outside their immediate family. Eddie was an average student but terribly shy and awkward. He enjoyed reading and rarely associated with other children when at school. When he did, his efforts to reach out were thwarted. His classmates teased the quiet and oddly effeminate boy. Augusta dashed any hopes he had of making lasting friends by barring him from spending time with his peers beyond the hours in school required by law. Eddie found his only escape from his loneliness and his mother's constant verbal abuse in pulp adventure tales.

When George Gein died in 1940, Augusta allowed Henry and Eddie to venture off the farm to supplement the family's meager income. Eddie took on odd jobs as a handyman and became one of Plainfield's most sought-after baby-sitters. No doubt because of his peculiar upbringing, Eddie remained childlike in many ways and had an instant rapport with the children he tended. As the brothers Gein appeared in town more frequently, they earned a reputation as polite and responsible workers.

As the years wore on after George's death, Henry apparently began to challenge Augusta's authority. Torn between his love for his brother and only friend and his idolization of his mother, Eddie began his pilgrimage into the annals of American crime. In the spring of 1944, a brush fire threatened the Gein farm. Henry and Eddie labored feverishly to extinguish the flames and, according to Eddie, separated from each other to attack the fire more efficiently. Hours later Eddie called local police to report that he could not find his brother and feared Henry had been consumed by the fire. Yet when police arrived at the farm, Eddie immediately led them to his brother's body. Henry Gein lay dead on ground untouched by the brush fire. His head was severely bruised. At the time, police never seriously considered that Henry may have been the victim of foul play; such a thought seemed ludicrous in a small town like Plain-field in the innocent era of the 1940s.

As Eddie grieved the loss of his brother and, most now suspect, his own role in his brother's death, Augusta suffered a series of strokes and died on December 29, 1945. Gein's primary biographer, Harold Schechter, notes in *Deviant*, that from that day forward Eddie Gein "was absolutely alone in the world."[8] Gein withdrew from all but two rooms of the farmhouse, living only in the kitchen and a small side room he used for sleeping. The rest of the house remained exactly as it had been at the moment of Augusta's death, a shrine to Eddie's love for her.

Few of us can conceive, thankfully, the depths of loneliness Eddie Gein must have felt following his mother's death. He never ventured out to make new friends. Never in his life did he approach a woman romantically or sexually. With all members of his family gone, Eddie's only companions were his books and magazines. He lost himself in adventure tales. He developed a particular fondness for stories of South Seas pirates and a particular fascination with reports of tribal customs in the area. Eddie studied anatomy books to better understand how some South Seas islanders shrunk the heads of their enemies and how others exhumed cadavers as part of elaborate death rituals.

Somehow, in some way we will never really understand, Eddie's twisted upbringing and his interests in death rituals converged on his loneliness: he sought solace at the local cemetery. For years, Eddie followed the obituary column in the local newspaper. Late in the night, under cover of darkness, Eddie would dig up the remains of newly deceased women. At first, Eddie simply would sit with a corpse in the silence of the graveyard, then gently replace the body and recover the casket. In time, he began to remove souvenirs from the bodies.

Not until after Gein became a household name across America did anyone in Plainfield know local graves ever had been disturbed. Neither did anyone suspect Eddie Gein's ghoulish late-night hobby. A neighbor boy was the first to notice something odd was going on in Eddie Gein's house. Yet when he told people he'd seen real shrunken heads in Gein's kitchen, they laughed at him and assured him Gein must have been teasing him with novelty items. As talk of the shrunken heads spread around the town, Eddie himself talked about his morbid collection at the town store. The people of Plainfield, of course, assumed their normally quiet neighbor must have been joking with them.

But the people of Plainfield and of the entire world soon realized that

Eddie Gein was not joking when he mentioned his collection. On November 17, 1957, local police arrived at the Gein farm to question Eddie about the disappearance of Bernice Worden and the robbery of her hardware store. Although no one had ever accused Eddie of a crime in his life, he was the last person seen entering the store; a receipt in his name was found near the cash register.

On arriving at the farm, Sheriff Arthur Schley visually surveyed the now dilapidated exterior of the house. Antique equipment, tools, furniture, and boxes lay about the yard and porch. Amid the unusual level of clutter, the Sheriff spied a typical sight during the peak of Wisconsin's deer hunting season: a headless carcass was drawn up by the feet, gutted, and hanging from the rafters of the porch to drain. When Sheriff Schley drew closer, he realized that the carcass was not that of a deer but of Bernice Worden.

Inside, police dug through years of accumulated filth in the two rooms Gein inhabited. They found cereal in a bowl fashioned from a human skull, lamp shades and wastebaskets formed from stretched human skin, and even an armchair upholstered in human flesh. As they continued their search, they uncovered four noses, a human heart, a head, a shoe box filled with vaginas, and a belt made of nipples. Finally, they made the most startling discovery of all, the one that defined the screen character Buffalo Bill: Eddie Gein had made himself a "woman suit." Gein later would explain to authorities that he would attire himself in the suit to feel as if he had breasts and female genitalia. Wearing nothing but the suit, he would wander about outside in the night.

Police found remains of ten people in the Gein house. Initially, Eddie admitted only to killing Bernice Worden, but he soon also confessed to having abducted and murdered Mary Hogan, a bartender from the nearby town of Wild Rose who had been missing for some time. Police were hesitant to believe Gein's claim that he actually had removed all the other bodies from their graves. After much controversy surrounding the ethics of the plan, police followed Eddie to the Plainfield cemetery where he pointed out which graves he had violated. Clear evidence of tampering was revealed on each coffin workers uncovered.

To this day, no one really understands how Eddie Gein managed to exhume eight bodies without raising suspicions. Some people believe he may have been assisted by a mentally handicapped man who worked at the cemetery, but no hard proof of that claim ever materialized. Gein himself claimed that he simply entered the cemetery after dark, dug quietly with a small spade and his hands, used various tools to open the coffins, removed the bodies to his truck, then quickly refilled the hole. Because he only desired fresh corpses, the ground covering the graves still was loose and bare; therefore, no one detected the graves had been violated.

In the end, prosecutors charged Eddie Gein with two counts of first-degree murder in the cases of Bernice Worden and Mary Hogan. The state of Wisconsin crime lab proved that remains of eight other victims found at his home belonged to bodies originally buried in the cemetery and thus that Gein could not have murdered the women. An eleventh body found buried on Gein's property was never identified. Police suspect Gein probably murdered several people who vanished in that area of Wisconsin in the 1940s and 1950s but have never been able to find their bodies. Gein himself stuck by his claim only to have murdered Worden and Hogan.

Not surprisingly, when police announced what they had uncovered in Eddie Gein's house, a media frenzy ensued. Reporters from all over the world descended on the tiny town of Plainfield. Although most local residents at first seemed hostile to the intrusion into their grief and dismay, many gradually warmed to the press and offered interviews. Newspapers and magazines worldwide told the story of Eddie Gein, the quiet little man who baby-sat for his neighbors yet was really a monster.

While his former neighbors talked about Eddie with the press, Eddie himself talked to psychiatrists at the Central State Hospital for the Criminally Insane. Gein was declared mentally unfit to stand trial. Doctors diagnosed Gein as a sexual psychopath, noting that his peculiar upbringing in general and his mother's near constant berating of him to avoid sexuality combusted in adulthood when he found himself alone on the farm. Eddie's need to create and wear his "woman suit" resulted from unchecked impulses toward transvestitism and fetishism as well as his limitless devotion to the mother who had abused him so horribly and polluted his thinking. Had he not been caught, it is unknown if Eddie would have killed again. The murders of Worden and Hogan may simply have been a means for him to acquire more materials for his woman suit when fresh graves were not available.

Eddie still was under care of the doctors at the Central State Hospital when his property went up for auction. Not since the case itself had broken had so many people traveled to Plainfield. The auctioneering company charged fifty cents admission of anyone who wanted to view the contents of the house. Outraged, the families of Gein's victims attempted to stop the sale. Although the auctioneer stopped charging the browser's fee, the sale itself went on as planned. The 1949 Ford truck Gein used to haul bodies to the farm sold for more than seven hundred dollars. For years, the truck toured America on the carnival circuit under the heading "Gein's Ghoul Car." Very early on the morning of March 20, 1958, the Plainfield Volunteer Fire Department was summoned to the Gein farm: the now empty house was ablaze. The firefighters and local townspeople watched quietly as Gein's house fell into ashes, an impromptu final eulogy for his victims.

In the late 1960s, Eddie Gein was finally declared fit to stand trial for the murder of Bernice Worden. After about a week of testimony, the judge found Gein guilty. However, Gein was soon acquitted on grounds that he had been insane at the time the murder itself took place. The court remanded Gein to the custody of doctors at the Central State Hospital for the Criminally Insane where he lived out his life.

Gein apparently was happier during his years at the hospital than he ever had been in his life. He remained largely to himself but was no longer alone. He chatted with his doctors, read books, and performed the various chores to which he was assigned. Never once did he cause any disruptions or require sedation. However, for the remainder of his years he did stare at female nurses in a peculiar manner and attempt to avoid most contact with them. Eddie Gein died of cancer on July 26, 1984. He was buried next to his mother, Augusta, in the Plainfield cemetery, a few paces away from the graves he had desecrated.

The Eddie Gein case riveted audiences in the 1950s and, through cinematic interpretations, continues to rivet audiences as we begin the twenty-first century. Yet what was it about Eddie Gein that made the whole world take notice? At the most basic level, we follow coverage of horrible crimes for the same reason we slow down to look as we pass the scene of a traffic accident: we humans seem to have an innate curiosity about the morbid. Perhaps because death is both inevitable and, largely, uncontrollable, we compulsively explore graphic displays of death.

On another level, cases such as that of Eddie Gein draw us in because they offer us a chance not simply to confront but to emasculate our fears. Just as little children fear invisible monsters lurking beneath their beds, we adults fear monsters living invisibly among us. Serial killers spark a particular fear in us not simply because of their horrendous acts of violence but because their ingenuity and stealth enable them to live in our midst, to prey on us without raising our suspicions. Serial killers only become *serial* killers because they successfully elude notice. Thus we fear a serial killer *may* be in our midst at any moment, just as a child fears a monster always *could* be hiding under the bed. On those rare occasions when police offer up an actual serial killer to public scrutiny, we are able to see the reality of the man instead of our nightmarish image of the monster. No matter how horrific the crimes, the serial killer once apprehended is a man, just a man, a beaten man, shackled and locked safely away from us forever.

Fictionalized accounts of serial killers in books and movies advance this process one step farther by allowing us not simply to see the killer but to control him. News media coverage of Eddie Gein in the 1950s exposed the monster; *Psycho* put him in a cage. Although movies such as *Psycho* terrify us, they also allow us safely to explore our greatest fears because they invite us, for a couple of hours, to encounter a serial killer in a way only his doomed victims normally do. Whether Norman Bates or Buffalo Bill is ready to stop his killing binge does not matter, because the director calls the shots. Movies about serial killers offer us a sense of control over the killers and, as a result, a sense of control over our own lives.

AMERICA'S NIGHTMARE: THE JEFFREY DAHMER CASE

Thirty years after police in Plainfield, Wisconsin, discovered Bernice Worden's butchered body hanging on Eddie Gein's porch, two officers patrolling Milwaukee's south side happened upon a young man fleeing down a darkened street with a handcuff dangling from one wrist. Terrified and barely able to explain the nightmare from which he had managed to escape, Tracy Edwards led the officers to the apartment of the "weird dude" who had held him captive and attempted to murder him. When the officers knocked on the door of apartment 213, Jeffrey Dahmer calmly invited them inside.[9]

Dahmer denied Edwards's allegations, instead claiming the two had been involved in mutually consensual sexual activities. He then politely offered to retrieve the handcuff key from his bedroom. But because Edwards warned the police that Dahmer had a knife in the bedroom, one of the officers entered the room himself in search of the key. Polaroid photos of corpses in various stages of evisceration and dismemberment lay scattered across a table and taped to the walls. The officer called to his partner to handcuff Dahmer immediately.

Suddenly, the calm and cooperative resident of apartment 213 transformed into the raging animal seen before only by the eighteen men he had killed. After a struggle, the officers managed to restrain Dahmer and began a preliminary search of the premises. They quickly realized that apartment 213 had been the scene of a hellish but tragically real nightmare. Human penises preserved in jars of formaldehyde lined a shelf. Filleted strips of human flesh nestled in the freezer. Human skulls formed a shrine in the living room. Decomposing body parts stewed in an acid bath in a fifty-five-gallon drum. A recently decapitated head stared out at investigators from a shelf in the refrigerator.

When America awoke to the Dahmer nightmare on July 22, 1991, no one imagined that the most inhuman elements of Dahmer's crimes had yet to be revealed. Neither could anyone conceive how Jeffrey Dahmer had managed to kill so many men for so many years without raising suspicions that a serial killer was active in the greater Milwaukee area. There are no satisfying answers to explain why Dahmer preyed on his fellow humans or why authorities allowed him to slip through their fingers so many times. But it is possible to find the key to understanding how media coverage of cases of extreme violence tend to make celebrities of the most repulsive members of our society.

Jeffrey Dahmer was born in Milwaukee on May 21, 1960, to Lionel and Joyce Dahmer. Joyce suffered from a variety of physical and emotional problems that often caused tension in the home. A chemist, Lionel used his work as an excuse to avoid his depressed and agitated wife and, as a result, his young son. Regardless of the tensions between his parents, Jeff seemed a normal and happy boy. When the family moved to Iowa so that Lionel could work toward his Ph.D., Jeff occupied himself with typical childhood pursuits like swimming and fishing. He loved spending time with the family pets and took great pride in having nursed an injured bird back to health.

Yet Lionel Dahmer believes, in hindsight, that evidence of Jeff's bizarre obsession with death surfaced very early. He recalls an occasion when he cleaned remains of some small animals from under the family's house. Four-year-old Jeff seemed transfixed by the bones. In *A Father's Story*, Lionel asks a question to which neither he nor the world ever will know the answer: was that the moment a future serial killer was born within the mind of a child?

Two years later Jeff was diagnosed with a double hernia that required surgery and a long recovery period. The ordeal changed the boy. The happy, rather outgoing lad began to withdraw into himself. When the family moved to Akron, Ohio, later the same year, the now shy Jeff failed to adjust to his new environment. He not only failed to make friends, he seemed reluctant even to approach other children.

Jeff finally started to come out of his shell in 1967 when the Dahmers moved to the suburb of Bath, Ohio. He quickly became friends with a boy named Lee and also developed a special attachment to his teacher. On one occasion Jeff presented his teacher with a bowlful of tadpoles, a heartfelt gift from a seven-year-old. Jeff was dismayed later to learn that the teacher in turn had given the tadpoles to his friend Lee. Jeff immediately visited Lee's house and killed the tadpoles. Perceiving the entire incident as a betrayal of his affections, Jeff reverted to his formerly reclusive ways.

After his arrest, Dahmer explained to investigators that it was around this time that he began to act on his fascination with death. Armed with plastic bags, he scoured the roads of Bath on his bicycle until he found the remains of dead animals. He enjoyed stripping flesh from the skeletons. He created his own secret animal cemetery in the woods behind his home. At one point he impaled the head of a dog on a stake and left it standing an ominous guard in the woods. In addition to his experiments on dead animals, Dahmer began to have sexual fantasies that troubled him deeply about committing a variety of sexual acts with other boys and with corpses.

Jeff became at once more lonely and more disturbed during his high-school years. An average student, Jeff had no real interest in school activities or his classmates. Unbeknownst to his parents, he began to consume enormous amounts of alcohol. His classmates considered him an alcoholic. Jeff binge drank frequently and even sneaked alcohol into school to guzzle during classes when his teachers were not looking.

During Jeff's senior year his already tumultuous life turned upside down when Lionel and Joyce divorced. The two engaged in an ugly custody battle over their younger son, David. Because Jeff had recently turned eighteen, he was not the subject of a legal contest. Yet as Joyce and Lionel avoided each other outside of court and concentrated their efforts on the fight for David, they seem almost to have forgotten Jeff. For weeks, Jeff lived alone in the family home with almost no money to buy food while Lionel resided with his new fiancée and Joyce took

David out of state. Truly alone for the first time, Jeff lost control of his dark impulses.

Shortly after he graduated from high school in the early summer of 1978, Jeffrey Dahmer killed for the first time. He had been out driving when he happened upon Steven Hicks, a hitchhiker close to his own age. He and Hicks returned to the Dahmer home where they drank heavily and had sex. However, when the hour grew late and Hicks prepared to leave, Dahmer flew into a rage, crashing a barbell down over Hicks's head. After his arrest in 1991, Dahmer explained that he had attacked Hicks to keep him from leaving; Dahmer simply could not bear being left alone in the house. No one knew Dahmer had killed Steven Hicks until he confessed to the crime in 1991. The night of the murder, Dahmer calmly dismembered the body and placed the pieces inside plastic bags, which he then sealed and buried in the woods behind the house. Steven Hicks's remains joined those of the many animals Dahmer had scavenged then buried in the yard as a child.

Dahmer lacked focus following the Hicks murder. He spent a semester at Ohio State University but flunked out. The few students who knew him later reported that he drank to the point of passing out virtually every day. He next tried the United States Army. Although he survived basic training with no major infractions, once stationed in Germany Dahmer became a problem for his fellow soldiers. Dahmer drank often and heavily. After a couple of years the Army discharged him because his alcoholism kept him from doing his job. Dahmer spent a brief period living in Florida following his discharge then returned to the house in Bath, Ohio. There he exhumed the already dismembered remains of Steven Hicks, pulverized the bones, then scattered the fragments in the woods.

When local police arrested Jeff on charges of drunk and disorderly conduct in the autumn of 1981, Lionel Dahmer lost patience with his listless and trouble-making son. Lionel arranged for Jeff to move in with his grandmother in the Milwaukee suburb of West Allis. Because Jeff had always been particularly close to his grandmother, Lionel hoped she could influence the young man to give up his drinking and settle into a more productive life. On the surface, it appeared the plan was working: Jeff found a job, spent many hours talking with his grandmother, and seemed to rein in his drinking. For several years the Dahmer family believed Jeff was finally turning his life around.

Then, in September of 1986, Jeffrey Dahmer had his first encounter with the Milwaukee police: he was arrested for masturbating in front of two young boys in a park. Because he had only the drunk and disorderly conduct charge on his record, the court only sentenced him to one year of probation. Within that year, Dahmer killed his second victim.

Dahmer met Steven Toumi in a gay bar in downtown Milwaukee. The two men talked and drank for many hours before checking into a hotel. Although Dahmer willingly confessed the most graphic details of his other murders, he told investigators in 1991 that he had no memory of murdering Toumi. According to Dahmer, when he awoke the next morning he discovered Toumi's bruised and bloody body next to him in the bed. He left the hotel, purchased a very large suitcase at a nearby store, returned to the hotel, and stuffed Toumi's body into the bag. He then checked out of the hotel with luggage in tow. Dahmer returned to his quarters in the basement of his grandmother's house where he had sex with Toumi's corpse and masturbated on the body. He then dismembered the remains and threw the pieces, sealed in plastic garbage bags, into the trash.

While nine years separated Dahmer's first and second murders, only a few months separated the second from the third. Dahmer's third victim, Jamie Doxtator, was only fourteen years old. Doxtator was well-known among regular patrons of Milwaukee's gay bars. The youth loitered in front of the bars hoping to forge relationships with the older men as they entered and exited. Doxtator made an easy target for Dahmer, who offered the boy money to pose for some photographs. Once he had Doxtator in his lair, Dahmer drugged the fourteen-year-old then strangled him to death. He sexually violated Doxtator's corpse before dismembering and disposing of the remains. By this time, the essential elements of Dahmer's pattern as a serial killer had become fixed.

By the summer of 1988, Jeffrey Dahmer had killed four people. Although his grandmother had no knowledge of his heinous crimes, she had become frustrated with his increasingly more frequent late-night carousing. As summer turned to fall, she asked Jeff to find another place to live. Dahmer moved into his own apartment in Milwaukee on September 25. On September 26 he offered a thirteen-year-old Laotian boy in his new neighborhood fifty dollars to pose for photographs. Soon after getting the boy into his new apartment Dahmer drugged and fondled him. When the boy returned home in an altered state of mind, his parents rushed him to the hospital where lab tests confirmed their suspicion that their son had been drugged. Milwaukee police arrested Dahmer while he was at work at the Ambrosia Chocolate Factory. Although he claimed he had no idea how young the boy was, Dahmer pled guilty to second-degree sexual assault.

Dahmer returned to his grandmother's house while awaiting sentencing. In the brief time he was there he killed again. Dahmer added a morbid new twist to his pattern with the murder of Anthony Sears: he began his collection of souvenirs. He first decapitated Sears and then boiled the head to remove all flesh from the skull. Fearing detection, he meticulously painted the skull gray so that anyone who saw it would assume it to be a plastic model. Yet he displayed the skull openly in his room. When alone he masturbated in front of the skull, which he apparently regarded as a sexual shrine.

Dahmer appeared before the judge on the second-degree sexual assault charge in May 1989. He argued that the crime resulted directly from his abuse of alcohol and vowed to control his drinking. Persuaded by Dahmer's rational appeals, the judge sentenced him to five years' probation beginning with one year in a work-release half-way house. Ten months later, having received no treatment for his alcoholism or counseling for his second sexual attack on young boys, Dahmer was released. Lionel wrote to the judge begging him to keep Jeff in custody until he had received some form of treatment. Lionel's plea fell on deaf ears.

Dahmer lived briefly again with his grandmother until moving into the now infamous apartment 213 on Milwaukee's south side. Finally completely on his own, Dahmer indulged all his impulses. From May 1990 to July 1991, he slaughtered twelve men inside his small apartment. With each murder, his rituals grew more elaborate. He used a Polaroid camera to document each stage of his crimes—from the seduction preceding the drugging to the dismemberment. No longer concerned his grandmother might walk in on him, he took his time with the bodies. He dissected many of the victims and later claimed he became sexually aroused by the heat given off by internal organs removed from a freshly killed corpse. Dahmer began experimenting with new disposal methods. He filled a fifty-five-gallon drum with acids that reduced the remains of his victims to a viscous liquid he could pour down the drain. He expanded his collection of sick souvenirs to include male genitalia, most of which he preserved in formaldehyde. He filleted the biceps of some victims and took sexual pleasure from eating their flesh.

Yet it was Dahmer's obsessive attempts to create what he called a "zombie" that finally caused at least a few of his neighbors to take notice. Dahmer believed he could keep his victims alive, but unable to leave him, by drilling holes in their skulls then pouring muriatic acid into their brains. His early zombie experiments failed horribly, resulting in the near instant death of the young men he tortured. On May 27, 1991, Dahmer lured fourteen-year-old Konerak Sinthasomphone to apartment 213 and drugged him. He took pictures of the boy, then preoccupied himself with preparations for the zombie procedure. When he returned to the living room, Dahmer realized Konerak had escaped.

On the street outside Dahmer's apartment building, a naked Konerak wandered aimlessly, bleeding from the anus. Two young women from the neighborhood realized something was terribly wrong and called the police. By the time officers arrived, Dahmer too was on the street. He claimed Konerak was over eighteen and had simply had too much to drink. He casually explained that the two were lovers and assured police he was in control of the situation. The police asked for Dahmer's identification but did not check it out for warrants. If they had, they would have discovered Dahmer's history of sexual molestation of young boys. If they had, they would have discovered that Dahmer then was on probation for having drugged and molested another Laotian child, Konerak Sinthasomphone's brother. But rather than doing so, the officers on the scene followed Dahmer and Konerak back to apartment 213. Still so drugged he was incapable of telling his side of the story, Konerak sat silently on the couch. The officers later explained that when Dahmer produced photographs of Konerak in sexually compromising positions, they believed Dahmer's claim that the two were lovers. The photographs, of course, had been taken within hours of the officers' arrival during the first stage of Dahmer's documentation of one of his crimes. Nevertheless, satisfied with Dahmer's story, the officers left the apartment where Tony Hughes's three-day-old corpse lay rotting on Dahmer's bed just off the living room. Dahmer then slaughtered Konerak Sinthasomphone almost immediately.

Following Dahmer's arrest two months later, the Milwaukee police came under fire for their handling of the Konerak Sinthasomphone incident. The media discovered that Glenda Cleveland, the mother of one of the girls who had called the police on Konerak's behalf, had followed up on the case when she heard news reports that a Laotian teenager was missing by calling law enforcement authorities to report what she and her daughter had seen. No officer ever returned her calls.

Investigations into the police department's handling of the incident also unearthed tapes of the radio call the two officers on the scene made the night they let Dahmer slip through their fingers. They joked that they had been dragged into the middle of a fight between two male lovers; one officer laughingly noted that as a result of having contact with Dahmer and Sinthasomphone he would need to return to the station to be deloused. Based on the time line Dahmer confessed to police a few months later, it became clear that Konerak Sinthasomphone lost his life within moments of the officers making that joke.

Dahmer's close call with the authorities did little to dampen his thirst for blood. If anything, his successful manipulation of the situation seemed to embolden him. He killed four more men in quick succession. Then, on July 22, Dahmer enticed Tracy Edwards back to apartment 213. Unlike Konerak Sinthasomphone, Edwards managed to escape *before* Dahmer had drugged him and was thus able rationally to counter Dahmer's cover story that the two were simply lovers having an argument. Police arrested Jeffrey Dahmer around midnight on July 22, 1991.

The next morning, America awoke to breaking news of the Dahmer case. The major networks broadcast video footage of investigators in HazMat suits wheeling the fifty-five-gallon acid bath down the steps of the apartment building. Cameras trailed another investigator carrying a large cardboard filing box: a close-up made possible by a zoom lens revealed a slight tuft of hair protruding through a small hole. Jeffrey Dahmer had killed eighteen men between 1978 and 1991. As viewers watched police cart evidence of the carnage out of apartment 213, they once again realized a monster had been living silently among them, this time for thirteen years.

Coverage of the Dahmer case dominated the world news media for several weeks then cooled slightly until the trial commenced on July 13, 1992. Because Dahmer had willingly confessed his crimes to authorities following his capture, he entered a guilty plea but also claimed that he was insane. The highly publicized trial invited onlookers into the life of a serial killer as Dahmer himself retraced his crimes in painstaking detail and psychiatrists and criminologists dissected his mind before the watchful eyes of the media audience. After listening to unbelievably graphic testimony and examining the horrific physical evidence in the long and complicated case, jurors deliberated for only five hours before returning a verdict: guilty and sane. Dahmer was sentenced to fifteen consecutive life sentences, or 957 years in prison.

The Wisconsin state prison authorities confined Dahmer in the Columbia Correctional Institute in Portage. He apparently adjusted rather well to prison life. He claimed to have been born again as a Christian. In interviews he gave to popular television programs like *Inside Edition* and *Dateline*, he professed to regret having committed his crimes, though many doubted, based on his manner in the interviews, that he felt true remorse. He admitted to interviewers that he still felt drawn by the impulses to kill and violate others and thus understood why he must live the remainder of his life in prison.

On November 28, 1994, Dahmer was placed on a cleaning detail with two other prisoners: Jesse Anderson, who had murdered his own wife, and Christopher Scarver, a delusional schizophrenic who believed himself to be Jesus Christ. For reasons no one seems to be able to explain, the detail guard left the men alone for a few minutes. Scarver attacked Anderson and Dahmer. When the guard returned, he found Anderson lying on the floor, fatally wounded. Jeffrey Dahmer was already dead. Scarver had crushed his skull, just as Dahmer had crushed Steven Hicks's skull sixteen years earlier.

TELLING DAHMER'S STORY

From the moment news crews set up camp outside Dahmer's apartment building to the time the trial ended more than a year later, the Jeffrey Dahmer story dominated American news media. If you turned on your television or radio or opened a newspaper, you simply could not avoid the story. So for most people, the story I just told is nothing new. All of us know about the murders. All of us remember the revelations about cannibalism. All of us recall seeing the investigators wheel the fifty-five-gallon drum down the stairs. All of us *know* Jeffrey Dahmer.

Yet what did we ever really know about his victims? At most, we remember Hicks as the first, Konerak as the one who nearly survived, and Edwards as the one who brought a halt to Dahmer's killing spree. But that is virtually all we know about them, and even that is tenfold more than we know of the other fifteen lives Dahmer brutally cut short by feeding his insatiable hunger for perverse sexual fulfillment.

Many people have pointed to our obsession with killings as one of the defining elements of our so-called culture of death. I think that notion is too simplistic. You see, it is not simply our obsession with killings, but rather the way we spin stories about killings that entrenches our ambivalence toward hatred. My recounting of the Jeffrey Dahmer story is not unique. In fact, I intentionally laid out the story as it has been told hundreds of times before in news reports and biographical and true crimes features about Dahmer. Now that the standard-issue narrative of the Dahmer story is fresh in our minds, let's examine very closely the ways in which the structure of the story itself reveals our love affair with hatred and violence.

While stories come in a variety of forms and encompass seemingly limitless themes and topics, all stories contain the same essential elements: plot, characters, setting, and motivation. When we tell stories, we manipulate those four elements to create our own unique telling of an event. A change in any one element can potentially effect the way the other three will develop. For example, if the plot of a story centers around a car crash, carefully describing the setting to include a dense fog and icy roads will shape listeners' understandings of the cause of the crash even if driver error was in fact to blame.

Because no story can tell all sides or perspectives of an event—the story would be so long and convoluted as to be unmanageable and also very boring—all stories are the by-product of choices made by the storytellers. Great novelists consciously and carefully make choices about how to structure their stories in order to achieve the best literary effect for their readers. But novelists are not the only storytellers in our society; they are simply the most *aware* storytellers. We are all storytellers. We all make choices about the structure of every story we tell, from how we explain to our friends how we got a fantastic bargain from the local car dealer to how we explain to a prospective employer how we accomplished a major goal in our career. By adjusting the way in which we develop a story, we can make ourselves appear as the hero or the villain, the witless victim of circumstances beyond our control or the king or queen of our own tightly controlled universe.

As we begin the twenty-first century, the mass media serves as a central storyteller for our society. Movies, sitcoms, and serial dramas flow through our television sets offering us instant access to complex narratives. While we all know that such fictional stories are crafted by writers and directors, we sometimes forget that the stories we see on the news are also the final product of a process of choices made by writers, directors, reporters, and editors. The nightly news, as well as CNN Headline News, absent commercials, runs only about twenty-two minutes. Rarely is any one story given more than three or four minutes coverage. Each day members of the news media must decide first which events even will be covered and then how the story of each event will be developed within the strict time limits of broadcast news or the strict column limits of print news. The stories we receive from the news media have thus been filtered through a decision-making process that, while absolutely necessary, also necessarily shapes the way we in turn come to think about events and people in our world.

When we take the time to stop and consciously consider that fact, most of us have the intellectual horsepower to take that process into account when reacting to news stories. However, most of us do not normally have our guard up and our critical thinking caps on when we sit down in front of the television after a long, long day tending to our families and jobs. As products of a media-driven culture ourselves, we comfortably accept all but the most glaringly obvious instances of bias in news reports. Yet I contend we are far more profoundly influenced by the most subtle manipulations of the elements of stories.

The media's development of stories about actual serial killing sprees offers an excellent example of this phenomenon. All major media accounts of serial killings overtly deplore the killers' actions. Because the act of serial murder so deeply assaults our values, the media is able and even expected to throw aside their normal objectivity: we viewers do not want to hear a news anchor being fair or unbiased toward a known serial killer. We want to hear the killer described as a "monster," as "sick," as "deviant." Yet while the media normally obliges our preference and appears to condemn the killer, many choices made by the media about how to tell the story of serial killings actually seem to glorify the killers. Although manipulation of any of the four narrative elements can impact a story's development, I will focus here only on plot and characters in order to understand how the standard-issue telling of the Jeffrey Dahmer story reveals another troubling example of our obsession with hatred and violence.

We are an action-loving people. From the warrior epics of the ancient Greek poets to the action-adventure blockbusters of today, Americans seem almost innately drawn to popular tales involving lots of plot movement. So it is not surprising that our news media too present stories to us with a premium on plot action: several thousand years of history prove human beings like our stories told in such a fashion and, of course, what we like, we watch and what we watch determines advertising prices. As

I've cautioned before in *Love to Hate*, we cannot allow ourselves off the hook by blaming the media because the media, as a business, is simply responding to our behavior as consumers. What impact then does the media's decision to feed our hunger for action-heavy plots have on our perceptions about a case such as the Dahmer killing spree?

First, action-heavy plots dictate how at least one character in a story must be developed. Narrative theorists distinguish between active and reactive characters: active characters drive the plot, literally causing the plot events to happen, whereas reactive characters respond to the plot. It follows then that for an action-heavy plot to develop in a way that makes sense to story-savvy audience members like us, at least one active character must be central to the telling of the story.

We need only to glance at the standard spin on the Dahmer story to realize that Jeffrey Dahmer himself is cast in the role of active character. Dahmer stalks. Dahmer drugs. Dahmer violates. Dahmer dismembers. Dahmer kills. Jeffrey Dahmer controls the plot. He acts on others—his victims, his family, the police.

This of course is, after all, the story of Jeffrey Dahmer. But what we all tend to lose sight of is that *that* is a choice made by the storytellers and expected by us as an action-loving audience. The standard telling of the Jeffrey Dahmer story casts Dahmer in the central role of active character in order to facilitate our preference for action-heavy plots. The Dahmer story with which we all are so familiar is the *standard* telling of the Milwaukee murders, but it is not the only possible way to tell the story. The story *could* begin with the birth of a precious Laotian boy. The story *could* trace his childhood, introducing us to his family and friends, his interests and his goals. The story *could* explore the pain he and his family suffered when a neighbor molested his brother. The story *could* help us imagine the terror he felt as he realized an evil man was trying to hurt him, the courage and strength he mustered up in order to escape from the man, the despair he felt as he sat on the couch, unable to speak, as two police officers left him alone with a killer. The story could be the Konerak Sinthasomphone story. Or the Tracy Edwards story. Or the Anthony Hughes story. Or the Jamie Doxtator Story. Or any of fourteen other stories of young men actively pursuing their lives for years until the one moment in which they encountered a killer. But those stories just do not seem to appeal to action-lovers like us. Those stories just do not pull in viewers, like us, in the same way *The Jeffrey Dahmer Story* does.

Because the standard telling of the Dahmer story is action-heavy and casts Dahmer himself in the active role, it also necessarily places him in the lead role. Normally, lead characters receive the most attention. In contrast, lesser characters, known in narrative theory as satellites, are explored only to the extent necessary for the story to make sense. Storytellers tend to develop lead characters as both dynamic and round, meaning that we learn enough about them to witness their growth over time (dynamic) and we learn enough about them so that they are multifaceted (round). Satellite characters are usually left static; we do not know enough about them to notice when or how they change. Storytellers also usually portray satellite characters as flat, reducing them only to the characteristics essential for fulfillment of their role in the plot.

In the standard telling of the Jeffrey Dahmer story, Dahmer is the only fully dynamic and round character. Because the story traces his life in search of clues to his madness, we all know Dahmer as a dynamic character: we have seen him grow from a lonely little boy into a disturbed teenager into a first-time killer into a serial killer. We also know Dahmer as a round character. Of course, we have intimate knowledge of his actual crimes—the rituals, the zombie experiments, the disposal methods, the cannibalism, and so on. But we know so much more about Dahmer. We know his parents, his brother, and his grandmother. We know what he liked to do as a child. We know that he flunked out of college, was kicked out of the Army, and ultimately held down a stable job in a chocolate factory. We know he liked to go to gay bars and bathhouses. We know he was an alcoholic. We know he enjoyed photography. We know he preferred his apartment to be very neat. We know he dabbled with satanism. We know he loved his childhood pets. We know he once loved a little boy named Lee. We know his sexual fantasies. We *know* Jeffrey Dahmer.

We know almost nothing about Dahmer's victims. All remain static and flat to us. Over the years, the media has given the most attention to Konerak Sinthasomphone, yet we know almost nothing of the boy. We know he was Laotian. We know he was one of the youngest of Dahmer's victims. We know he nearly escaped. We know he had a brother. Yet we know these things only because they are critical to the story of Dahmer not because they are essential to Konerak's own story. We know *nothing* about Konerak separate from his relationship to Dahmer. We know nothing about *any* of the eighteen men separate from their relationship to Dahmer.

When an action-hungry audience demands to be fed the story of a killing spree, storytellers reduce victims to satellite status and thus sentence them to an eternity of being nothing more than the victim of their killer. Jeffrey Dahmer took the lives of eighteen men between 1978 and 1991. Since then, we all have condemned those men to an eternity as "Dahmer's victims" because we have not bothered to remember anything else about them. In the case of most of them, we have not even bothered to remember their names.

Since the Eddie Gein story broke in 1957, the American audience has greedily devoured stories about serial killers. From classic movie villains such as Norman Bates and Buffalo Bill to real-life monsters such as Charles Manson and Jeffrey Dahmer, we have elevated the image of the serial killer to iconic status in our popular culture.

Our response to serial killers provides telling evidence of our obsession with hatred and violence. On the one hand, we publicly deplore serial killers, ostracize them, and, in some states, even kill them. On the other hand, we eagerly listen to *their* stories. We purport to despise serial killers and their extreme sprees of violence and depravity. Yet we offer serial killers one of our most valuable cultural commodities: celebrity.

Unlike serial killers who stalk their victims one by one, mass murderer Timothy McVeigh killed 168 people in a matter of a few moments when he blew up the Murrah Federal Building in Oklahoma City in 1996. The site of the bombing now stands as a chilling shrine to the memory of each life lost. Yet from the moment he was apprehended in 1996 until and even after his execution in 2001, we focused our attention on McVeigh and not on his victims. Kathleen Treanor, who lost three family members, including her five-year-old daughter, Ashley, in the blast, spoke directly and poignantly to the consequences of our fascination with hatred and violence in a press conference immediately following McVeigh's execution.[10] She implored the media to remember that the Oklahoma City bombing was not McVeigh's story but the story of the 168 people who died, of the hundreds of others who were injured, and of the thousands of people who lost friends and family members. We consumers of media also need to heed her words.

Pope John Paul II has called our culture a "culture of death." Central to our culture of death is a cult of celebrity. We no longer distinguish much between the famous and the infamous. Too frequently we only distinguish between those who are known and those who are invisible. In America at the beginning of the twenty-first century, simply being known is a critical component of status within society. Jeffrey Dahmer has been dead for more than six years. We still know him. We never will forget him.

We can't forget the eighteen men he killed either. We can't forget people we never took the time to know in the first place.

CHAPTER 6

Organized Hatred:
Supremacy Movements

I was seven when I joined The Avengers. The secret club convened in near total darkness on a hot summer evening inside my dad's tool shed. After much secretive planning we formalized our eternal bond by reading a verse from the Bible while drinking blood (okay, so it was cherry Kool Aid). We vowed to tell no one of our covert activities. Then we all went home. It's hard to sustain lifelong loyalty on a Dixie Cup of Kool Aid, especially when you have an 8:30 curfew.

Joining a secret club is a childhood ritual almost all of us have experienced. But for some people, the lure of membership in a covert organization continues into adulthood where it often takes on a sinister purpose. For example, members of the Supreme Order of the Star-Spangled Banner, one of America's first organized hate groups, solemnly vowed to reply "I know nothing" to any questions about their clandestine activities and also to despise newly arrived Catholic immigrants. Likewise, members of groups such as the Ku Klux Klan (KKK) and the Knights of the White Camellia originally wore elaborate robes and hoods not only to shroud the identity of members but also to look like terrifying ghosts as they rode through African American neighborhoods in the dead of night.

While hate groups of the past carefully hid their membership and most of their activities from the rest of society, today some hate groups seek out publicity as a way to further their cause. Members of some Ku Klux Klan klaverns and certain skinhead gangs cavort about on talk-show stages offering audiences glimpses of hatred in its most sensationalistic forms.

We reassure ourselves when we assume that the sometimes inane characters we see on television are no threat to us. Of course, in doing so we make one critical—and potentially lethal—mistake: we assume that the goofy guests on a talk show represent the reality of organized hatred in America. The hate groups that pose serious threats to our society are not those whose members agree to make fools of themselves on syndicated talk shows. By treating hate groups like sideshow attractions, we display a flirtatious attitude toward hatred that, in this case, threatens the safety of each and every one of us.

In this chapter I explore the reality of organized hatred in America as we begin the twenty-first century. Once I have discussed the beliefs, history, and plans (revealed on the public Web sites) of some of the key hate groups currently active in the United States, I will explore the complicated challenges hate groups pose to our principles. First, I consider how the hate groups' persuasive tactics rely on the destructive thinking patterns I first mentioned in chapter 1: absolutism, stereotyping, scapegoating, and dehumanization. I then look at seemingly contradictory responses to media coverage of hate groups. Finally, I unpack the particular tensions between our hatred of hate groups and our love of freedom.

THE AMERICAN HATE SCENE: THE CURTAIN OPENS

Ironically, in a nation built on a foundation of tolerance, intolerance itself must be tolerated. As a result, when a group of people determine that they "hate" some other group, the American system of liberty secures their right to form an organization that celebrates their hatred. American history is littered with a succession of organized hate groups that have targeted Catholics, African Americans, Jews, Hispanics, gays, and many other minorities. Sadly, members of organized hate groups have killed thousands of people in America over the years and have seriously impaired the social and economic well-being of millions of others.

Ultimately, two historical lines produced the current hate group scene in America: the domestic line of nineteenth-century white Protestant supremacy groups and the influential line of German Nazism in the first part of the twentieth century. Because most hate groups maintain some level of secrecy, only by understanding their lineage is it possible to begin to understand what they are plotting today behind closed doors.

Because the Ku Klux Klan has received so much media attention (and self-promoted so efficiently), many people believe it to be the first significant hate group. However, hate groups existed in the world long before the Klan formed in 1866.[1] In fact, the history of hate groups in Europe influenced early hate group activity in America. Although the European colonists who settled America were often fleeing religious oppression, they themselves arrived on American soil with centuries-old religious prejudices. Specifically, many of the Protestant colonists clung to the anti-Catholic and anti-Semitic beliefs with which they had been raised in Europe. The early history of the American colonies and, later, the United States is a history of substantial religious intolerance.

This religious intolerance crystallized into a vast and fully organized social movement in the 1830s in response to rapid changes in immigration patterns.[2] Throughout the 1830s and 1840s what had been a small stream of Irish Catholic immigrants became a raging river due to the Irish potato famine and political and religious conflicts in Britain. By the mid-1840s, nearly a million poverty-stricken victims of the famine were landing on United States soil every year. Because immigrants could become naturalized American citizens after only five years, the rapid change in the flow of immigration rapidly changed the face of the American political, social, and economic scene. Native-born Americans—some displaced from their jobs by Irish who would work for lower wages, some watching politicians cater to the so-called Catholic vote—began to view the Irish Americans not as newly naturalized countrymen but as enemies within the borders of the United States.

In the mid-1830s propagandists added fuel to the smoldering fires of anti-Catholic sentiment. Although remembered today as the inventor of the telegraph, in his own time Samuel F. B. Morse was hailed as the intellectual leader of the anti-Catholic movement. In *Foreign Conspiracy Against the Liberties of the United States*, he claimed to reveal details of a Vatican-based plot to overthrow American liberty.[3] According to Morse, the plot involved using the votes of newly naturalized Irish Catholic Americans to vote democracy out of the American system. A puppet government representing the alliance between the Pope and the Emperor of Austria would then rule America.

Around the same time a young woman calling herself Maria Monk appeared in New York City hawking her tale, *Awful Disclosures of the Hotel Dieu Nunnery at Montreal.*[4] Monk claimed to be a nun who had escaped the Hotel Dieu Convent in order to save the life of her unborn child, a child fathered by one of several priests who routinely raped the nuns in the convent. Monk fled because, she alleged, the many children born of the priests and nuns were murdered within moments of their birth to hide the evidence of sexual promiscuity behind convent doors. Monk also told of sadistic, even deadly, punishments practiced on the nuns and elaborate secret rituals within the Catholic Church that no doubt appeared pagan to most of her readers. Monk warned American Protestants that the Catholic Church was a corruption of all things moral, Christian, and democratic. Significantly, Monk's *Awful Disclosures* was one of the top selling books of the mid-nineteenth century, even though it was most probably a hoax.

The conspiratorial rantings of Morse, Monk, and hundreds of other anti-Catholic propagandists stirred many American Protestants to action. By the early 1840s, several national religious missionary unions formed to save Catholic immigrants from the Pope and protect American liberty in the process. Groups such as the Order of United Americans, which drew many members from the merchant class, organized efforts to protect Protestant jobs and, in turn, deny immigrant Catholics opportunities to earn a living. Perhaps most important, the Native American Party (NAP) formed around a platform of denying immigrants the right to naturalize for twenty-one years. Later called the American Republican Party and then simply the American Party, the NAP also demanded the use of overtly Protestant readings—such as the King James Bible and writings by Martin Luther—as standard texts in public schools. By the mid-1850s, anti-Catholic politicians had won control of the government of Massachusetts and held a substantial sway vote in the United States Congress.

While thousands of American Protestants used such legitimate channels to argue their case against Catholics, others adopted a more dramatic—and more dangerous—approach. In the early 1840s, some Protestants formed what today would be called gangs that defended turf against immigrant Catholics. Gangs such as the Wide Awakes, the Blood Tubs, and the Dead Rabbits also attacked Catholics who tried to vote. In the early 1840s, violence attended virtually every election in major East Coast cities. A three-day riot in Philadelphia's Kensington District left thirteen dead, hundreds injured, and razed an entire sector of the town.

Yet it was not until the late 1840s that anti-Catholicism took on its darkest form. In 1849 James Barker took over leadership of a group called the Sons of the Sires of '76. Barker renamed the group the Supreme Order of the Star-Spangled Banner (SSSB) and thus ordained one of the most hateful groups in American history. Members of the SSSB vowed to work against Catholics at all levels — to deny them jobs, to strip them of their vote, and, if the need arose, to use violence to ensure Protestant dominance in America. Reportedly 1.3 million members strong at its peak in the early 1850s, the SSSB operated in near-total secrecy. Members used elaborate codes to identify each other in public and to plot their attacks on Catholics.

The anti-Catholic movement died out in the late 1850s as the North-South tensions leading to the onset of the Civil War demanded all Americans' primary attention. Yet in the three decades of anti-Catholic agitation that had passed, much damage had been done. Arsonists so frequently targeted Catholic churches, seminaries, convents, and schools that no American insurance company would sell policies on Catholic-owned structures. At the hands of anti-Catholic school board members, many American public school districts became so overtly anti-Catholic that the Catholic Church had no recourse but to establish parochial schools in which Catholic children could study without being attacked. And, tragically, several hundred lives were lost in violence motivated by religious intolerance.

While the Civil War distracted American anti-Catholics, it did not destroy the anti-Catholic sentiment among some Americans. Rather, when the smoke cleared, anti-Catholics found new allies among whites who feared that the recently freed black population of America posed a serious threat to the American way of life. Hate groups formed throughout what had been the Confederate states in the years immediately following the Union's victory. Organizations such as the Knights of the White Camellia, the Citizens Council, and the Ku Klux Klan promised to protect white Protestant dominance at all costs and labeled blacks, Catholics, and Jews their primary targets for intimidation.

The Ku Klux Klan, the most notorious of the nineteenth-century supremacy groups, traces its origin to Pulaski, Tennessee, in the year

1866.[5] Bored and disillusioned by life in their small town, six former Confederate soldiers decided to form a club that could provide them a social and intellectual outlet. Initially the young men devoted themselves to the study and discussion of history. Having all been college students before the war, they enjoyed delving into research as a means of entertainment.

Soon after forming the club, the men moved their meetings from the rather staid offices of a local judge to an abandoned house outside Pulaski that was rumored to be haunted. There the men devised elaborate initiation rituals and crafted costumes for themselves to wear while meeting. They even developed a coded language to describe the hierarchy of their organization. The group gradually adopted a policy of near total secrecy about both its membership and its activities. As local interest in the club grew, the first Ku Klux Klan den sent emissaries to neighboring areas to help establish new chapters.

The Ku Klux Klan staged its first night ride on July 4, 1867, through the area of Pulaski that was inhabited primarily by blacks. Knowing most of the former slaves clung to superstitions about ghosts, the Klansmen outfitted themselves in white masks, pointed hats, and flowing robes before galloping silently through the neighborhood. In time, the Klan expanded its repertoire of terror to include pulling "bloody" artificial limbs or heads from their bodies as they rode past frightened blacks.

While such early Klan activities no doubt terrified blacks in the area, the Pulaski den of the Klan apparently did not cross the line into violence. Rather, the second den, based in Athens, Alabama, moved the Klan farther in the direction of a full-fledged hate group when its members lashed out in reaction to the opening of a new school for black children. The Athens Klansmen tracked down one of the male students late one night and tossed him into an icy creek for being too friendly with the white female teacher at the school.

As word of this event spread throughout the South, the Ku Klux Klan gained a reputation for, as it was called in those days, "keeping the Negroes in their place." The Klan's active racism quickly lured new members from the thousands of former Confederate soldiers struggling with the new social, economic, and political climate being forced on the southern states by the postwar reconstruction policies of the federal government. Local newspapers hailed the Klan as the savior of the Old South. Soon, Klan dens were forming throughout the eleven former Confederate States.

The Ku Klux Klan reorganized itself to better meet the needs of its rapidly growing membership. The group established a more complex hierarchy to facilitate the spread of the Klan throughout the nation. Offices with names such as Grand Dragon and Imperial Wizard — names now familiar to the general public — entered Klan protocol. The Klan also standardized their key icons, such as the flying dragon, and formally color-coded their robes and hoods to reflect members' status within the leadership system. Capping this critical period in the Klan's development, Confederate hero General Nathan Bedford Forrest vowed allegiance to the Nashville klavern, the newly agreed upon code word for a local den.

The Ku Klux Klan divides its history into eras. The First era of the Klan's presence in America extends from the formative years immediately following the Civil War to the end of the nineteenth century. During this time Klansmen preoccupied themselves with blocking the effects of the passage of the Thirteenth, Fourteenth, and Fifteenth Amendments to the United States Constitution that, taken together, enfranchised blacks as American citizens. The Klan seems to have been resigned to the fact of the amendments; instead of focusing on repealing the amendments, the Klan instead launched a concerted effort to circumvent them. The Klan played a critical role in passing and enforcing the so-called Jim Crow laws that had the effect of denying blacks the right to vote without discriminating on the grounds of race per se. In addition to the passage of Jim Crow legislation, the Klan stepped up its regimen of intimidation, burning crosses in the yards of those blacks who could not be legally shunned from the polls as a warning that Klansmen would seek vengeance on any black who challenged the system. Publicity surrounding lynchings served as a chilling reminder to all that the Klan of the First era followed through on its threats of violence.

The Ku Klux Klan and other hate groups began to spread across the nation during this period. As racial tensions in the South mounted, thousands of blacks migrated north. The second great wave of Catholic immigration into America, this time from Italy and other Southern European countries, occurred in the last decades of the nineteenth century. The combination of black migration and Catholic immigration created new social, economic, and political pressures in most northern cities. Confused and frustrated by the changes, some northern white Protestants allied themselves with supremacy groups.

Yet even though organized hatred was spreading around the nation by the end of the nineteenth century, the frequency and intensity of its activities—both political and physical—seem to have tapered off. Were it not for two critical events, the Klan and its kin may never have evolved past the First era and survived into the twentieth century. In 1905 Thomas Dixon published *The Clansman*, a sympathetic account of the Klan and the Confederacy that brought renewed public attention to the group.[6] Then, in 1915, filmmaker D. W. Griffith transformed *The Clansman* into *Birth of a Nation*, the first feature-length film in American cinema history.[7] *Birth of a Nation* drew huge public audiences, grossing over eighteen million dollars in admissions at theaters. Although most audience members no doubt attended simply to experience a motion picture, all who viewed the film also experienced the powerful emotions of the epic tale that glorified the Ku Klux Klan.

Claiming he was inspired by the film, the Reverend William Joseph Simmons sponsored a cross-burning atop Stone Mountain in Georgia on the eve of Thanksgiving in 1915. In the wake of the Stone Mountain rebirth of the Klan, the group intensified recruiting efforts as it moved into the period now defined as the Second era. By the early 1920s, more than two million Americans called themselves Klansmen. And many Klansmen held key leadership positions in society: around this time the governors of Georgia, Alabama, California, and Indiana were exposed as Klansmen, as was multiterm United States Senator Earl Mayfield from Texas. In 1925, forty thousand members of the Ku Klux Klan donned full ceremonial robes and hoods and marched in front of the White House as a show of strength and unity. However, with the onset of the Great Depression in 1929 the Klan all but disappeared from public view.

The Third era of the Ku Klux Klan began on May 17, 1954, when the United States Supreme Court handed down its decision in the case *Brown v. Board of Education*, thus mandating desegregation of American public schools. The Court's decision marked the beginning of the end for the Jim Crow laws that had upheld systematic racism for more than eighty years. As the Civil Rights movement gained strength and racked up more and more victories in the late 1950s and early 1960s, the Klan reemerged from the shadows of history. From 1954 to 1964, the United States federal government investigated more than one hundred and fifty bombings, as well as several hundred cases of arson and murder, with particular Klan klaverns as primary suspect groups. No doubt due to the Klan's extremely covert nature during its brutally violent Third era, very few Klansmen were ever prosecuted successfully by the

government. Yet even though they largely succeeded in escaping criminal prosecution, the Klan suffered defeat after defeat as the Civil Rights
movement gradually chipped away the entire system of Jim Crow laws
the First-era Klansmen had worked to pass.

In the 1970s, white supremacy entered the Fourth era when it
assumed a new public image largely as a result of one man's rise to
prominence within the Ku Klux Klan. Young, college-educated, and
very media-savvy, David Duke publicly proclaimed the dawn of a "new"
Klan, a Klan that was prowhite, not antiblack. Duke coined the term
"racialist" as a reference to the supposed new-Klan mentality of preserving and celebrating white heritage. But while Duke publicly claimed
the Klan had changed, United States Federal Bureau of Investigation
agents who infiltrated the Klan revealed that, in private, Duke not only
maintained the old racist attitudes but even elevated those ideas to levels more akin to Nazism than to nineteenth-century Klan ideology.

It was at this moment in history that America's home-grown hatred
intersected with a style of supremacy that some leaders had been
importing from Europe for several decades. As Duke moved the Klan
more into alignment with Nazism, he also moved the Klan into alliance
with the followers of Adolf Hitler. Although America and the Allied
forces had defeated Hitler's Third Reich in World War II, Nazism not
only survived but found a small group of loyalists on American soil.

Ironically, the first and most legendary American Nazi served as a
pilot in the United States Navy during World War II.[8] George Lincoln
Rockwell spent the years following World War II developing himself as
a commercial artist and advertising executive on the East Coast. When
United States troops engaged in the Korean War, Rockwell again vol-
unteered for service, rising to the rank of Commander. Following his
return stateside in the early 1950s, Rockwell engrossed himself in the
conspiracy theories of the McCarthy era. He quickly became not only
an ardent anti-Communist but also an anti-Semite. Rockwell came to
believe that the Jewish people were responsible for the spread of com-
munism and what he perceived to be the impending downfall of Western civilization. Although Rockwell found himself persuaded by theories of communist/Jewish plots, he remained dissatisfied with the vague
solutions touted by other conspiracy howlers. Then he opened a copy of
Mein Kampf, Adolf Hitler's autobiographical statement of Nazism.
Rockwell's conversion to Nazism was almost immediate. Later in life,
the former Navy pilot would explain that he founded the American

Nazi Party in order to repair the damage he felt he personally had done to Hitler's forces during World War II. For George Lincoln Rockwell, Nazi activism in American was not simply political but deeply personal.

In 1954 Rockwell moved to Washington, D.C., and insinuated himself into right-wing political circles. He frequently delivered speeches and circulated pamphlets that fell just short of publicly embracing the National Socialist philosophies of Hitler's Third Reich. While Rockwell was able to draw audiences for his ideas, he failed to find any right-wing groups willing to take action. Thus, with financial backing from the very wealthy and controversial Harold N. Arrowsmith Jr., Rockwell inaugurated the National Committee to Free America from Jewish Control. The National Committee embodied many principles of Nazism but, initially, was not devoted fully to the National Socialist agenda.

Nevertheless, Rockwell and his National Committee rapidly drew media attention and government scrutiny. On July 29, 1958, Rockwell and his followers led their first public demonstration at the White House against alleged Jewish control of the United States. In October of the same year Rockwell and Arrowsmith were identified as prime suspects when a bomb destroyed an Atlanta synagogue. Although neither man was ultimately charged, the pressure was more than Arrowsmith could bear: he withdrew his financial support of the National Committee.

In the aftermath of the Atlanta bombing, Rockwell claimed to have had a mystical experience. Like Hitler before him, Rockwell believed that a supernatural force instructed him in the truth of Nazism. This religiopolitical awakening steeled Rockwell's resolve: no longer would he try to mask his faith in National Socialism. As Rockwell prepared to salvage what was left of his organization after Arrowsmith's departure, he did so with a firm and public commitment to a Nazi agenda.

By March 1959, Rockwell had retooled the National Committee at all levels. The former advertising executive applied his knowledge of mass persuasive campaigns to his own cause. The National Committee to Free America from Jewish Control became the American Nazi Party, a named changed again in 1967 to the National Socialist White People's Party (NSWPP). Members were dubbed "storm troopers" and costumed for public appearances. Rockwell himself began regularly delivering pro-Nazi speeches on the Mall in Washington, D.C. Joined by his stormtroopers, Rockwell often scheduled counterdemonstrations in areas where he knew Martin Luther King Jr. would be rallying members of the Civil Rights movement.

No doubt drawing on Rockwell's experiences in the advertising and publishing fields, the American Nazi Party developed a variety of communication media. Early in 1960, the group released the first edition of *National Socialist Bulletin*. Rockwell's autobiography, *This Time the World*, hit the market later that year. In the fall of 1961 he published the first *Rockwell Report*, a periodical update of the actions of the alleged Jewish conspiracy and the American Nazi Party's response.

Although he founded the Nazi Party in America, Rockwell did not view the rebirth of National Socialism as a uniquely American phenomenon. In August 1962 he traveled to Europe to meet with representatives of the fledgling Nazi parties then organizing on that continent. The representatives signed what is known as the Cotswold Agreement, committing themselves and their followers to the goal of Pax Aryana, or the Aryan Peace. Rockwell and the other Nazi leaders argued that only when all Aryans (whites of Northern European descent) united could they focus their collective efforts on the annihilation of other races, the ultimate goal of National Socialism since the mid-1960s. An NSWPP legend maintains that Rockwell himself once bluntly stated, "I will kill every Jew, Catholic, and Negro."

George Lincoln Rockwell defined one form of hatred in the middle of the twentieth century and shaped the development of the white supremacy movement for decades to come. Although followed by a relatively small group of devotees, Rockwell provoked most other Americans. Supposedly under pressure from some Jewish groups, the United States Navy forced Rockwell to accept a formal discharge in 1960 because his ideas were considered so incendiary. Even among the ranks of supremacists Rockwell inspired anger as often as he inspired loyalty. Ultimately, neither the Civil Rights movement nor the federal government silenced George Lincoln Rockwell; a former member of the American Nazi Party assassinated him on August 25, 1967.

THE CONTEMPORARY AMERICAN HATE SCENE

Since the 1970s, both the tradition of American white Protestant supremacy groups and the influence of European and American Nazi leaders have colored the hate scene in America. While a few groups seem particularly loyal to one branch of the hateful history over the other, most contemporary hate groups reflect aspects of both traditions.

According to watchdog groups such as the Southern Poverty Law Center and the Anti-Defamation League of B'nai B'rith, the number of organized hate groups grew rapidly in the late 1980s and throughout the 1990s. It is not possible to know with certainty how many Americans belong to hate groups because so many of the groups operate covertly. We do know, though, that, in 2000, hate groups operated in forty-nine of the fifty states.[9] Several thousand United States citizens now hold official membership in hate groups. Thousands of others are being targeted as recruits by the sophisticated propaganda machines of twenty-first-century American hate groups. In this section I want to look at the basic structure of a few of the most significant hate groups currently active in America.

Although the National Socialist White People's Party floundered in the years immediately following Rockwell's death, another group quickly arose to fill the void. William Pierce, a former comrade of Rockwell's, established the National Alliance in 1974.[10] Drawing most of its members from the National Youth Alliance, the National Alliance admitted members of all ages and thus expanded to reach a wider audience.

The National Alliance today serves a critical role as a communications hub for the supremacy movement. The organization has published *National Vanguard*, perhaps the premier hate-group periodical in the United States, since 1975. National Vanguard Books, the publishing arm of the group, is one of the largest suppliers of supremacist books, videos, and paraphernalia. Recently, Pierce purchased Resistance Records, America's top producer and distributor of skinhead music. The National Alliance/National Vanguard Books/Resistance Records Web site provides to all visitors a vast, comprehensive catalogue of thousands of resources.

Yet the National Alliance's greatest claim to fame and National Vanguard Book's all-time best seller remains founder William Pierce's novel, *The Turner Diaries*.[11] First published serially in *National Vanguard*, *The Turner Diaries* traces the development and activities of a small cadre of white Protestant men who lash out at minorities and the government. The climax of the book sees its hateful heroes make a gigantic bomb using ammonium nitrate fertilizer and a rented moving truck as their tools. They detonate the truck in front of a federal building in a midwestern city shortly after nine on a workday morning.

Sound familiar? When police apprehended real-life Oklahoma City bomber Timothy McVeigh, copies of pages from *The Turner Diaries* were found in his car.[12] The literature popular among members of hate groups may not be something most people encounter at their local bookstore. It may seem far-fetched, silly, or offensive to most Americans. But while it is taken seriously only by a very small audience, it nevertheless has a quality most Pulitzer prize-winning novels do not have: it provides the inspiration and the instructions for the commission of mass murder.

If William Pierce is the "mind" of the contemporary hate scene in America, Richard Butler is the "soul." Butler is the self-ordained high priest of the Church of Jesus Christ Christian, the primary pulpit for a theology called Identity.[13] In the nineteenth century, Anglo-Israelism, which claimed Anglo-Saxons were the chosen people (Israel) of God, became popular for a time in Britain. Shortly after World War II, Dr. Wesley Swift revived and expanded Anglo-Israelism theories into what now is called Identity theology. Swift, a virulent anti-Catholic and anti-Semitic Klansman, argued that non-Aryans are "mudpeople," born without souls. Satan, not God, creates mudpeople who are on earth to test Aryans. In Identity teachings, then, non-Aryans are not human and not of God. According to Swift's interpretation of the biblical book of Revelations, Aryans must prove themselves to God by eradicating the mudpeople, the children of Satan, in order to bring about the apocalypse and eternal salvation. Clearly, such a belief system has the potential to create extremely violent crusaders for the cause.

When Swift died in 1970, Richard Butler assumed leadership of the crusade. A former Klansman himself, Butler apparently sought a more focused philosophy on which to center his ideas about white supremacy. In the past thirty years, Butler has emerged as one of the most important leaders of the white supremacy movement. Those drawn to the movement quickly discover his Identity-driven sermons and pamphlets in the catalogues and on the Web sites of almost all supremacy groups. Most significantly though, Butler has managed to wed his religion to a political vision. Butler's greatest impact on the supremacy movement is this marriage of divine inspiration with militant activism: a combination thousands of years of world history warn us is almost always deadly.

In addition to the Church of Jesus Christ Christian, Richard Butler also heads up Aryan Nations, one of the largest and most notorious white supremacy groups active in America today. Aryan Nations per se is the paramilitary core unit of adult male followers of Butler. Politically, Aryan Nationalists envision the formation of an actual Aryan national state, modeled on the Third Reich, in America. The Aryan Nationalists are not alone: Butler also sponsors several other groups allegiant both to Identity theology and a goal of Aryan political dominance. Aryan Youth Action serves all young people interested in the supremacy movement, though it caters particularly to the interests of skinheads. Aryan Youth Action regularly sponsors concerts by skinhead bands, education and physical training programs, and festivals such as the Aryan Olympics and the Adolf Hitler Youth Camp. Female followers of Butler unite under the banner of Aryan Women's League to discuss their role as mothers in preserving the purity of the Aryan bloodline and to function as something of a women's auxiliary for the Aryan Nationalists. Finally, Aryan Brotherhood, Butler's Identity outreach program in the United States prison system, is considered by police and prison authorities to be one of the most vicious gangs operating in the United States at this time.

Because Butler's followers tend to be among the most ardent and extreme white supremacists, they have received significant press coverage in the wake of major incidents. In the mid-1980s, the contemporary supremacy movement attracted national media attention for the first time when Bob Matthews and The Order pulled a multimillion dollar bank robbery to fund the Aryan Nationalist cause. Matthews and The Order assassinated Alan Berg, a well-known Jewish talk radio personality. Matthews himself was finally killed by law enforcement agents in a bloody shoot-out. Almost all known surviving members of The Order remain in federal maximum security prisons.

More recently, Aryan Nationalist Randy Weaver hunkered down in his cabin near Butler's Idaho compound during a standoff with agents of the Federal Bureau of Alcohol Tobacco and Firearms (ATF). The incident, which came on the heels of the ATF's disastrous encounter with David Koresh and the Branch Davidians in Waco, Texas, drew extended media attention. Ultimately, federal agents shot Weaver's wife and young son before they apprehended Weaver himself.

Although not known to be members of Aryan Nations, Oklahoma City bombers Timothy McVeigh and Terry Nichols were known to be supporters of Aryan Nationalist beliefs. Shortly before the bombing, for example, McVeigh visited Elohim City, a paramilitary training camp in the south whose leaders preach Identity theology.

In the summer of 1999, Aryan Nationalist affiliate Buford Furrow

attacked a Jewish community center in California. Furrow's undiscrim-
inating rage left three kindergarten students, a teenage helper, and a
teacher bleeding in the hallway as he prowled farther into the building.
Later the same day Furrow fatally shot a postal worker before being cap-
tured. Not long after Furrow's arrest the media uncovered an interesting
twist of history: Furrow's wife is the widow of Aryan Nation's martyr, Bob
Matthews.

Most recently, Aryan Nations topped the nightly news when the
courts effectively bankrupted the group by ordering it to pay more than
six million dollars in damages to Victoria Keenan and her son, Jason.
Aryan Nations security guards had shot at and ultimately beaten the two
up for driving along a road near the group's twenty-acre compound in
1998. The settlement forced Butler to turn the entire compound over to
the Keenans who, in turn, sold it to Greg Carr, a millionaire who plans
to transform the longtime headquarters of hatred into a center devoted
to the promotion of antihate/antiviolence initiatives. But Reverend Butler and the Aryan Nationalists have not disbanded. In fact, they have
redoubled their focus on the Internet and will soon debut two new white
supremacist shows on public access television. One of Butler's wealthi-
est supporters donated a house for Butler to use as an interim base of
operations as he rebuilds the infrastructure of Aryan Nations with an
eye toward cyberspace as the compound of the future.[14]

While supremacists affiliated with Aryan Nations and Identity theology have garnered the most media attention in recent years, the media's
favorite supremacist of the late 1980s and early 1990s remains every bit
as active today as he used to be. Tom Metzger, a television repairman
from a suburb of San Diego, California, is the founder and undisputed
leader of White Aryan Resistance, or WAR. Metzger's son, John, runs
Aryan Youth Movement (AYM), an organizational and communication
hub for skinhead gangs from around the nation.[15]

The Metzgers seem to have an affinity for media attention of all sorts.
They themselves intermittently operate a cable talk show catering to the
interests of white racialists. They also publish a detailed periodical,
manage a telephone hotline, offer a variety of items for sale through
their own catalogue business, and maintain one of the most up-to-date
and complex Web sites of all the hate groups.

But ultimately, the Metzger's claim to fame derives from their appearances on other people's talk shows, appearances that seem to have set the
standard for over-the-top behavior by supremacists for a decade now. Tom

and John Metzger, joined by several followers, led the onstage riot in which a chair hurled by one of the WAR members broke the nose of syndicated talk show host Geraldo Rivera. Around the same time, Tom Metzger appeared on Oprah Winfrey's show, demanding the creation of whites-only regions in the United States. Accused by an audience member of masterminding violence against minorities, Metzger sidetracked the issue and challenged anyone to prove he'd ever had a hand in violence.[16]

The courts took Metzger up on his challenge a few years later. The Metzgers drew serious media attention in the early 1990s when they took center stage in a Portland, Oregon, courtroom in an action for wrongful death and racial intimidation.[17] Tom and John Metzger stood accused of inspiring members of the skinhead gang East Side White Pride to murder Mulugeta Seraw, an Ethiopian immigrant. The skinheads bludgeoned Seraw so severely with a baseball bat that members of his own family were not able immediately to identify his remains. Ultimately, the court found against the Metzgers, assessing nine million dollars of punitive damages against Tom Metzger, John Metzger, and the WAR organization plus an additional $2.5 million in damages for Seraw's unrealized future income and the pain and suffering he experienced during the attack. Tom Metzger lost his home and most of his personal property as a result of the lawsuit, although by all accounts he and WAR have since recovered financially.

While Tom and John Metzger's brush with the law in Portland seemed a high-profile victory for antihate group activists, the case did little to quiet their skinhead followers. If anything, most supremacists—skinheads included—came to view the Metzgers as martyrs: the Portland case became a reason to evangelize.

Although the Metzgers gave skinheads their first real publicity in the United States, skinhead gangs have existed in America for several decades.[18] The skinhead movement traces its roots to Britain in the 1960s where a split occurred within the Mod subculture associated with mainstream rock groups such as the Rolling Stones. A splinter group called "hard mods" formed around their shared lower-economic background and penchant for drinking and rowdiness. The hard mods cropped their hair very, very short and wore a uniform of sorts: work shirts, cuffed denim jeans, suspenders, and heavy black Dr. Marten boots. The hard-mod hairstyle, of course, later gave rise to the term "skinhead," while their attire remains the standard for members of most skinhead gangs.

The British skinheads quickly earned a wide-reaching reputation. Organized into crews, or gangs, the skinheads supported local soccer teams. When rival teams played, rival crews met up in the stands. Much of the legendary violence surrounding British soccer games can be attributed to the skinheads' legendary propensity for violence. More often than not, British skinhead violence was fueled by a liberal supply of alcohol, another central feature of the skinheads' reputation.

Beyond their rowdy support of soccer teams, most British skinheads involved themselves in local music scenes. The punk revolution of the 1970s appealed to the renegade spirit of the skinheads. Yet even though bands such as The Sex Pistols, The Clash, and Generation X bellowed rage into their microphones, they were not prepared for the very real rage their music could unleash in a club packed full of skinheads. Almost as quickly as the skinheads discovered punk music, they found themselves banned from entering most nightclubs. Left outside the scene, some skinheads formed their own bands, which tended to fuse punk music with heavy metal and ska influences. The resulting genre, called oi!, has been described by one skinhead source as "music to riot by."[19]

The first organized skinhead group appeared in America in 1984. Calling themselves Romantic Violence, the group, which still exists, more closely resembles a traditional American inner-city street gang than a British hard-mod skinhead crew. Like most American gangs, Romantic Violence uses graffiti to mark their territory: the gang's identifying tag is a swastika.

In 2000 Romantic Violence was only one of thirty-nine known skinhead gangs operating in the United States.[20] The largest group, Hammerskin Nation, which formed in Dallas in the early 1990s, now claims members not just across the nation but across the globe. As organized skinhead associations continue to move into more and more areas of the United States, the movement is likely to grow even more rapidly in the first years of the twenty-first century than it did in the last years of the twentieth.

Still, many people seem to dismiss the threat of skinheads because the members are so young. Some write the entire skinhead phenomenon off as nothing more than a phase, a temporary rebellion. While that undoubtedly may be true for some skinheads, it does not make even temporary skinheads any less dangerous *while* they are committed to racist violence. The skinheads' commitment to violence is so intense that they brazenly document their crimes on their bodies: a skinhead's spiderweb tattoo symbolizes his or her participation in the serious assault or murder of a member of a targeted group; each inky creature entangled in the web represents additional attacks. Joining the gang means earning the right to wear a web tattoo. Today, several thousand young Americans, both male and female, wear the web.

Perhaps more significant in the long run, though, is the new crop of leaders emerging from the skinhead fold. Not long ago a street-level gang member himself, Eric Hawthorne (a.k.a. George Burdi), then lead singer of the skinhead band Rahowa, founded Resistance Records, the largest importer, producer, and distributor of racist music in America.[21] Matt Hale began his association with neo-Nazi skinheads as an eighth grader; now a law school graduate approaching age thirty, he operates the racist World Church of the Creator, one of the more popular spiritual associations among white supremacists.[22] National Alliance founder William Pierce's likely successor is Bruce Alan Breeding, the charismatic Florida Alliance leader who has yet to turn thirty-five.[23] And, of course, we must not forget the heirs to a couple of the hate-group thrones: Tom Metzger has for years been grooming his son to move from leadership of AYM to leadership of White Aryan Resistance; likewise, Knights of the Ku Klux Klan national director Tom Robb appears ready to vest leadership in his daughter.

Those who dismiss the skinhead threat are right about one thing: not all skinheads stay in the movement. For many it truly is a youthful rebellion that ends almost as quickly as it begins. Yet for the few weeks or months or years a young person is involved with a skinhead gang, they open themselves up wholly to theories about Jewish plots, black and Hispanic inferiority, and mudpeople. They learn that racially targeted violence is not just a viable but a *preferred* solution to social tensions and personal fears. How long do remnants of these ideas remain in the minds of a former skinhead? Do skinheads have to stay in the movement to pose a danger? Not according to Tom Metzger. Having just learned the verdict in the Portland case, he said, "The movement will not be stopped in the puny town of Portland. We're too deep. We're imbedded now. Don't you understand? We're in your colleges, we're in your armies, we're in your police forces, we're in your technical areas, we're in your banks. Where do you think a lot of these skinheads disappeared to?"[24]

BRINGING IN THE SHEAVES . . . AND THE SHAVEN

Smart recruiting strategies employed by the larger white supremacy groups account for much of their growth in recent years. New technologies—specifically the Internet, desk-top publishing, and computer databases used for direct mailings—allow hate groups affordable and sophisticated access to potential members. Yet while contemporary hate groups are moving into new avenues for conveying their messages, the messages themselves remain virtually identical to the messages hate groups have spread for centuries.

What must be of greater concern to us, though, is that the hate groups' sales pitches rely on some of the same faulty reasoning that we allow ourselves to use all too frequently. In chapter 1 I explored four potentially dangerous thinking patterns: absolutism, stereotyping, scapegoating, and dehumanization. In what follows, I demonstrate how hate groups use these as tactics to attract new members.

Absolutism

Absolutists see the world only in stark black and white. White supremacists are the ultimate absolutists: they literally view the world as a contest between black and white—that is, black and white people. Supremacists who believe the teachings of Identity theology elevate the contest to a supernatural level, dividing the world not simply by human races but, rather, into the categories of human (Aryan children of God) and mudpeople (non-Aryan children of Satan.) Even those supremacists who do not follow Identity read world history as the story of racial conflict in which the purity of the Aryan bloodline is the Holy Grail.

As I showed in chapter 1, absolutist thinking patterns make compromise impossible. The extremely polarized worldview of hate group members simply will not allow them to consider compromise as a possibility. Especially for those who practice Identity, efforts to find common ground with Jews and blacks would be seen as bargaining with the devil's children: compromise itself would violate what they feel is God's plan.

With compromise ruled out, only two courses of action remain for those in the grips of absolutist thinking patterns. First, they may simply give up. No evidence indicates that such a concession should be expected from the white supremacy movement. Now well into the Fourth era, by Ku Klux Klan calculations, adherents to the movement are as devoted to the cause today as their forefathers were following the Civil War. Hate group activity has waned occasionally over the past hundred years; but each time it appears that the movement has lost momentum another groundswell of interest crosses the United States.

The rather rapid increases recently in both the number of active and organized hate groups and the size of their membership rosters suggest that today's white supremacists are unlikely to give up their cause any time soon.

Which leaves us with the only other option for those who fall into absolutist thinking patterns: a trend of escalating attacks on those they perceive to be evil. Tragically, the bloody history of American and European hate groups supports this claim. From anti-Catholic SSSB convent burnings, to early KKK lynchings, to the Holocaust itself, hate groups have demonstrated their willingness to lash out violently at those they target.

Most of the hate groups active in America today admit in publicly accessible documents that they will take whatever means they feel are necessary to protect the Aryan bloodline.[25] Skinhead gangs enact this creed directly and somewhat randomly by attacking minorities they encounter in public. Other groups, including many branches of the Ku Klux Klan, claim they will not rest until the United States of America returns to a state of segregation, even if that means another civil war to divide the country. The most extreme incarnations of hate group planning come from leaders such as Richard Butler, who insists that only a genocidal race war can satisfy the biblical prophesies of the God of Identity. Butler's Aryan Nationalists have discussed on their publicly accessible Web site their belief that by instigating race riots in major urban areas they will be able to justify the escalation of violence against minorities.

Stereotyping

Stereotyping occurs when we prejudge people based on biases or on inadequate or inaccurate information. The prejudging involved in stereotyping is the root of prejudice. Not surprisingly, stereotyping is common among groups whose members unite around their shared hatred of other groups in a society.

The major contemporary hate groups particularly stereotype Jews and blacks as part of their ideas about a conspiracy to destroy what they believe is the pure Aryan bloodline. The theory casts Jews as the sinister leaders of the secret plot. The Jewish conspirators control blacks who mongrelize the Aryan bloodline through interracial relationships and who generally destabilize the traditional American (read that as "white Protestant American") way of life.

The stereotypes white supremacists hold about Jews and blacks thus derive from the theory of a conspiracy and also feed the theory of a conspiracy.[26] Jews are described in supremacist literature as tricky, secretive, and cunning. To the extent that the Aryan bloodline is believed superior, only a highly intelligent opponent could pose a true threat: as a result, the stereotype of Jews credits the Jewish people with great minds but alleges those great minds are working toward an evil goal. In contrast, blacks are portrayed as dupes of the Jewish conspirators. Blacks are described as ignorant and primitive in hate group documents. Blacks also are accused of being highly sexual: black women seek to seduce white men; black men rape white women who cannot be seduced. Significantly, these same stereotypes about black people were used as justification for the institution of slavery in the nineteenth century when southern slave owners claimed that blacks were too wild to be free and posed a safety risk to whites.

Yet while it is no surprise that white supremacists stereotype the groups they hate, it must be remembered that they also stereotype whites. A closer look at the overt racism in the literature the groups distribute and on the Web sites they open to the public reveals that the ultimate stereotype in supremacist thinking is "Aryan." As I noted in chapter 1, stereotyping is dangerous not only because it is based on inadequate or inaccurate information but also because it reduces those stereotyped to nothing more than the content of the stereotype. Even though the Aryan stereotype is supremely positive among members of hate groups, it nevertheless prompts them to reduce their understanding of themselves and each other to nothing more than their racial identity. More subtle issues of character, intelligence, personality, and morality disappear under the all-encompassing cloak of the label "Aryan."

Clearly, members of targeted minority groups are at the greater immediate risk due to hate groups' stereotypes of them. However, the hate groups' implicit stereotyping of Aryans also carries a risk—one that is almost never discussed in popular media: if simply being Aryan is the ultimate good, then being an Aryan who in any way betrays the cause no doubt would be the ultimate evil. According to Identity teachings and even historical theories of conspiracy, Jews and blacks are destined at birth to fill their roles in the grand drama between absolute good and absolute evil. Whites, on the other hand, are free agents. Only whites have the power to choose to raise the banner of Aryan pride and work toward the cause of Aryan supremacy. Conversely, only whites have the power to choose not to embrace the white supremacy movement. Whites who involve themselves in interraccial relationships, whites who work on behalf of civil rights for all, whites who try to silence the hate groups, and even whites who simply do not care are the most profound enemies of true Aryan loyalists.

Scapegoating

Scapegoating, or falsely assigning blame for our problems onto others, lies at the very center of hate group recruiting tactics. Even a cursory examination of hate group Web sites and pamphlets reveals that hate group writers fully understand the power of scapegoating as a lure for potential members.

To understand how today's white Protestant supremacy groups target particular audiences through scapegoating, it is necessary to understand the "logic" of the theory of the Zionist Occupational Government (ZOG), the most popular explanation of an anti-Aryan conspiracy circulating among white supremacists in recent years.[27] According to most contemporary supremacists, the United States is now controlled by a powerful but covert group of Jewish masterminds. The group, referred to by supremacists as the ZOG, now controls all aspects of the American political and economic system, directing social policy, determining spending and taxing decisions, etc. Those who believe in the ZOG feel that American democracy is a sham and that, in fact, the majority of American politicians and judges answer to this powerful cabal.

Because they accuse Jews of manipulating both politics and the economy, the hate groups set the Jewish community up as responsible for all problems now facing whites. Other minorities, especially blacks, emerge from the conspiracy theory as puppets of the Jewish plot and beneficiaries of Jewish efforts to destroy Aryan dominance. Thus, from the perspective of hate group thinking, social programs such as affirmative action help blacks and Hispanics *in order to hurt whites*—it's all part of the master plot of the Jewish conspirators. *Everything* is part of the master plot of the Jewish conspirators.

The ZOG theory allows hate group members to scapegoat all of their problems onto the Jewish conspirators and their supposed allies in other minority communities. If a white man cannot find employment to support his family, it is because Jewish corporate executives have given all the good jobs in the area to Hispanic workers; it is not because he lacks appropriate job skills or because he has not actually applied for any jobs. If a white women cannot win a scholarship to college, it is because Jewish academics have earmarked all the good scholarships for blacks; it is not because she chose not to take college prep courses in high school or because her family has no financial need. In placing the blame on someone else, the thought patterns of scapegoating also absolve those who buy into them of blame for their own lot in life.

Contemporary white supremacists make brilliant strategic use of scapegoating thought patterns in their recruiting efforts. The groups carefully target potential recruits based on their likely fit with the scape-goating patterns implied by the ZOG theory. On college campuses, fly-ers disseminated by hate groups usually speak directly to students' fears about securing employment after graduation. They also invite white male students, in particular, to unleash their frustration at skyrocketing tuition bills by suggesting that all the minority students on the campus attend school virtually for free even though they are not as intelligent or as hardworking as the white male students no doubt are. Likewise, hate groups often move into a town to begin recruiting during times of major economic turmoil such as the closing of a factory that had employed a large portion of the community. The groups' representatives plant the seed of ZOG theory in the minds of the recently unemployed: "It's not your fault your family is financially strapped. It's not a coincidence either. Someone is doing this *to* you." The scapegoating thought process turns confusion and fear into a focused hatred and, in the process, effi-ciently produces a new member for the hate group rosters.

Clearly, some people are more susceptible to such appeals than oth-ers. People who are, in general, content and happy are not likely sud-denly and unexpectedly to fall for appeals to join any kind of intense group, whether the group is a hate group or cult or whether the group is a mainstream church or a branch of the military. Normally people join groups that will demand substantial amounts of their time, thoughts, and emotions *only* when they feel a compelling need. Many young people join the military to meet their need to move away from home with the security of a guaranteed job, shelter, clothing, and food. Likewise, the decision suddenly to join a church after years of religious inactivity is most often is prompted by a life-altering event: the birth of a child or the death of a loved one can create new mental and emo-tional needs for spiritual fulfillment.

Hate groups pick up where such mainstream organizations usually stop: they offer potential members not only a safe place and a new faith but also an explanation for the failures in their life. By using scapegoating techniques, hate groups are able to convince potential members that the conditions of their lives are not their fault. For a person who feels powerless in the face of personal, social, or economic difficulties, the reassurance that "it's not my fault" fills a deep emotional need.

Dehumanization

Dehumanization, or reducing other people to a status somehow less than human, marks the final step in the classic thinking patterns associated with hatred. Dehumanization also marks the pinnacle of white supremacist ideology today as well as in days gone by. While absolutism, stereotyping, and scapegoating pose serious dangers alone and in combination, only when they build to the crescendo of dehumanization does the risk of violence become imminent.

White Protestant supremacists have dehumanized people of other races, religions, and ethnicities for centuries. Early nineteenth-century anti-Catholics labeled members of the Catholic clergy "demonic." Slave owners and the Klansmen who succeeded them referred to blacks as "animals" to be owned and managed in the same manner as cattle. In the twentieth century the rise of Identity theology within the supremacy movement dehumanizes all non-Aryans into the category "mud."

As I have pointed out in chapter 1, a process of dehumanization must precede violence. When otherwise sane people lash out violently they do so not at another "person" but at a being they have dehumanized to the status of monster, animal, devil, or "mud." Killing such a creature is not murder, for murder implies that the victim was human. Inflicting pain on such a creature is not cruel, for cruelty implies that the victim was innocent. According to the elaborate theories of the ZOG conspiracy and Identity theology, acts of violence against non-Aryans are a matter of self-defense, a matter of the survival of the pure Aryan bloodline.

At no time in the past two hundred years have American white Protestant supremacists been so forthcoming about their plans for using violence against minority groups as they are today. The public Web sites of established groups such as Aryan Nations and White Aryan Resistance envision a bloody race war in America that will result in the annihilation of all non-Aryans.[28] Aryan Nations and many other hate groups openly rehearse paramilitary maneuvers in preparation for the coming war. White Aryan Resistance and the National Alliance now work closely with a variety of skinhead gangs to disseminate literature, music, and Internet links that encourage the skins to unleash their rage. Over the next few years we will measure the effectiveness of the hate groups' mastery of dehumanization techniques in the only way it can be measured: by the death toll.

A FINAL NOTE ABOUT THE THOUGHT PATTERNS OF HATRED

It is very easy to condemn hate group members for their flawed thinking. For those of us who do not buy into ideas like the ZOG conspiracy theory or Identity theology, the fallacies of absolutism, stereotyping, scapegoating, and dehumanization shine clearly through the sometimes convoluted rantings of hate group activists.

Yet if we look a bit more closely a bit closer to home we may find that we use the exact same thought patterns in reaction to hate groups. We cannot understand how supremacists can hold the beliefs they hold when their ideas are so obviously wrong and immoral and our ideas so obviously are right and good. We find it easy to recognize hate group members for what we *assume* they really are: ignorant little bullies who lack self-esteem. We want our communities to be rid of hate groups because we do not want our children corrupted by their kind. Let's face it, we *know* hate group members are scum; they do not deserve the attention, let alone the sympathy, of Americans like us who are committed to principles of freedom and justice.

Perhaps the only thing easier than seeing the fallacies inherent in hate group thinking is to fall into exactly the same patterns of flawed thinking ourselves when we react to these groups. Certainly, we could write the whole problem off quite easily with an ends-justify-the-means argument such as "it's okay to use absolutism, stereotyping, scapegoating, and dehumanization so long as I use them against people who *really are bad.*" Of course, that is exactly how hate group members justify their arguments to themselves.

When we rely on the thought patterns of hatred to react to hate groups, we really are no different from such groups. We are simply shooting the same gun at a different target. We all need to remember that the next time we unload our loathing for hate groups in front of our children. Regardless of who is the good guy and who is the bad guy, regardless of how convinced we are that the ends justify the means on this issue, at the heart of our diatribes against hate groups is one very clear message to our kids: hate is okay, so long as you hate the right people. Same gun, different target.

WE ARE WHAT WE WATCH

Americans love to watch PBS. Just ask us. When queried face-to-face by a pollster, most of us claim we devote most of our television viewing hours to PBS, CSPAN, CNN, and other news and educational channels. It's a wonder the likes of NBC, ABC, CBS, ESPN, and MTV can stay in business with such an intellectually demanding national audience. Although we do not like to admit it, most of us *are* watching popular television—and not just in our choice of channels but, within channels, in our choice of shows. The ratings clearly prove that a great many of us favor "real" crime shows such as COPS, infotainment magazines such as *Inside Edition*, and talk shows such as *Jerry Springer*.

Whereas all hate groups once carefully concealed the identity of their members, some now regularly appear on popular national television programs. Members of certain Ku Klux Klan klaverns and some skinhead gangs show up on television quite frequently. Talk shows pit white supremacists in face-to-face debates with minorities and garner huge audiences with the free-for-all brawls that ensue. Both infotainment and news magazine programs produce feature stories with titles such as "Women of the Klan" and "Children of Hatred."

We need to regard the increasing media coverage of hate groups as a double-edged sword. On the one side, media coverage undoubtedly raises general public awareness of the existence and growth of the supremacy movement. But on the other side, the nature of much of the coverage of hate groups is itself dangerous.

Even though the ratings indicate that many of us watch infotainment programs and talk shows, we do not necessarily take seriously the stories and guests featured on them. When Jerry Springer, for example, hosts "women who are leaving their lesbian lovers for their father's gay boyfriend's uncle's boss's ex-wife," we watch it as a contemporary farce. The exaggerated uses of regional dialects and urban slang and the flamboyant physical posing and posturing—not to mention the now predictable chair throwing, hair pulling, and face slapping—display the participants not as real characters but, rather, as caricatures. On the basis of past encounters with such shows, American audiences now expect such shenanigans when they sit down to watch such programs. We also presume, based on those same past encounters and expectations, that the guests are somehow artificial.

When we encounter hate group members on talk shows, those same expectations kick in and influence our thinking. We read their behaviors, their speech patterns, and their uniforms as part of an elaborate performance for the cameras. The caricatures are so extreme that we assume—for our own peace of mind—that the people themselves cannot be real. Whether the few who actually appear on television are real or not misses the more important point: they are not typical. The hate group members who appear on television do not represent the norms of behavior and attitudes within the contemporary white supremacy movement.

I usually show a documentary film called *The California Reich* in a class I teach about social movements in American history.[29] Produced in the 1970s, *The California Reich* traces the activities of members of a neo-Nazi organization in preparation for a rally. The filmmakers introduce not only the group's leader but also some of the members and their families. Men wearing SS-styled uniforms dance the polka with women in traditional German dresses in a meeting hall adorned with pictures of Adolf Hitler. A rather typical-looking middle-aged man leads the camera on a tour through his rather typical middle-class house, culminating in the arsenal in the basement. A boy about nine years old wearing swastika arm patches complains about how much time Nazi meetings take away from playing sports, then breaks into singing a racist song. Prompted by his mother, a much younger boy, perhaps three or four years old, declares he wants to be a police officer when he grows up so he can kill "niggers."

My classes fall silent while watching *The California Reich*. In discussion following the film, two reactions always emerge. First, college students are shocked at how deeply engrained prejudices are in the children shown in *The California Reich*; they wonder where the little boys are now; they wonder if the little three year old, who now would be in his mid-thirties, actually has become a police officer. Second, and in many ways even more troubling, the college students admit they are surprised at how "normal" the Nazis seem in the film. One of my students recently expressed it this way: "I thought they would be stupid. They aren't like the guys you see on television."[30]

The mass media is giving us exactly what we want by showing us goofy hate group members: such caricatures allow us to feel safe by encouraging us to dismiss all hate group members as nothing more than sideshow attractions in today's media circus. The televised supremacists' exaggerated displays of prejudice seem too outrageous to be a real threat. Their flamboyant hatred just does not ring true to the reality of our daily lives. As a result, we conclude that if these guys are what hate groups are all about then no one in their right mind would listen seriously to such inane characters.

And we would be right to draw such a conclusion if the hate group members shown on television were in fact typical of the reality of the white supremacy movement today. But of course they are not. Except for a few publicly known leaders and spokesmen, serious supremacists guard their identity for the good of the cause. They hold down jobs, own homes, and raise children. They may live in our towns, even in our neighborhoods. They cruise supremacist Web sites and read supremacist literature, raise their children with racist attitudes, contribute substantial amounts of money to organized hate groups, attend out-of-town rallies clad in swastikas or white robes, and, possibly, commit acts of violence against those they hate. But we do not suspect them. Thanks to the appearances of "crazy" Klansmen and skinheads on shows such as *Jerry Springer*, we *know* "normal" people like our neighbors—like us—never would be involved with a hate group. The false assumption that hate group members all must be talk-show freaks is the most fundamental danger of our mass-mediated flirtation with the contemporary white supremacy movement.

A different kind of danger lurks in the media coverage given to hate groups by serious programs, including high-caliber talk shows such as *Oprah* and newsmagazines such as *60 Minutes, Dateline*, and *20/20*. These shows are often able to secure interviews with the official spokespeople of major supremacy organizations. White Aryan Resistance's Tom Metzger, for example, has made notorious appearances on shows hosted by both Geraldo Rivera and Oprah Winfrey. Metzger has also given interviews to most of the major network newsmagazines and to documentaries produced by cable networks. Various newsmagazines have also aired interviews with Aryan Nations' leader Richard Butler, the National Alliance's William Pierce, and Tom Robb, national director of the Knights of the Ku Klux Klan. David Duke, of course, secured substantial network airtime on both magazine programs and the nightly news during his runs for political office.

Although mass media portrayals of white supremacist leaders are always slanted against racism and hate group activity, they nevertheless serve as a forum from which the leaders may spread their messages. Tom Metzger won no points with Geraldo and Oprah fans as a result of his antics on their nationally televised programs, but he earned something few other Americans ever had: several minutes of free airtime during which he could preach his ideas before an audience of millions. During his appearance on the *Oprah Winfrey Show*, he even managed to advertise the mailing address for White Aryan Resistance. No matter how overtly the media displays its bias against hate groups, covering them at all gives them free access to the American public.

Television is not the only medium that provides free publicity for hate groups. You have another example of it in your hands at this moment. Hate groups draw not only viewers but also readers. Thanks to our fascination with hatred, hate sells. And to the extent that I write about that phenomenon, I too am selling it. While my intent is to dissect the seductive appeal of hatred—whether in music videos or on the publicly accessible Web sites of hate groups—my effect, nevertheless, is once again to parade hatred and violence before the public eye.

HANDLING HATE GROUPS

Where there are hate groups, there are opposition groups. Throughout American history hate groups have encountered varying degrees of resistance from the victims of hatred, from the government, from organized countermovement groups, and from the general public. That white Protestant supremacists do not control the United States today proves that resistance has been successful at some levels over the years. Yet, that hate groups still exist and once again are growing in numbers and strength tells us that opposition efforts ultimately have failed.

The idea of handling hate groups is extremely complex in a free society. In order to understand the special challenges involved, we need to consider the tensions between freedom and tolerance in the American system of rights.

"Ambivalent" perhaps best describes America's official reactions to hate groups. Federal, state, and local governments rarely act directly to quell hate group formation and propaganda. Usually hate groups must cross the line of violence before a branch of the government takes action against them. For many Americans, the government's failure to suppress hate group agitation *before* it proliferates to violence is a crime in itself.

Yet our system was designed to prevent the government from suppressing the rights of those who hold different opinions. The same constitutional guarantees that prevent a Democratic president from outlawing the Republican Party prevent Congress from outlawing groups such as the Ku Klux Klan. In 1787 James Madison authored *The Federalist* paper Number Ten in which he warned the citizens of the young nation to beware the dangers of a tyranny of the majority.[31] Although the Revolutionary War had freed Americans from the rule of the British monarchy, Madison believed that an unchecked majority of the public could become equally oppressive. As a result of Madison's warnings and those of other political thinkers of the era, the framers of the United States Constitution built checks on the power of the majority into our systems, as well as protections for the rights of minority opinions. These checks and protections are the very heart of liberty in America.

When we strongly disagree with a particular minority position, we find it more difficult to embrace wholeheartedly the constitutional guarantees of that group's right to publicize their controversial ideas. However, if we fail to protect the rights of those with whom we disagree, we erode the integrity of the system that protects *our* rights as well. Thus if we deny white supremacist church leaders the right to preach the teachings of Identity theology, we compromise the security of religious freedom not only for Identity practitioners but for Christians, Jews, Muslims, Buddhists, and followers of all other religions. Likewise, if we silence Tom Metzger or William Pierce or Richard Butler or any white supremacist, we risk our own ability freely to speak our opinions, including our opinions about hate groups. We must always remember that the price we pay for our own freedom is tolerance of the freedom of others. Hate groups whose members hope to strip minorities of their rights are able to exist in America because most Americans refuse to strip hate group members of their rights. In this case, our ambivalence toward hatred reflects our crystal-clear commitment to political freedom.

Since the first Europeans settled on American soil, prejudices based on religion, race, and ethnicity have characterized the so-called American way of life. The history of America has been the history of the sometimes hostile, sometimes cooperative, but always complex relationships between and among the many groups that make up our great American society. Yet even deciding which groups have been victims and which have been guilty of championing hatred is itself a very complex task. For as I have shown in this chapter, while hate groups may overtly employ the thought patterns of hatred—absolutism, stereotyping, scapegoating, and dehumanization—we too sometimes rely on exactly the same faulty ways of thinking when we react to hate groups. Further, by continuing our dangerous flirtation with the caricatures of hatred we see on popular television shows, we risk underestimating the depth of hatred embraced by most active hate group members and the height of violence they plan to unleash in the coming years.

Hate groups challenge our commitment to the principles of freedom on which our nation was founded. To secure our own rights, including our right to speak out against hate groups, we must ensure the rights of hate group members to voice their ideas. We simply cannot draw a line in the dirt and assert that some "good" opinions will be protected while other "bad" opinions will not be allowed.

As Americans, we draw a different kind of line. Protecting the rights of all Americans to hold and express whatever opinions and beliefs they choose does not mean protecting the rights of even one American *to act* on his or her beliefs. Morris Dees, chief trial counsel for the Southern Poverty Law Center, explains it simply: "In America we have the right to hate, but we don't have the right to hurt."[32] The problem, of course, is that in the instant of time when hate turns to hurt, we lose yet another innocent life.

Conclusion:
Freeing Ourselves of Our Obsession
with Hatred and Violence

Hatred and violence now infuse virtually every aspect of our culture. The movies we watch, the games we play, the music we listen to, the television programs we follow, and even the newscasts we rely on for information provide us with daily exposure to levels of graphic violence unthinkable only a few generations ago. While many critics blame the sheer saturation of violent images for the reality of violence in American life, I contend that the problem is far more subtle. As I have demonstrated throughout *Love to Hate*, violence per se is merely a symptom of a more fundamental issue: namely, our ongoing obsession with hatred.

Violence does not arise spontaneously. Violence results from hatred. And while we publicly profess to despise hatred, our behavior as a society gives the lie to our claims of tolerance. From our fascination with hate groups and serial killers to our casual reliance on the thought and language structures that enable hatred and violence, we tolerate not only intolerance in others but also the seeds of intolerance in ourselves.

I want now to take a look at the process of freeing ourselves from our obsession with hatred and violence. First, I consider a case study of the power we actually have to stand up against hatred and violence. The movement against hatred inspired by the murder of Matthew Shepard is a ray of hope and love in our dark and dangerous world. I caution readers that my discussion of Matthew Shepard's murder is graphic; the reality of hate-motivated violence is graphic. Second, I offer a series of specific changes you can incorporate into your own ways of thinking and interacting with the world that will help us all become less vulnerable to hatred's seductive appeal.

AMBIVALENT NO LONGER: THE LEGACY OF MATTHEW SHEPARD

Matthew Wayne Shepard was born on December 1, 1976, in Caspar, Wyoming.[1] Matthew was a typical kid in many ways. He enjoyed outdoor pursuits like swimming, camping, fishing, and skiing. He expressed his artistic flair in both dance and theater. He regularly attended St. Mark's Episcopal Church where he served as an acolyte. Matthew also loved spending time with family and his many friends. The Reverend R. W. Brown describes Matthew as "a really nice kid."[2] The Reverend Anne Kitch adds, "What was important to Matt was to care, to help to nurture, to bring joy to others in his quiet, gentle way."[3]

As a teenager, he traveled to Switzerland to complete his junior and senior years in high school. Like many recent graduates, Matthew had a bit of trouble finding his path. He attended a few different colleges before settling in as a political science major at the University of Wyoming. Not one to limit his interests to the confines of books, Matthew became actively involved in campus political organizations. A gay man himself, Matthew took particular pride in his work with the campus gay and lesbian rights group.

On the evening of October 6, 1998, Matthew Shepard went out for dinner with friends from the University of Wyoming's gay student group, then headed to the Fireside Lounge. He was doing the same thing tens of thousands of other college students do every night: he was hanging out at a bar near his campus, enjoying a few drinks and socializing with other young people. Matthew struck up a conversation with a couple of guys who seemed friendly enough. Russell Henderson and Aaron McKinney told Matthew they too were gay. Shortly after midnight, they invited him to leave the bar with them. Henderson and McKinney drove Matthew Shepard to a remote area outside Laramie, Wyoming. They tied Matthew to a split-rail fence. They pistol-whipped Matthew with a .357 Magnum. They tortured Matthew. Matthew begged for his life as Henderson and McKinney savaged him. Only when his body showed no signs of life did they leave him for dead, tied to a fence in the middle of nowhere.

But Matthew was not dead. For eighteen hours he clung to life, alone. Finally, a passing cyclist noticed the figure draped over the fence. The cyclist initially mistook Matthew for a scarecrow, but upon closer investigation realized that the seemingly lifeless, misshapen figure actually was a person, a person still clinging tenuously to life. Matthew's head and face were so bloody that his bruised skin was visible only in the trails left by his tears.

Emergency medical teams transported Matthew to Poudre Valley Hospital in Fort Collins, Colorado. Doctors determined his skull was fractured from the middle back all the way to the front of his right ear. He had suffered massive damage to his brain stem. Matthew's injuries were so severe the doctors concluded they could not operate. News of the vicious attack hit the national media.

While Matthew Shepard's family and friends maintained a vigil around his bedside, a small group of students at nearby Colorado State University entered an original float in the homecoming parade. A scarecrowlike figure hung loosely from a makeshift fence. A sign on the figure's chest proclaimed, "I'm gay." An obscene remark decorated its back. The students who constructed the float later claimed they had not meant to be insensitive: they were just making a joke.

With their dying son hanging in effigy as a "joke" in a local parade and national media swooping down on them, Dennis and Judy Shepard watched helplessly as their beloved Matthew lay comatose in the hospital. On October 9, prosecutors formally charged McKinney and Henderson with the attack. Three days later, in the early morning hours of October 12, Matthew Shepard died without ever having regained consciousness.

As media coverage of Matthew's murder accelerated, outrage spread across the nation. Gay and lesbian rights groups were among the first to rally. Parents groups, antihate crime lobbies, and political and religious leaders soon joined in the call for an end to senseless violence. Vigils were held in major cities and small towns to remember the gentle spirit of Matthew Shepard, to remember yet another life cut short by hatred. On October 14, a vigil in Washington, D.C., drew thousands of mourners. Of the many speakers that night, perhaps none spoke the feelings of the crowd more eloquently than actress Ellen Degeneres who said simply, "I can't stop crying. I am so devastated by this." In her nationally tel-evised speech she implored "heterosexuals to see this as a wake-up call to please stem the hate."[4]

Sadly, members of at least one organization viewed Shepard's death as a rallying cry for hatred. Under the direction of Fred Phelps, mem-bers of the Westboro Baptist Church staged a protest at Matthew's funeral. As Matthew's family and friends grieved inside the church, Phelps's crew marched around outside with placards declaring God Hates Fags and Matt Shepard Is in Hell. At one point, a group of Matthew's friends, dressed as angels, peacefully paraded down the street and among the protesters.

No matter how many accounts of the Matthew Shepard story I hear, I cannot really conceive the pain Dennis and Judy Shepard must have felt. To lose a child under any circumstance is any parent's worst night-mare. But to learn that your child was tortured simply for being who he was. To sit helplessly by as your child lingers in a coma while an image of his broken body hangs in effigy as a "joke" on a homecoming float. To walk past a protest line to enter your own son's funeral. To know that as you try to say the impossible—to say good-bye—the national media is airing footage of a poster announcing that your son is in hell.

Anyone, especially anyone who is a parent, would understand if Judy and Dennis Shepard harbored rage for the remainder of their lives. Rage at the two men who savaged Matthew and left him hanging on a fence to die. Rage at Phelps and others who have turned Matthew's death into a morbid grandstand for their hateful theories. Rage at a society that for too long has tolerated open, violent hatred of people who are different.

Yet the Shepards have not shown rage: they have shown compassion. In November 1999 Dennis and Judy Shepard beseeched the court to show mercy on Aaron McKinney. McKinney will not be put to death; he will serve a life sentence, along with Russell Henderson, because his victim's family showed the mercy the killers themselves refused to show Matthew as he begged for his life that fateful night. When asked recently if she has forgiven Matthew's killers, Judy Shepard explained, "Forgive-ness hasn't been an issue. To me, forgiveness follows rage. There never was that."[5]

Instead of giving themselves over to rage, the Shepards have set out on a campaign against hatred. They realize—more profoundly than most of us—that rage will only beget more rage. The killers' rage cost Matthew his life. The Shepard's compassion saved the killers' lives.

Dennis and Judy broke the cycle of hatred. They refused to allow themselves to hate their son's killers, even though that hatred may seem justifiable to us. The Shepards took a clear stand—No Hatred Is Justifiable. In doing so, Dennis and Judy Shepard have paid the highest tribute imaginable to their son: they have helped launch a movement against the hatred that took Matthew's life. As Judy says, "I just wasn't going to let Matt's death be only an act of violence."[6]

Shortly after Matthew's murder, Judy and Dennis founded The Matthew Shepard Foundation, a not-for-profit organization designed to support diversity programming in education and to establish places where young people can feel safe being themselves. The Shepards now travel the nation educating people about the very real consequences of violence. They also advocate for the passage of hate-crimes legislation. Through both their activism and the towering example of their compassion, Judy and Dennis Shepard have shown all of us that it is not just possible but imperative to get rid of our obsession with hatred. They also have secured for future generations the memory of Matthew Shepard, a caring, loving, and beloved young man. The work of The Matthew Shepard Foundation guarantees that Matthew will be neither forgotten nor remembered only as just another victim of violence. The spirit of Matthew Shepard survives because his parents refused to let it be killed.

The murder of Matthew Shepard and the living legacy of love carried forth by his parents have inspired many people to join the drive to eradicate our obsession with hatred and violence. Brent Scarpo and Martin Bedogne, both Hollywood filmmakers, had been discussing ideas for a joint project about hatred for some time when news broke of the brutal attack on Matthew Shepard.[7] When the two men met up at a vigil for Matthew in October 1998, they resolved to take action. As Scarpo recalls, "The pain, anger, and disbelief were loud and clear in the faces of the 3000 mourners on that powerful night. Each person was searching for answers, and asking, 'Why?' We decided that we should be the ones to provide the answer."[8]

Scarpo and Bedogne's answer has taken the form of a documentary film entitled *Journey to a Hate Free Millennium* and a not-for-profit multimedia company called New Light Media. Dennis and Judy Shepard endorsed the project during its planning phase and provided the filmmakers full access to their home, their memories, and their unique understanding of the power of hatred. The family of James Byrd Jr., the man who was dragged to death by racist extremists in Texas, also agreed to work on the project. Ironically, shortly after Bedogne and Scarpo set up the New Light Media offices in Denver, Eric Harris and Dylan Klebold opened fire in nearby Columbine High School. Darrell Scott, whose daughter, Rachel, died in the Columbine massacre, quickly signed on to support the New Light Media project. Major celebrities, including Elton John, Kathy Najimy, John Dye, and Olivia Newton John, also contributed their support.

The film itself is a gripping account of the aftermath of hatred. Interviews with the Shepard, Byrd, and Scott families accomplish what standard media coverage of murders normally does not: they bring the victims alive in the audience's mind. As I described at length in chapter 5, too often media coverage of killings focuses on the killers and reduces victims to nothing more than convenient tags such as "gay student" or "black male." *Journey to a Hate Free Millennium* forces us to realize that *people* are being killed by hatred. The film also seeks solutions to the hatred and violence now plaguing our society. The families and friends of Shepard, Byrd, and Scott provide insights, as do several celebrities and T. J. Leyden, a former neo-Nazi who now works to educate people about hatred. Ultimately, though, *Journey To a Hate Free Millennium* does not simply offer answers; rather, it invites viewers to ask themselves the most critical questions of all: how does hate affect my life and what can I do to overcome hatred?

Brent Scarpo, Judy Shepard, and other members of the New Light Media and Matthew Shepard Foundation teams now travel the country showing *Journey to a Hate Free Millennium* and leading discussion sessions. They guide audiences to a better understanding of the nature of hatred itself and help people feel the anguish and sorrow violence always leaves in its wake. As more and more audiences watch the film and participate in follow-up discussions, more and more people are taking a stand against our society's casual tolerance of hatred and violence.

I am one of those people. I first saw *Journey to a Hate Free Millennium* in September, 2000 when Brent Scarpo visited Ripon College. I almost skipped the event; I was tired and just wanted to stay home with my family that night. But I determined to go because several of my students and co-workers who had planned the event were anxious for me to attend. I also wanted to see the angle Scarpo and Bedogne took on the topic of hatred. I had just finished writing the first draft of the book you now are reading and, to put it bluntly, I wanted to check out the competition.

Brent Scarpo began his presentation by asking each of us in the audience to turn to the person sitting next to us and say, "You are here tonight for a purpose." Now, I am a professor of speech communication; I've listened to *thousands* of speeches over the years. So I took Brent's request with a grain of salt, thinking, "Oh great, yet another speaker with yet another cute attention-getting device." Speech professors make tough audiences! Nevertheless, I complied with his request. "You are here tonight for a purpose" I said to the student on my right. "You are here tonight for a purpose too" she replied with a giggle.

As it turns out, I was there for a purpose. I will be forever thankful to all the forces that conspired to seat me in Brent Scarpo's audience that night. I learned then that until that night I had *understood* the dynamics of our love affair with hatred and violence, but I no longer really *felt* very much about them. Somewhere along the line, over the many years I had spent studying hate groups and killers, I had become emotionally numb; to enable myself to analyze and evaluate the most graphic accounts of extreme acts of violence, I had developed an immunity to *feeling*. Brent's film hit me like a bolt of electricity—it shocked me into *feeling* again. As I mentioned in the introduction to this book, the birth of my daughter made me react to the Columbine shootings with more emotion than I'd felt in myself in years. Yet my reaction to Columbine was very selfish—Please God never let this happen to my child. *Journey to a Hate Free Millennium* forced me to move beyond my own emotional self-interest and into a genuine state of outrage about the pervasiveness of hatred and violence in America. Brent's presentation inspired me finally and fully to put my heart—not just my mind—into *Love to Hate*. In the course of about two hours I was transformed from a professor who writes about hatred as part of my job into a person who writes about hatred because I am sick to death of living in a world where reports of slayings, killing sprees, and school shootings still sadden us but no longer shock us.

I hope *Love to Hate* will help my readers to better understand the dynamics of hatred in our society. And I hope *Love to Hate* will open my readers' eyes to the mixed messages we all send and receive about hatred everyday. But, most fundamentally, I hope something I've written here will give my readers what Brent Scarpo and *Journey to a Hate Free Millennium* gave me—the passion required actually to take the first steps on the journey to a hate-free millennium.

I now invite everyone who reads this book to consider some of the steps we all—individually and together—can take to make our world a safer and saner place to live.

FREEING OURSELVES FROM OUR OBSESSION
WITH HATRED AND VIOLENCE: THE CRITICAL STEPS

It is not possible to solve a problem without really understanding the problem. In the aftermath of tragedies like the Columbine shooting or the Shepard murder, we too often allow our first wave of emotions to cloud our understanding of the nature of the problem and thus propose well-intended but nevertheless flawed solutions. For example, within days of the Columbine shooting, voices around the nation called for enhanced security systems in schools and stricter gun control laws. While these proposals have merit, they don't actually speak to the real problem: what is it in our society that prompts two teenage boys to dehumanize their classmates, to scapegoat all their problems onto others, to know that by committing mass murder they instantly would become the most famous kids in the world? School security systems and gun control laws may make the next massacre more difficult to plan, but they will not prevent it.

To prevent another Columbine, another Matthew Shepard murder, or any other act of violence, we have to target solutions at the fundamental processes of hatred that ultimately give rise to violence. The overwhelming majority of Americans are kind, loving, nonviolent people. Our problem is not that we, as a society, are intrinsically violent. Rather, our problem is that we, as a society, passively tolerate the thought and language processes of hatred that lead some among us to violence. And we passively tolerate popular culture icons, themes, images, and story lines that entrench hatred and violence not simply as norms but as values.

The problem is not that our society is violent but, rather, that we are carrying on a twisted love affair with hatred and violence. Like a teenage girl drawn to the neighborhood bad boy, we enjoy the thrill of flirting with danger. And like that dangerous boy, hatred and violence are very seductive—they offer us easy ways to blame our problems on others and, whether real or fictional, they offer us exciting entertainment as a break from our sometimes boring everyday lives. Our challenge then is not to make ourselves loving and nonviolent—we already are—but, rather, to make ourselves stop falling for the seductive appeal of hatred and violence. Getting rid of our fascination with hatred and violence will not make hatred and violence go away completely, but it will make it infinitely harder for those who hate and behave violently to find an audience, to find followers, and to find defenders.

Clearly, changing our attitude toward hatred and violence will take time and hard work. Our society took centuries to get where it is; we are foolish if we believe we can fix things overnight. But we can *start* right now. The sooner we begin, the sooner we'll see the onset of change. As Brent Scarpo and Martin Bedogne remind their audiences, like any journey, the journey to a hate-free millennium must begin with a single step. Without a doubt, the critical first step we must take is to own up to the role each of us plays in continuing to be obsessed with hatred. Second, we must follow through on that awareness by becoming intolerant of our own intolerance. Specifically, we must no longer allow ourselves casually to use the flawed thought and language processes that enable hatred and passively to accept messages in popular culture that glorify violence. Third, we must find ways to help children avoid falling into an obsession with hatred and violence in the first place. And, finally, we need to lend our support to some of the national and even international organizations that are on the front line of the war against hatred and violence.

STEP 1: OWNING UP TO OUR OBSESSION WITH HATRED

Accepting responsibility for the problems we face is a tough pill to swallow. Taking blame hurts; it means admitting to ourselves that we were wrong or lazy or closed-minded or, in some cases, just plain dumb in how we handled a situation. When we take blame onto ourselves, we feel embarrassed and our fear of embarrassment (even in our own eyes) too often keeps us from admitting our culpability.

Yet, only by embracing our role in causing a problem do we empower ourselves to solve it. Victims cannot solve problems. Fortunately for all of us, we are not victims in this obsession with hatred and violence. So long as we have flipped on the television, purchased the compact disc, played the video game, or followed news of a real-life tragedy as if it were our favorite soap opera, we have been willing, even eager parties to the affair. If the media has seduced us, we certainly have been fully consenting adults in showing up again and again for subsequent trysts. We are not victims of the mass media and popular culture.

We are their cohorts. We too hold responsibility for the dangerous flirtation with hatred that characterizes our society and gives rise to outrageous acts of violence. We are to blame.

Thank heavens we too are to blame. For in admitting our blame we find our power. If our obsession with hatred truly were forced upon us by the media and other cultural influences, we really would be in dire straits: we would be hapless and helpless victims. But we are not. Once we admit to ourselves our own role, we can see the truth: the obsession cannot continue unless we allow it to do so. The media will stop selling violence if we stop buying it. Hateful icons will disappear if we stop propping them up. It only takes one side to call off a two-party affair. We are to blame and, therefore, we are powerful.

STEP 2: BECOMING INTOLERANT OF OUR OWN INTOLERANCE

Once we admit we hold at least half the blame, we have the power to call off our obsession with hatred. But simply learning that we have the power does not change anything. If we truly want to make our world a safer and more tolerant place, we must determine to take action, and that action absolutely must begin with changes in our own ways of thinking and behaving. We don't need anyone else's support and we don't need acts of Congress to make substantial changes in our own hearts and minds. All we need is knowledge and the determination to change.

As I have demonstrated repeatedly in *Love to Hate*, all of us fall prey too easily to the flawed thought patterns that give rise to hatred. Too often we fail to realize when we cross the line dividing normal comparative thought (us and them) from the dangerous realm of "us versus them" thinking. Too often we ourselves fall into the easy, but ultimately false logic of absolutism, stereotyping, scapegoating, and dehumanization. Even more often, we passively accept such ideas as they float around our popular culture. We also thoughtlessly misuse language in ways that can demean and degrade others. Misuse of powerful language structures such as naming, metaphors, diminutives, and reduction facilitates us versus them thinking.

Our tolerance of these flawed thought patterns and misused language structures allows hatred to flourish. We never will reject our obsession with hatred and violence until we first equip ourselves to fight against the underlying, unreasonable thought patterns of hatred. To do this, we must put our critical thinking skills to work for they are our first line of defense in this battle.

By critical thinking I mean the package of mental skills we use when we evaluate and categorize information, draw reasonable conclusions, formulate ideas, and analyze and solve problems. Critical thinking skills allow us actively to navigate our world. Without actively using our critical thinking skills we float aimlessly, passively through life, always reacting, never taking control. Critical thinking skills are our tools of survival in the complex world of the information age.

Each one of us can make grand strides toward ending our personal obsession with hatred and violence simply by learning about the flawed thought patterns behind hatred and then raising the standard we set for our own thinking process. Having read this far in *Love to Hate*, you now understand how some thought patterns can be misused to foster hatred. You have also learned how common language structures can be abused to divide us. You have developed an appreciation for the power of cultural icons and narratives to shape our perceptions. You have become more aware of the mechanics of our complex relationship with hatred and violence.

Your task now is to marshal that awareness toward personal change by refusing to participate any longer in this obsession with hatred. This task does not require isolating yourself from popular culture and interactions with other people; rather, it requires you actively and rationally to engage popular culture and other people according to a new set of standards you establish for yourself. I challenge you to become your own toughest critic. No longer tolerate your own intolerance. Do not let yourself get away with sloppy and dangerous mental leaps such as absolutism and stereotyping. Make more rigorous demands on your own mind-language connection: do not allow yourself casually to use language structures such as diminutives or reduction without first considering the weight of your words. Challenge yourself to critically assess popular culture: reassess your own role models and heroes; think about how a news story was shaped and edited not simply to fit the time or page limits but also to draw in an audience for advertisers; notice when stories are told with the killer as the lead character, leaving the victims all but unknown to the audience. Reflect on the messages you send to others and to yourself through your choices in movies, music, games, and reading materials.

I ask you honestly to assess what you now do. In the appendices you'll find some tools to help you get started. With your new awareness of our national obsession with hatred, are you still comfortable with the way you are living your life? Are you content with your reactions to popular culture? Are you proud of the logic behind your words? If you are, then I congratulate you. But if *Love to Hate* has made you uncertain about your own relationship with hatred and violence, then you need to make some changes. Your uncertainty is telling you something: you are ready to raise the standards by which you measure your own thought patterns and language usage and, in the process, to make an end to your personal fascination with hatred.

You may by now be wondering when I'm going to start focusing in on the "real" issue: what we need to do to stop the people who produce the "big" messages about hatred and violence—the producers of graphically violent video games and movies, the hate groups, even the teenagers who operate Web sites that glorify school shooters or gang members. How do we change them? My answer is very simple: by changing us.

Remember, it only takes one party to call off a two-party affair. When we change our ways of thinking, we fundamentally change the audience for messages about hatred and violence. In a mass-mediated information society such as ours, the power of the audience is enormous. If the national audience is content passively to accept messages steeped in hatred, messages that glorify violence, then the people who produce those messages have no motivation to make changes. To put it another way, so long as we continue to buy the bill of goods they're selling, why should they change their products? But if we begin to behave differently as an audience, the people creating messages full of hatred and violence will have to react if they want to continue to get our attention and, in most cases, our money.

I want to consider the media separately for a moment as a producer of messages about hatred and violence. We cannot overlook the fundamental fact that media is a business. If a television program does not draw a significant audience share, the price of advertising during that show drops. If the audience share drops far enough, the network drops the show because it is no longer profitable. Likewise, when a certain type of movie fails to bring in sufficient revenues, production companies stop making that type of movie; they are businesses and are thus unwilling to bet on a financial loser. The same analysis applies to video games, cartoons, many Internet sites, music, magazines, even books. The people who produce the content of today's mass media are business people seeking to make a profit. They will stop producing items that do not result in profit. The best strategy we can adopt for changing the media, therefore, is to change ourselves: when our behavior as consumers stops making violence profitable, we will see a sharp decline in violent images in media. I realize that sounds simplistic. But it really is that simple. We get exactly what we pay for—so long as we continue to pay for violence, it only makes sense for profit-motivated corporations to continue to provide us with violent products.

In the face of giant media corporations, most of us feel a lot like David facing off against Goliath. And, in truth, any one of us really is dwarfed by a giant corporation. But all of us together are not. I recently heard a broadcast journalist explain how his station views audience feedback about programming: one letter is a letter, ten letters are a stack, but a hundred letters are a serious problem. We need to let the media know that more and more of us are becoming dissatisfied consumers. We need to tell media executives that we are not going to buy any more products that glorify hatred and violence. And, then, and this is the key, we actually have to stop buying those products.

Hate groups, as well as some individuals, pose a different kind of challenge. Unlike the media, these people are not normally motivated by profit but by a sincere belief that their theories are true and that violence actually is the answer. I have no easy solution for dealing with these people. I think what we must remember is that they currently represent a relatively small minority of our population. Clearly, even with small numbers they have the potential to do great harm as we've learned painfully through several recent incidents. However, we must concern ourselves more with the threat they will pose in the future if they succeed in recruiting new members. We can make that task infinitely more difficult for them in a couple of ways. First, if we can succeed in using our power as an audience of consumers to influence the content of media, we will help create a more tolerant, less violent climate in society overall. While this clearly is a long-term solution, we must remember that the small steps we take now to change our society's relationship with hatred and violence will, in the long run, result in a society less prone to falling for the flawed thought patterns that almost always lie at the core of such groups' recruiting pitches. Second, those of us who are or plan someday to be parents need to teach our children to recognize the holes in the theories espoused by hate groups. Many hate groups target teens, in particular, with their recruiting plans. By helping our children become resistant to the rhetoric of hatred, we literally undercut the future of organized hatred. The hate groups need to look to today's children as recruiting targets in order to secure the existence of their organizations in the future. We need to remember that *our* children are *our* future and raise them to embrace the values of love and reject appeals rooted in hatred.

I disagree strongly with those who advocate censorship as a way to combat hate groups. First and foremost, we have to hold the First Amendment sacred because it can only protect our right to advocate for tolerance if it also protects the rights of those who advocate for intolerance. Second, I fear that censorship might actually backfire. When we make something taboo, we imbue it with a sense of mystery and danger that is especially appealing to young people. Think about alcohol for a moment. Teens experiment with alcohol for a lot of reasons. That they are not supposed to experiment with alcohol often tops the list. If we censor hate groups, we may inadvertently make them more interesting to our children. We also probably would make them more violent. Most hate groups operating in America today believe a conspiracy is afoot to strip them and the people they claim to represent of their rights. If we actually strip them of their right to freedom of expression, we may be throwing a match into an open tank of gasoline.

Although they are very different in nature, ideas for censoring hate groups, enhancing school security systems, and tightening gun control laws all have one thing in common—they miss the root cause of the problem. They are quick fixes that may or may not work in the short term but will not work over the long term. For real, lasting solutions to the problem of hatred and violence in our society, we must always return to the fundamental fact that until we rid ourselves of our obsession, our society will not change. If we ever want to achieve a hate-free millennium, we must prepare ourselves for a long and difficult journey. We must be brave enough to take that first step and also determined enough to take many, many more after it.

STEP 3: PROTECTING OUR CHILDREN

I hope you will decide to extend your crusade against hatred and violence beyond your own life. If you do, I encourage you to begin your efforts with the children in your life. For a couple of reasons, children are particularly vulnerable to being caught up in our society's fascination with hatred and violence. First, children learn by watching and imitating. If the adults in their lives use or even tolerate the flawed thought and language patterns of hatred, children learn to use and tolerate the same flawed patterns. This process carries the obsession with hatred across generations. Second, today most children spend a lot of their waking hours watching television, surfing the Internet, and playing video games. They are heavy consumers of media who rarely have been taught how to evaluate media messages.

In the appendices you'll find a collection of specific strategies you can employ to help children avoid repeating our own mistakes. I want to consider here some of the key steps we can take for the sake of the children in our lives. Obviously, the first change we can and should make on their behalf is to become role models of clear thought and language. By minding our own ideas and how we express them, we embed legitimate patterns of thought and word choice in the minds of the children who hear us. If you've spent much time at all around small children, you know that they are the world's best mimics. Children learn language by listening, then repeating. That's why they pick up not only words from their parents but also accents, speech styles, and the attitudes toward others coded into adult language. The thought and language patterns we use in front of children are the thought and language patterns they will adopt. Thus when we change the ways we think and the ways we express those thoughts, we literally are changing the way children will understand the world as they grow up.

Further, when we refuse passively to accept others' reliance on the flawed thought and language patterns of hatred, we model for children the process of listening carefully and thinking critically. We demonstrate that it is not okay blindly to accept all statements. We can use such situations to show children it is possible to compassionately question flawed ideas without attacking the speaker as a person. For example, we might say to another adult in front of the child, "I usually agree with a lot of your ideas, Bob, but I don't agree with this one. You're a very bright guy. That's why it surprises me to hear you suggesting that all minorities behave in a certain way because of something one person did." We then can reinforce the lesson with our children later by talking with them about why we disagreed with Bob. In such private interactions, age-appropriate language and examples they can relate to will help the lesson stick. For instance, you might explain to a preschooler that just because one of his stuffed bears has a crooked ear, that doesn't mean all stuffed animals, or even all stuffed bears, have crooked ears: people are a lot like animals, what's true about one person isn't necessarily true about all people, even about all people who look similar or live in the same place. You might even turn the lesson into a fun game by having the child gather all his stuffed animals and examine each one's ears. He will see that not all the animals, not even all the bears, have crooked ears.

Of course, in an age when television markets programs to children below the age of two, we also need to equip the children in our lives to understand as much as possible about what they see and hear via mass media. To make our children media literate we must not simply dictate what they can and cannot watch on television or what music they can or cannot listen to on the stereo. If we really want to raise media-literate children we have to make the time to watch television with them, listen to music with them, play games with them, and explore cyberspace with them.

Simply sitting alongside a child and enduring an episode of *Barney* will not foster media literacy. You will need to engage the child. Think of how you read to a child, the way you pause in following the story to point out some interesting aspect of the illustration or to connect the story to the child's life. That is how adults prepare children to be literate. Engaging children in media along the same pattern will help them become media literate.

You can use the ideas I have introduced throughout *Love to Hate* in age-appropriate ways to help children better navigate the mediated world in which they live. For example, you can help even very young children to understand that there are different kinds of stories—funny stories, exciting stories, sad stories. As the child grows, you can begin to explain that some stories are complicated, containing sad and funny and exciting parts all at once. In time you can introduce the child to the notion that the same series of events can be made to seem sad or funny or exciting by how we choose to tell the story: let children try their own hand by rewriting one of their own tales. By the time children reach the late grade school years, they are ready, with your help, to question the motivations behind the choices made in the telling of a particular story: is it supposed to get me to watch the next episode? buy the action figure? Draw middle-schoolers and high-schoolers into discussions about the ways the kids in their school are influenced by media: do members of some cliques all wear clothes of a particular brand? what image does that particular company promote in its advertisements? do students try to conform to the images of people portrayed in music videos?

You do not need any special training to start to equip the children in your life with media literacy. Your own critical thinking abilities and awareness of some of the issues raised in *Love to Hate* should be plenty of preparation at least to begin. Remember that the way you read to children is a great model for how you should watch television, surf the Net, play games, and listen to music with them. You do not need to hover over children every time they approach the TV, computer, or stereo; even a little bit of time devoted to active, engaged interaction with media each week will help children become media savvy. Up to now we have role-modeled passive ambivalence toward hatred and violence for our children; from now on we must be their models for active, critical intolerance of the seeds of intolerance in mass-mediated popular culture and in our own ideas as they are shaped by that culture.

Education is a lot like charity and, as the saying goes, it begins at home. But if we really want to turn away from our society's obsession with hatred and violence, we also need to use our influence to make changes beyond the walls of our own homes. Specifically, we need to rally our power as involved citizens to encourage initiatives in schools that will hasten the journey to a hate-free millennium.

Let's begin by exploring some of the educational initiatives we can support that promise to make a real difference in America's future. First, any plan for education that increases the focus on developing critical thinking skills will help future generations of Americans be less susceptible to the seductive appeal of thought patterns such as stereotyping, scapegoating, absolutism, and dehumanization. As I explained in chapter 1, these patterns are easy to fall into under the best of circumstances. The more refined people's critical thinking skills become, the more resistant they will be to sliding into such careless and potentially dangerous thought patterns.

While virtually all educational initiatives hope to improve students' critical thinking abilities, one idea deserves special consideration in our mass-mediated world. The idea is generally called "media literacy," formal instruction in the schools to prepare our children for life in a world now largely lived in mediated situations. Quite a few states now include media literacy units at some level in K–12 education. Proposals for the mandatory inclusion of media literacy in the curriculum are on the horizon. You can help bring media literacy to schools in your area by raising the issue at school board meetings, in a letter to the editor of the local newspaper, or in discussions with teachers and school administrators.

Of course, we can improve our children's overall education very significantly by adding special programs and events to the school calendar. Unlike curricular reforms and initiatives, special events usually do not require major resource commitments of time, money, training, and staffing. They can provide an immediate impact on children's education while larger, more comprehensive programs are being developed. As you may recall from your own school days, the arrival of an outside speaker is a big occasion for students because it is an exciting event in their otherwise rather monotonous schedule. That fact alone makes kids really tune in to guest speakers. In addition, an experienced special program speaker knows how to excite and engage students. Many excellent speakers are available to address students of various grade levels about issues ranging from intolerance among children to school violence to violence in the media. In the appendices you'll find a list of resources that includes information about organizations that sponsor educational programs. I encourage you to share that information with school officials in your area.

Sadly, local public school board elections draw very few voters to the polls even though they probably impact our lives more than elections for most other offices. If you feel the schools in your area are doing a good job of equipping students with critical thinking skills and the ability to survive in a mediated world, then by all means show your thanks by turning out at the polls and keeping wise board members in office. But if you feel your local schools could be doing better, then do whatever you can do to improve things. Learn where candidates for the school board stand on important initiatives and then be sure to show up and vote in the next election. You might also consider organizing a group of parents to work with administrators on bringing special programs and presentations into the schools. Too often we all assume somebody else will take care of things. We have to remember that *we* are the "somebody else" that everybody else is depending on.

STEP 4: SUPPORTING THOSE ON THE FRONT LINE

When Dennis and Judy Shepard set up the Matthew Shepard Foundation, they joined a long tradition of Americans who have organized to combat hatred in our society. For example, in the nineteenth century people united to fight prejudice against Catholics and, of course, to lobby against the institution of slavery. In the twentieth century, groups such as the National Association for the Advancement of Colored People (NAACP) and the Anti-Defamation League of B'nai B'rith (ADL) have worked to challenge long-standing prejudices that lie at the very heart of much hatred and violence.

In addition to such large, national organizations, many smaller organizations now provide services designed to combat hatred and violence in our society. At the back of this book you will find a list of many of these groups along with contact information. Because I now work closely with New Light Media, The Matthew Shepard Foundation, and a new organization called Students Talking About Respect (STAR), I'm going to use them as examples of the ways new, relatively small organizations are participating in the movement against hatred and violence. Please understand that my focus on these three groups is based simply on my access to information about them and in no way implies that their work is more important than the work being accomplished by other similar organizations.

The Matthew Shepard Foundation was created to "replace hate with understanding, acceptance, and compassion."[9] Toward this end, the Matthew Shepard Foundation sponsors public awareness and educational programs nationwide. Judy Shepard volunteers much of her time to speaking on behalf of the organization. Her public appearances, including appearances on national television, before Congress, and in the documentary film *Journey to a Hate Free Millennium*, have brought the foundation's message to millions of people. Additionally, the foundation provides information to individuals and groups working toward similar goals and sponsors the development of educational materials and programs designed to combat hatred in our society. The Matthew Shepard Foundation also raises money to support the establishment of places, such as youth clubs and campus meeting areas, where people can feel safe in our too often dangerous world.

While New Light Media shares the goals of the Matthew Shepard Foundation, it focuses specifically on developing multimedia works and educational tools that enable people to resist the lure of hatred and violence. The production of the documentary film, *Journey to a Hate Free Millennium*, was the first major project of New Light Media but clearly not the last. Members of the New Light Media team travel around the nation talking about the dynamics of hatred and leading discussion sessions about what each of us can do to combat hatred. New Light Media has developed special age-appropriate presentations for students at the elementary, middle-school, and high-school levels, as well as training seminars for educators committed to making our world a safer and more tolerant place in the future. Significantly, New Light Media and The Matthew Shepard Foundation collaborate on project development, pooling their resources to bring programs such as *Journey to a Hate Free Millennium* to schools that otherwise could not afford outside speakers. As such, the two organizations role model for all of us the type of cooperative spirit we will need actually to usher in a hate-free millennium.

Students Talking About Respect is a brand-new, extracurricular educational initiative that directly involves high school students in the fight against hatred and violence. Headquartered on the campus of Ripon College, STAR invites high schools from all over the United States to participate in an antihate initiative that also fosters the development of students' critical thinking and communication skills. STAR chapters in the high schools provide opportunities for teenagers to openly discuss their thoughts about hatred and violence in the media, in music, and even in their schools. Through a variety of interactive training programs, STAR also equips high school students with advanced communication skills they then can use to bring presentations about compassion and nonviolence to K–8 students in their community.

If you would like to support the Matthew Shepard Foundation, New Light Media, STAR, or any of the other organizations dedicated to driving hatred and violence out of our society, you have many options for becoming involved. First, you can simply get on the Internet and learn about some of these organizations (Web site addresses are provided in the appendices of this book) and then spread the word to people you know. A great way to do this, if you have a personal Web page, is by creating links so your friends and family members have an easy way to check out the Internet sites of groups you support. You also can gather brochures of some of the organizations who provide educational programs and make sure school administrators and teachers in your area know about the services available. Along the same line, you can encourage groups or clubs in your area to consider sponsoring a visiting speaker from a group such as New Light Media. Just by helping get the word out you can become an important part of the public relations chain.

Second, you can sign your name to the membership rosters of many of these organizations. Joining often requires nothing more than a signature or a click of the mouse. By signing on to the group's mission, you add your name to the growing list of names of people who are committed to change. The simple act of lending your name can help these groups demonstrate to policy makers that *many* Americans want to see change.

Third, you can volunteer time with a group in your area. All organizations need as many volunteers as they can get. By donating even an hour on one occasion, you can help a group prepare for a fund-raiser or get an important mailing ready to go. If you are willing to make a long-term time commitment, you may be able to train to become a spokesperson for the group, a discussion leader, a counselor, or program developer.

Finally, even if you choose not to work directly with a group, you can facilitate their work with financial support. Your monetary donation — no matter how small — will join with other people's donations to underwrite educational programs, the printing of teaching materials, and even the construction of safe houses for the victims of all forms of violence.

No matter how you choose to get involved, any support you give to the organizations on the front line of the fight against hatred and violence will make a difference. It doesn't matter which organization you choose either. I learned this lesson recently myself. As you may recall one of my motivations for attending Brent Scarpo's presentation of *Journey to a Hate Free Millennium* was to "check out the competition." I showed up that night thinking I was in a race in which I was pitted against all the other people who are writing books and producing films about hatred and violence. In a sense, I myself had fallen right into the middle of "us versus them" thinking. I learned a lot that night about the importance of working together to change our world. And the more I work with others, including people from New Light Media and the Matthew Shepard Foundation, the more profoundly I realize that cooperation, not competition is what we need now.

We *are* in a race, a race toward the hate-free millennium. It's like a relay race in which all of us who are committed to making our world a better place constantly pass the baton back and forth to each other. There is room on our team for anyone who's ready to run in the same direction. So long as they are ready to race. Because we are racing. But we are not racing against each other; we are racing against time so that we can lay claim to the next millennium before it too is corrupted by America's love affair with hatred and violence.

Western civilization has spent centuries becoming obsessed with hatred and violence. We cannot expect to free ourselves of our obsession abruptly. By becoming aware of our ambivalence we have taken the all important first step toward someday making our society a more tolerant and safer place to live. By holding ourselves to high standards of critical thought—especially when we interact with mass-mediated popular culture—we can declare our personal freedom from the seductive embrace of hatred. By entrenching the development of critical thinking skills and media literacy into our homes and our educational system, we can prepare our children to resist hatred's temptations. And, finally, by supporting organizations dedicated to making our world better, we too can be part of the team effort required ultimately to end this obsession.

But we cannot change our society overnight. When the Pope labeled America a "culture of death," most of us agreed. However, too many of us immediately blamed the media, the schools, the government—the other—for our society's fall.

We cannot scapegoat this one. It is *our* problem. We have done this to ourselves. Every one of us is to blame. And until we finally and profoundly accept that fact, our obsession with hatred and violence will persist.

So long as it does, I will not wonder if there will be another school shooting or another multistate killing spree. Until we give up our obsession with hatred, none of us need to wonder if, only when, where, and how many more innocent lives will be lost.

Appendixes

Appendix 1: The Five Most Critical Resolutions Each of Us Can Make to Free Ourselves from Our Obsession with Hatred and Violence

Resolution 1: I will own up when I lapse into one of the flawed thought processes or language patterns that underlie hatred. If I lapse in front of other people, especially children, I will have the courage to call myself on my error.

Resolution 2: I will consume popular culture critically. I will refuse to be a passive consumer of popular culture. I will think about what I am seeing and hearing. I will make a conscious choice about what I want to support as a consumer of media.

Resolution 3: I will not tolerate hatred silently. When someone in my life stereotypes or dehumanizes others, I will speak up. I will remember that passive tolerance of intolerance is at the very heart of our society's love affair with hatred and violence.

Resolution 4: I will encourage media literacy, critical thinking, and anti-hate initiatives in schools in my area. I will make the effort to find out how these issues are handled now and where school board members (and candidates) stand on these issues. Then I will vote.

Resolution 5: I will donate some money or some time (and skills) to an organization that works to rid our society of hatred and violence. I know that even a small financial contribution or an hour of volunteer time can make a huge difference when combined with the dollars and hours of many other people.

Appendix 2: Self-Assessment Tools

The purpose of the following questions and exercises is to raise your awareness of your own participation in America's obsession with hatred and violence. You may find it useful to write down your answers. As you begin the process of changing, you then will be able to revisit your initial responses to see how your ideas and actions have altered over time. These self-assessment tools are designed for use by individuals but can also be used in a small group setting so long as all members of the group agree to open discussion and to respect each other's privacy. Although not suitable for younger children, many of the self-assessment tools are appropriate for teenagers: parents and/or teachers should use their knowledge of particular teens to determine which questions/exercises might be useful.

One: What is your first memory of feeling hatred toward another person? In hindsight, what made you hate? Fear? Rejection? Etc.?

Two: What was your "clique" in high school? What were some of the other cliques? How did your clique stereotype members of other cliques? What cliques are you in now (socially, at work, in church, etc.)? In what ways do you still stereotype members of other cliques?

Three: What is your favorite "bad name" to say—or think—about someone when you are mad at them? What kind of language pattern do you rely on when saying your pet bad name (i.e., "bitch" is a metaphor). Take a moment to consider the implications of your use of such language—does it dehumanize, encourage absolutism, etc.? As you reflect on this now—not in the middle of a heated argument—are you comfortable standing behind the implications of the words you sometimes spit out in anger?

Four: Have you ever crossed the line to violence, or even for a split second fantasized about it? What in the situation brought you to that point? What were you thinking about/feeling toward the other person (your victim) at that moment? How did you feel, what emotions did you experience other than rage? What emotions came immediately prior to the desire to lash out physically? How do you feel about that moment now?

Five: Who were your icons for "cool" when you were growing up? What did they subtly say about hatred and violence? Who are your icons as an adult?

Six: For one week, watch your favorite television programs like a critic. Do you see evidence of the thought processes of hatred? How are the characters and plots developed to guide your reactions as a viewer? What alternative character and plot developments could there be? How would those alternatives change your reactions?

Seven: What celebrities fascinate you? Do you secretly scan the tabloid headlines in the grocery store checkout to see the latest scandals about certain stars? What are the public images (persona) of celebrities you find fascinating? What do those images say (if anything) about issues related to hatred and violence? How far do you believe a particular celebrity's image is from the reality of their life?

Eight: What are your public images (personae) at work, at home, with friends? Do your various personae react differently to fundamental issues tied to hatred and violence? For example, do you laugh along, uncomfortably, but audibly, when your boss tells a stereotyping joke, but scold your children for doing the same thing?

Nine: What group in society (i.e., racists, sexists) do you "hate"? When thinking of that group, how do you allow yourself to fall into the flawed thought patterns of hatred—absolutism, stereotyping, scapegoating, dehumanization? No matter how "right" you are, take a minute to consider how similar in pattern your thoughts about that group are to the "wrongness" you detest in their thinking.

Ten: How much financial incentive do you give to the corporations that produce violent fare? Take a stroll through your home and count the videos, CDs, games, and books that feature hatred and violence as themes. How much money have you spent telling media corporations that violence sells? In a typical week, how many hours of television do you and your family watch? How many of those hours subtly or overtly condone hatred and violence? Multiply those hours by sixteen, the minimum number of commercials in a typical hour of television broadcasting. That's how many times per week you are reinforcing the media's profit-motive to produce programs that feed into our obsession with hatred and violence.

Eleven: Who is your "us" at home, at work, socially, economically, politically? Who are your "thems" in each context? In each context, do you live your life in an "us and them" or an "us versus them" mindset?

Twelve: What is your "hot button"? What issue makes you see the world in absolutist terms of "I'm right; you are wrong!"? When you allow yourself to view the other side as an enemy, as wholly "other," what actions do you leave open to yourself when encountering your opponents? In what ways might you be able actually to improve the situation if you did not allow yourself to perceive the other side as the enemy but instead as misguided, misinformed, or even misunderstood?

Thirteen: Who are your scapegoats (boss, spouse, children, Internal Revenue Service, etc.)? For a few minutes, take the blame onto yourself for a problem you recently scapegoated onto someone else (even if it really was their fault). By taking the blame onto yourself, what do you then empower yourself to do in response to the situation? Do your options open up or narrow?

Fourteen: Who uses you as a scapegoat? How do you feel when you are blamed unfairly?

Fifteen: Make a list of five skills you use frequently at home or at work (i.e., writing, filing, cooking, operating a drill press). How could you put each of those skills to work to assist an organization devoted to the promotion of compassion and the prevention of violence?

Appendix 3: Twenty-Five Small Steps Toward Freeing Ourselves from Our Obsession with Hatred and Violence

The problem of hatred and violence in our society seems so vast that it is tempting to believe we are incapable of solving it. Certainly, we cannot rid our society of these phenomena overnight. And, frankly, we never will completely drive hatred and violence out of human existence. But we can make our world more compassionate and less violent. Every small step each one of us takes makes our world just a little bit less hateful. While a world free of hatred and violence may be ideal, a world even a little less hateful and violent would be a better world. The following list offers some ideas for relatively simple steps you can take to make our world safer and more compassionate. If you commit to doing even one thing on this list on one occasion, you will have made a difference, you will have moved us all one step closer to eradicating our national obsession.

Fine yourself a dollar (or whatever you can afford) each time you fall back into the dangerous thought and language patterns you've learned about through reading *Love to Hate* that promote hatred and violence. Then donate your fines to an organization that works to make our world a safer place (see resource list in appendix 5).

The next time you see a news report of a hate crime, take the time to learn at least one thing about the victim beyond their status as a victim.

Donate one copy of a book about fighting hatred and violence to a school in your area (see resource list in appendix 5).

Educate yourself on candidates' positions on issues such as critical thinking, media literacy, and antihate initiatives for schools, then vote in the next school board election in your district.

Do not laugh at jokes based on stereotypes, no matter who tells them and no matter what group is stereotyped. Remember, whether its deadly serious or "all in fun," whether aimed at racial minorities or "dumb blondes," the process of stereotyping always reinforces "us versus them" thinking at some level.

Check out the Web site of an organization that promotes compassion and antiviolence initiatives (see appendix 5). Then create a link to that site on your personal or family Web page.

Take a child (or an adult) to an exhibit or play about the consequences of hatred and violence.

The next time you're faced with a gift-giving occasion, give a biography of a person who devoted their life to fighting hatred and violence.

Invite a local teacher out for coffee to discuss their thoughts on how schools can help children resist hatred.

Finally forgive the bully you "hated" as a child.

Ask the children in your life to explain to you why they think a particular movie, song, or celebrity is "cool." They may never have stopped to ask themselves "why?"

Through a program like Big Brothers/Big Sisters, become a real-life role model of compassion and nonviolence for a child.

Include in your holiday card a suggested book or Web site about making our world a more loving place—could any message be more appropriate during the holidays?

Resist the temptation to hate people who hate. Remember: same gun, different target.

Refuse to participate in the cult of celebrity that too often surrounds killers.

If you see signs of hate group activity in your area (racist or homophobic leaflets are often a first presence), alert the police. Do not assume they already are aware an organized hate group is targeting your area.

Expose yourself, your friends, and your family, to music, movies, and foods from cultures other than your own.

Talk about what you see on television and in movies, about the messages narrative choices and editing techniques send about hatred and violence.

Always report threats of violence to the appropriate authorities. In this era of school shootings and hate crimes, never dismiss even a rumor—let the authorities who are trained in investigation know what you have heard.

Remember that at the heart of popular culture is media and that media is a business. Your behavior as a consumer either challenges or reinforces media corporations' profit motives.

Whenever you become angry with another person, get in the habit of saying aloud (even if you are alone in the room) at least one good thing about that other person. Absolutism and stereotyping are very difficult to fall into if you force yourself to see even a tiny speck of goodness in other people.

Shed the tough skin we've all developed. Be outraged whenever even one life is lost to violence. Don't wait for another Columbine to demand your attention—give your attention each day.

Actively seek evidence to debunk the stereotypes you were exposed to as a child. Finally disprove to your own satisfaction the deep-seated biases that you were socialized to believe.

Suggest that your employer make a corporate donation to an organization that takes antihate/antiviolence programs into schools.

Don't take children's compassion for granted. Reward them with lots of positive attention when they behave with kindness, empathy, and love toward others.

Appendix 4: Tips for Parents (and Teachers): Raising Hate-Free and Hate-Proof Kids

As you've learned by reading *Love to Hate*, American popular culture—and each one of us—tends to send mixed messages about hatred and violence. These mixed messages are especially confusing to children who look to popular culture, adults, and also peers for cues about how to think, feel, and act in all kinds of situations. The following activities can help you help your children develop a better understanding of the flawed thought processes that allow hatred and violence to flourish. Some of the activities are designed specifically to make children more critical consumers of media/popular culture messages about hatred and violence. The activities are divided into two groups: Activities for Younger Children and Activities for Teens. Use your own knowledge of the children in your life to determine which particular activities might best suit their needs for growth and their learning styles.

Activities for Younger Children

1. CHALLENGING ABSOLUTIST THINKING

Children tend to view the world in absolute terms—right or wrong, happy or sad, nice or mean. Such concrete labelling is normal for children. However, when we allow (or encourage by our own examples) children to apply absolute labels to people, instead of to actions, we are subtly guiding them toward acceptance of one of the flawed thought patterns of hatred. You can help children avoid absolute labeling of people in a couple of ways. First, when speaking to children or even within their earshot, avoid phrases such as "you are naughty." Instead, explain that "throwing things at your brother is naughty." This subtle shift in language defines the action absolutely but not the person. Second, help children redirect their own language along the same pattern. When a child proclaims "Jonny is mean!" ask "Is Jonny mean or is hitting mean?" While these suggestions may seem like very small changes in the total scope of a child's life, they in fact introduce children to fundamental principles of critical thinking that will help them detect flawed thinking (hateful or otherwise) as they grow older.

Another way to combat absolutist thinking in young children involves asking children to see a person, animal, or character in a story from another angle. For example, if a child declares a snake at the zoo to be scary, ask the child what else the snake is? Shiny, scaly, sleeping, a mommy or a baby, etc. These questions draw the child's attention to other qualities of the snake (or person) and thus make absolutist labeling far more difficult. You might also ask the child if other animals would think the snake is scary? Would the elephant or the zebra call the snake scary? Would a dinosaur be afraid of the snake? Such questions encourage children to realize there are different perspectives on everything and, of course, different perspectives undercut the power of absolutist thinking. When applied to characters in a storybook or on a television program, the same kinds of questions can offer children an early lesson in the differences between round and flat characters.

2. CHALLENGING THE TENDENCY TO STEREOTYPE

Use a child's favorite toys to get them thinking about the inherent flaws in stereotypes. Gather up a group of stuffed bears or toy cars or whatever particular kind of toy your child loves. Ask them to pick one of the toys and describe it in lots of detail. Then look to see if the other toys of that type meet the same description. You can make this really fun for children by exaggerating your reactions as you search and inspect the other toys. "Your bear is brown. This thing is tan. This must not be a bear!!! You go over there, you silly toy, you aren't a bear!" Most children quickly will join in the fun—either helping you banish bears or coming to the other bears' defense. Either way, you are engaging your child in a relatively complicated sorting game the point of which is to realize that bears (or toy cars or people) all share some things in common and all have differences that make them special. And, of course, what's true of one bear isn't true of all bears. A fun variation on this game replaces the bear with a neighbor or relative. Ask the child to describe Uncle Joe, then investigate the other uncles in your family to see if they all fit Uncle Joe's description.

3. CHALLENGING SCAPEGOATING

Kids provide a wealth of opportunities for adults to talk about scapegoating, but you can really stimulate them to think critically about scapegoating if you yourself are the one doing the scapegoating. The next time you cause a small spill in the kitchen, blame the dog or the baby or even the toaster. Ham it up as much as you need to to inspire your child to come to the defense of your scapegoat. Follow your child's lead and you'll find ample ground for discussing why it's not fair to blame somebody or something else for your own wrongdoings.

4. CHALLENGING DEHUMANIZATION OF OTHERS

Very young children rarely dehumanize; in fact, they are more likely to humanize everything around them than to dehumanize anything. However, as children enter school they often partake in (or fall victim to) name-calling and teasing that is an early form of dehumanization. Parents have very little control over what transpires between seven year olds during recess. However, you probably do know from casual observations which children in your son or daughter's class tend to be teased by others. You can help insulate your child from the tendency to tease by exposing them to more information about the children who are teased. On a drive or walk, point out the other child's house. Mention in the car on the way to school that you thought the dress Mary wore yesterday was really pretty. You might even ask your child to speculate on Mary's favorite color or if she likes cats. In other words, find ways casually to work Mary into your child's thoughts. Every detail of Mary's life you plant in your child's mind makes it that much harder for your child not to empathize with her. And, of course, empathy makes dehumanization impossible. If your child is the frequent target of teasing at school, I encourage you to talk to your child's teacher or school counselor for suggestions on how to handle this most difficult situation.

5. DEVELOPING UNDERSTANDING OF NARRATIVES

Whether in fairy tales, video games, television sitcoms, the evening news, or a trip down memory lane with grandma, children encounter thousands of narratives. You can help your children understand the ways narratives shape how we think about people and events by making them aware that stories are created, that choices are made by the narrators. One of the most effective ways to teach this fundamental principle involves rewriting stories. When children are very young, you can rewrite stories for them by changing the ending when you read a favorite bedtime story. As they grow a bit older, put their imaginations to work on rewriting their favorite tales, adding other characters, twisting the plot in a new direction, or changing the setting. You might even have your child make their own storybooks, telling the same story from two different perspectives (the cat's version and the mouse's version, for instance). When teaching children about narratives, how you alter stories is irrelevant; any alteration demonstrates to the child that stories are crafted, which is the key concept we need to teach our kids. As children enter the middle elementary school years, you can transfer your work on fiction to "real" stories. Ask kids to consider how a newspaper story could be told from a different angle or how the video images accompanying a story on the evening news make them feel about the topic. Invite children to speculate as to why a writer or editor decided to tell a story in the way they did. While you can use some of the theories about narratives introduced in *Love to Hate* to guide you through these discussions with your children, you don't need to worry about specific terminology or coming up with the correct answers. So long as your child is picking up on the notion that somewhere someone makes a decision to tell a story in a certain way, you are preparing your child to think critically about all the thousands of stories they are going to encounter in their lifetime.

Activities and Discussion Topics for Teens

Before explaining specific activities and discussion topics you can use with teenagers, let me add a few words of advice that I'm sure will ring true to anyone who ever has been a parent to, or, for that matter, has ever been a teenager. Unlike young children who still think their parents are "cool" and eagerly participate in any activity that remotely resembles a game with mom or dad, teens by their nature tend to resist parental advances. As such, don't try to preach the messages in *Love to Hate* to the teenagers in your life. Instead, provide opportunities (in disguise, if need be) that allow teens to explore these issues on their own and come to their own conclusions. The goal is not to give them the answers but to encourage them to ask the questions for themselves. Talk about issues from *Love to Hate* with your teens if they'll let you, of course. If they won't, talk about issues of hatred and violence with someone else, but in earshot of your teen. They are listening even when they don't look like they are. Following are some ideas for how you can directly and indirectly get teens thinking about America's obsession with hatred and violence, the ways it impacts their lives, and the ways they want to react. Consider your teenager's learning style, openness, and interests when selecting activities and discussion topics that will be most successful in your family.

1. CHECK THE MAIN ROLE MODELS

As much as every teen wants to deny it, the adults in their lives—in particular their parents—are their primary role models. Your attitudes toward hatred and violence have a direct influence on your teens' attitudes and actions. If not for your own sake, for your teen's sake, honestly self-assess where you stand on hatred and violence. Are you sending mixed messages about hatred in your own home? How do you currently respond to violence on television? Do you cringe, turn away, express sadness or anger? Do you laugh, cheer for the star? Or do you simply watch passively while also flipping through a magazine or paying bills? Before even considering changing your behaviors, watch your teen's reactions to your reactions to violence in the media. Do they seem to notice your reactions at all? Is it possible they've stopped noticing your reactions because you have stopped having obvious reactions? Are you role-modeling passive consumption of hatred and violence? Have your children learned this behavior at home? How could you change your viewing behavior, your reactions in ways that would make your teen notice issues of hatred and violence in media?

2. IF YOU AREN'T COOL, WHO IS?

While teens really do look to their parents as role models, they do not think their parents are "cool." Who does your teen think is cool? Start decoding this one by looking at the walls in their room—the posters and magazine clippings are ready evidence. Make the time to learn something about the public images of these celebrities. As a gift, buy your teen a biography of their idol to help them see more of the person behind the persona. If your teen thinks you're at least a little bit cool, ask him or her if you could read the bio too, then start a discussion about the things in the bio that "surprised" you—specifically raise points about the person's history or opinions that seem out of sync with their public image.

3. TO BANISH OR NOT TO BANISH

Most teens have at least one video game or CD that their parents would like to banish from the house (or the planet). Of course, most parents of teens also are shrewd enough to know that making something taboo only makes it more tantalizing during the teenage years. Instead of simply banning a game or CD you find offensive, ask your teen to introduce you to it, explain why they enjoy or value it, and give their reactions to your concerns. Whether you ultimately decide to allow your teen to have the item is, of course, up to you. But by engaging them in explaining it to you, you have already forced them to think critically about the item, about the nature of their desire for it, and about their own behavior as a consumer of media. In other words, you've already shaken them out of passive consumption and thus drastically reduced the potential for a game or CD to influence your teen in negative ways.

4. OLD ENOUGH TO SAY IT, OLD ENOUGH TO OWN IT

At some point in time, children are old enough to take responsibility for their words and actions. There is no magic date on which this occurs, but most parents know when their own child is mature enough to be held accountable. For the most part, high-school-aged teenagers are old enough to bear responsibility for their choice to use hateful language *if* parents and/or teachers have explained to them how certain language structures and thought patterns promote hatred. If you are not sure your teen knows about the flawed thought patterns and language structures at the root of hatred, take the time to teach them. Then, when you catch them carelessly (or intentionally) using such patterns, call them on it. Point out the implications of their thoughts and words. Ask them if they are willing to stand by those implications. Challenge them to defend their positions. You are not telling your teenager what to think; rather, you are demanding that your teenager be aware of and responsible for the implications of his or her thoughts and language.

5. MEDIA LITERACY

Even if your child is lucky enough to attend a school where media literacy is promoted, you can enhance your child's media savvy by providing opportunities for learning outside the classroom. Watch "the making of" specials and videos with your teen. MTV regularly offers behind-the-scenes specials on the production of popular music videos. Documentaries chronicle the making of feature films. Educational television, and even network news programs, sometimes explore how broadcast news stories are crafted. These behind-the-scenes glimpses at media help people of all ages understand that even "real" images in popular culture are enhanced and edited to convey particular themes and messages. You can provide your teen with a hands-on encounter with media literacy by attending the taping of a television program. Some teens may enjoy devoting a week or two of their summer to a print or broadcast journalism camp where they can explore media careers and also get a crash course in the real ins-and-outs of media as a force in popular culture. You can provide a home-based lesson about the impact of editing and story design by putting your teen in charge of creating a family Web site or videotaping a family function. To get your teen to think critically about media, ask that they produce two Web sites or two videos: one based on a list of criteria/outcomes you (the producer) demand; another to meet their own standards. They will quickly realize the power of editorial decision-making to shape how a "real" event appears on television or the Internet.

6. VISIT THEIR WORLD

I myself would not encourage anyone over the age of nineteen to dress like Britney Spears, but parents need to realize that you don't have to act like a teen, or even enjoy what teens enjoy, in order to have some clue about what teens are into watching, buying, listening to, and emulating. Here's the good news: you do not have to monitor MTV twenty-four hours a day to know what kind of music may be influencing your teen. Nor do you need to follow your teen around all the time (which would no doubt drive both of you crazy). You can get a bird's-eye view of youth popular culture in a few minutes each week by checking out MTV Web sites (www.mtv.com and www.mtvnews.com), flipping through a magazine such as *Teen People* or *Seventeen*, or tuning in to watch your teen's favorite television programs. There's a great deal of truth in the old saying "forewarned is forearmed." By educating yourself about the dominate themes, issues, and trends in youth popular culture, you provide yourself with an arsenal of topics of interest to your teen that you can use to initiate conversations about hatred and violence in our society, in media targeted toward teens, and in your teen's everyday life.

Appendix 5: Resources

The organizations and publications listed below represent only a small fraction of those currently available. Please view this list only as a starting place as you seek out additional information about hatred and violence in America and what we all can do to make our world more compassionate and safer.

Organizations Dedicated to the Prevention
of Hatred and Violence

American Civil Liberties Union, www.aclu.org
Anti-Defamation League, www.adl.org
Center for the Prevention of School Violence, www.cpsv.org
Center for the Study and Prevention of Violence,
    www.colorado.edu/cspv
Children's Safety Network, www.edc.org/hhd/csn
Civil Rights Organization, www.civilrights.org
Collaborative To Advance Social and Emotional Learning,
    www.casel.org
Connect for Kids, www.connectforkids.org
Family Education Network, www.familyeducation.com
Family Violence Prevention Foundation, www.fvpf.org
Gang Resistance Education and Training,
    www.ncl.org/anr/partners/great.htm
Hamilton Fish National Institute on School and Community
    Violence
www.hamfish.org
Hate Hurts, www.hatehurts.org
Hate Monitor, www.hatemonitor.org
Hate Watch, www.hatewatch.org
Healing the Heart of Diversity (Fetzger Institute), www.fetzger.org
Institute for the Study and Prevention of Violence, www.kent.edu/
    violence
Keep Schools Safe, www.keepschoolssafe.org
Matthew Shepard Foundation, www.matthewshepard.org

Mothers Against Violence in America, www.mavia.org
National Alliance for Safe Schools, www.safeschools.org
National Children's Coalition, www.child.net/ncc.htm
The National Consortium on Violence Research,
      www.ncovr.heinz.cmu.edu
National Education Association Safe Schools Now Network,
      www.safeschoolsnow.org
National Organizations of Youth Safety, www.noys.org
National Parent-Teacher Association, www.pta.org
National Safe Kids Campaign, www.safekids.org
National School Safety Center, www.nssc1.org
National Youth Gang Center, www.iir.com/nygc
New Light Media, www.newlightmedia.org
The Nizkor Project, www.nizkor.org
Not In Our Town, www.pbs.org/niot
Parents, Family, and Friends of Lesbians and Gays,
      www.pflag.org
Partnership Against Violence Network, www.pavnet.org
Peace Builders, www.peacebuilders.com
Peace Center, www.comcat.com/peace/peacecenter
Resolving Conflict Creatively, www.rcci.org
Safe Youth, www.safeyouth.org
The Simon Wiesenthal Center, www.wiesenthal.org
Southern Poverty Law Center, www.splcenter.org
Student Pledge Against Gun Violence, www.pledge.org
Students Talking About Respect, www.starespect.org
Teaching Tolerance, www.teachingtolerance.org
United Against Hate, www.unitedagainsthate.org

Organizations That Promote Development of Critical Thinking Skills

Center for Critical Thinking, www.criticalthinking.org
Foundation for Critical Thinking, www.criticalthinking.org/fct
Institute for Critical Thinking, www.chss.montclair.edu/ict
National Center for Excellence in Critical Thinking, www.critical-
      thinking.org/ncect

Organizations That Promote Development
of Media Literacy

Action for Media Education, www.action4mediaed.org
Assignment: Media Literacy, www.assignmentmedialit.com
Center for a New American Dream, www.newdream.org
Center for Media Literacy, www.medialit.org
Center for Research on the Effects of Television, www.ithaca.edu/cretv
Get Net Wise, www.getnetwise.org
Just Think/Twenty-First Century Literacy, www.justthink.org
Media Literacy Clearinghouse, www.med.sc.edu:/1081
Mediascope, www.mediascope.org
National Institute On Media and the Family, www.mediafamily.org
Project Look Sharp, www.ithaca.edu/looksharp

Publications

Alibrandi, Tom. *Hate Is My Neighbor*. Ellensburg, W.Va.: Stand Together Publishers, 1999.

Aronson, Elliot. *Nobody Left to Hate: Teaching Compassion After Columbine*. New York: Freeman, 2000.

Bailie, Gil. *Violence Unveiled: Humanity at the Crossroads*. New York: Crossroad, 1995.

Baumeister, Roy F. *Evil: Inside Human Cruelty and Violence*. New York: Freeman, 1997.

Beane, Allan L. *The Bully Free Classroom: Over 100 Tips and Strategies for Teachers K-8*. Minneapolis: Free Spirit Publishers, 1999.

Beck, Aaron T. *Prisoners of Hate: The Cognitive Basis of Anger, Hostility, and Violence*. New York: HarperCollins, 1999.

Begun, Ruth Weltmann and Frank J. Huml. *Ready-To-Use Violence Prevention Skills: Lessons and Activities for Elementary Students*. West Nyack, N.Y.: Center for Applied Research in Education, 1999.

— —. *Ready-To-Use Violence Prevention Skills: Lessons and Activities for Secondary Students*. West Nyack, N.Y.: Center for Applied Research in Education, 1998.

Bell, Derrick. *Faces at the Bottom of the Well: The Permanence of Racism*. New York: Basic Books, 1992.

Berzon, Betty. *Setting Them Straight: You Can Do Something About Bigotry and Homophobia in Your Life*. New York: Penguin Books, 1996.

Bianculli, David. *Teleliteracy: Taking Television Seriously*. New York: Simon & Schuster, 1994.

Blue, Rose and Corrine J. Naden. *Working Together Against Hate Groups*. New York: Rosen Publishing Group, 1994.

Bok, Sissela. *Mayhem: Violence As Public Entertainment*. Reading, Mass.: Perseus Books, 1999.

Brookfield, Stephen D. *Developing Critical Thinkers: Challenging Adults to Explore Alternative Ways of Thinking and Acting*. San Francisco: Jossey-Bass, 1987.

Browne, M. Neil and Stuart M. Keeley. *Asking the Right Questions: A Guide to Critical Thinking*. Upper Saddle River, N.J.: Prentice Hall, 2001.

Cappello, Dominic. *Ten Talks Parents Must Have with Their Children About Violence*. New York: Hyperion, 2000.

Christensen, Loren. *Skinhead Street Gangs*. Boulder, Colo.: Paladin Press, 1994.

Cohn, Janice. *The Christmas Menorahs: How a Town Fought Hate*. Morton Grove, Ill.: Whitman, 1995.

Cortese, Anthony J. *Provocateur: Images of Women and Minorities in Advertising*. New York: Rowman and Littlefield, 1999.

Dees, Morris and Steve Fiffer. *Hate on Trial: The Case Against America's Most Dangerous Neo-Nazi*. New York: Villard Books, 1993.

DeGaetano, Gloria and Kathleen Bander. *Screen Smarts: A Family Guide to Media Literacy*. Boston: Houghton Miflin, 1996.

Dyson, Michael Eric. *Race Rules: Navigating the Color Line*. New York: Vintage Books, 1997.

Ferber, Abby L. et al. *Hate Crime in America: What Do We Know?* Washington, D.C.: Spivack Program in Applied Social Research and Social Policy, American Sociological Association, 2000.

Flannery, Raymond B. Jr. *Violence in America: Coping with Drugs, Distressed Families, Inadequate Schooling, and Acts of Hate*. New York: Continuum, 1997.

Fowles, Jib. *The Case For Television Violence*. Thousand Oaks, Cal.: Sage, 1999.

Fried, SuEllen and Paula Fried. *Bullies and Victims: Helping Your Child Survive the Schoolyard Battlefield*. New York: Evans, 1996.

Garbarino, James et al. *Children in Danger: Coping with the Consequences of Community Violence*. San Francisco: Jossey-Bass, 1992.

Garbarino, James. *Lost Boys: Why Our Sons Turn Violent and How We Can Save Them*. New York: Free Press, 1999.

Garbarino, James. *Raising Children in a Socially Toxic Environment*. San Francisco: Jossey-Bass, 1995.

Gedatus, Gus. *Hate*. Mankato, Minn.: LifeMatters, 2000.

Gilligan, James. *Violence: Our Deadly Epidemic and Its Causes*. New York: Grosset/Putnam, 1997.

Gilovich, Thomas. *How We Know What Isn't So: The Fallibility of Human Reason in Everyday Life*. New York: Free Press, 1991.

Gilroy, Paul. *Against Race: Imagining Political Culture Beyond the Color Line*. Cambridge, Mass.: The Belknap Press of Harvard University Press, 2000.

Goodman, Greg. S. *Reducing Hate Crimes and Violence Among American Youth: Creating Transformational Agency Through Critical Praxis*. New York: Lang, 2001.

Grossman, Dave and Gloria DeGaetano. *Stop Teaching Our Kids to Kill: A Call to Action Against TV, Movie, and Video Game Violence*. New York: Crown, 1999.

Hamilton, James T. *Channeling Violence: The Economic Market for Violent Television Programming*. Princeton: Princeton University Press, 1998.

Hecht, Michael L., ed. *Communicating Prejudice*. Thousand Oaks, Cal.: Sage, 1998.

Heumann, Milton and Thomas W. Church, eds. *Hate Speech on Campus: Cases, Case Studies, and Commentary*. Boston: Northeastern University Press, 1997.

Hooks, Bell. *Killing Rage: Ending Racism*. New York: Holt, 1995.

——. *Where We Stand: Class Matters*. New York: Routledge, 2000.

Howard, Sue, ed. *Wired-Up: Young People and the Electronic Media*. London: UCL Press, 1998.

Huckabee, Governor Mike. *Kids Who Kill: Confronting Our Culture of Violence*. Nashville, Tenn.: Broadman and Holman, 1998.

Huston, Aletha et. al. *Big World, Small Screen: The Role of Television in American Society*. Lincoln: University of Nebraska Press, 1992.

Jacobs, James B. and Kimberly Potter. *Hate Crimes: Criminal Law and Identity Politics*. New York: Oxford University Press, 1998.

Jenness, Valerie and Ryken Grattet. *Making Hate a Crime: From Social Movement Concept to Law Enforcement Practice*. New York: Russell Sage, 2001.

Kaplan, Jeffrey and Tore Bjorgo. *Nation and Race: The Developing Euro-American Racist Subculture*. Boston: Northeastern University Press, 1998.

Krueger, Ellen and Mary T. Christel. *Seeing and Believing: How to Teach Media Literacy in the English Classroom*. Portsmouth, N.H.: Heinemann, 2001.

LaFrance, Edward. *Men, Media, and Masculinity*. Dubuque, Iowa: Kendall/ Hunt Publishing Company, 1995.

Lawrence, Frederick M. *Punishing Hate: Bias Crimes Under American Law*. Cambridge: Harvard University Press, 1999.

Leonard, John. *Smoke and Mirrors: Violence, Television, and Other American Cultures*. New York: New Press, 1997.

Levin, Diane E. *Remote Control Childhood? Combating the Hazards of Media Culture*. Washington, D.C.: National Association for the Education of Young Children, 1998.

Levine, Madeline. *Viewing Violence*. New York: Doubleday, 1996.

Matsuda, Mari J. et al. *Words That Wound: Critical Race Theory, Assaultive Speech, and the First Amendment*. Boulder, Colo.: Westview Press, 1993.

McNeal, James U. *Kids as Customers: A Handbook of Marketing to Children*. New York: Lexington Books, 1992.

Muse, Daphne, ed. *Prejudice: Stories About Hate, Ignorance, Revelation, and Transformation*. New York: Hyperion Books for Children, 1995.

Namka, Lynne. *The Mad Family Gets Their Mads Out: Fifty Things Your Family Can Say and Do to Express Anger Constructively*. Tucson, Ariz.: Talk, Trust, and Feel Therapeutics, 1995.

Nicoletti, John, Sally Spencer-Thomas, and Christopher Bollinger. *Violence Goes to College: The Authoritative Guide to Prevention and Intervention*. Springfield, Ill.: C. C. Thomas, 2001.

Noble, Kerry. *Tabernacle of Hate. Why They Bombed Oklahoma City*. Prescott, Ontario: Voyageur, 1998.

Osofsky, Joy D. *Children in a Violent Society*. New York: Guilford Press, 1997.

Perry, Barbara. *In the Name of Hate: Understanding Hate Crimes*. New York: Routledge, 2001.

Potter, James W. *Media Literacy*. Thousand Oaks, Cal.: Sage, 2001.

Roleff, Tamara L., ed. *Hate Crimes*. San Diego: Greenhaven Press, 2001.

Rowan, Carl T. *The Coming Race War in America: A Wake-Up Call*. Boston: Little, Brown, 1996.

Shiell, Timothy C. *Campus Hate Speech on Trial*. Lawrence: University Press of Kansas, 1998.

Silverblatt, Art, Jane Ferry, and Barbara Finan. *Approaches to Media Literacy: A Handbook*. Armonk, N.Y.: M. E. Sharpe, 1999.

Singular, Stephen. *The Uncivil War: The Rise of Hate, Violence, and Terrorism in America*. Beverly Hills, Cal.: New Millennium Press, 2001.

Smith, Donald E. P. et al. *Critical Thinking: Building the Basics*. Belmont, Cal.: Wadsworth, 1998.

Stern-LaRosa, Caryl and Ellen Hofheimer. *The Anti-Defamation League's Hate Hurts: How Children Learn and Unlearn Prejudice*. New York: Scholastic, 2000.

Strum, Philippa. *When the Nazis Came to Skokie: Freedom for Speech We Hate*. Lawrence: University Press of Kansas, 1999.

Suttie, Ian D. *The Origins of Love and Hate*. London: Free Association Books, 1988.

Twesigye, Emmanuel K. *The Global Human Problem: Ignorance, Hate, Injustice, and Violence*. New York: Lang, 1988.

Tyner, Kathleen. *Literacy in a Digital World: Teaching and Learning in the Age of Information*. Mahwah, N.J.: Erlbaum, 1998.

Walsh, David. *Selling Out America's Children: How America Puts Profits Before Values—and What Parents Can Do*. Minneapolis: Fairview Press, 1995.

West, Cornel. *Race Matters*. 2d ed. New York: Vintage Books, 2001.

Winn, Marie. *The Plug-In Drug: Television, Children, and the Family*. Rev. ed. New York: Penguin Books, 1985.

Zimring, Franklin, E. *American Youth Violence*. New York: Oxford University Press, 1998.

NOTES

INTRODUCTION

1. Catholic World News, "Jovial Pope Encourages American Youth," cwnews.com, no. 9476, January 27, 1999.

2. Arab-American Anti-Discrimination League, "Hate Crime Hotline Established," www.adc.org/action, September 17, 2001.

1. US VERSUS THEM

1. Richard Hofstadter, "The Paranoid Style in American Politics," in D. B. Davis, ed., *The Fear of Conspiracy: Images of Un-American Subversion from the Revolution to the Present* (Ithaca, N.Y.: Cornell University Press, 1971), p. 6.

2. J. Wallis, "Whites' Racist Attitudes Are a Serious Problem," in W. Dudley, ed., *Racism In America: Opposing Viewpoints* (San Diego: Greenhaven Press, 1991), p. 30.

3. John Hughes, *The Breakfast Club* (1985).

4. Adolf Hitler, *Mein Kampf*, James Murphy, tr. (London: Hurst and Blackett, 1939).

5. Kenneth Burke, "The Rhetoric of Hitler's Battle," in C. R. Burgchardt, ed., *Readings in Rhetorical Criticism* (State College, Penn.: Strata, 1995), pp. 206–221.

6. Sut Jhally, *Dreamworlds* (1991).

2. HATE TALK: THE MIND/LANGUAGE CONNECTION

1. Charles J. Stewart, Craig Allen Smith, and Robert E. Denton, *Persuasion and Social Movements*, 2d ed. (Prospect Heights, Ill.: Waveland Press, 1989), p. 123.

2. Neil Miller, *Out of the Past: Gay and Lesbian History from 1869 to the Present* (New York: Vintage Books, 1995), p. 58.

3. Miller, *Out of the Past*, pp. 44–51.

4. Ibid., p. 49.

5. Ibid., p. 51.

6. Jonathan Ned Katz, *Gay/Lesbian Almanac: A New Documentary* (New York: Carroll and Graf, 1994), pp. 152, 16.

7. Heinz Hegler, *The Men with the Pink Triangle: The True, Life-and-Death Story of Homosexuals in the Nazi Death Camps* David Fernbach, trans. (Boston: Alyson Publications, 1994).

8. Katz, *Gay/Lesbian Almanac*, p. 14.

9. Miller, *Out of the Past*, p. 100.

10. Katz, *Gay/Lesbian Almanac*, p.15.

11. Herbert Aptheker, *Afro-American History: The Modern Era* (Secaucus, N.J.: The Citadel Press, 1971), pp. 213–217.

12. Aletha C. Huston, et al., *Big World, Small Screen: The Role of Television in American Society* (Lincoln: University of Nebraska Press, 1992), p. 70.

13. "National News Briefs: Jury Gives Canoeist New Reason to Curse," nytimes.com, June 12, 1999.

14. Wayne Brockriede, "Arguers As Lovers," *Philosophy and Rhetoric* 5 (Winter 1972): 1–11.

3. HATE IS COOL

1. Theodore T. Herbert, *Dimensions of Organizational Behavior*, 2d ed. (New York: Macmillan, 1981), p. 304.

2. Bob Clark, *A Christmas Story* (1983).

3. Dennis Hopper, *Easy Rider* (1969).

4. George Miller, *Mad Max* (1979). George Miller, *Mad Max 2* (1981). George Miller, *Mad Max Beyond Thunderdome* (1985).

5. Joel Coen, *Raising Arizona* (1987).

6. Laslo Benedek, *The Wild One* (1954).

7. Anthony DeCurtis, "The Eighties," in Anthony DeCurtis, ed., *Present Tense: Rock and Roll and Culture* (Durham, N.C.: Duke University Press, 1992), p. 4.

8. Biographical information and discography for Tupac Shakur compiled from listings entitled "Tupac Shakur" on rollingstone.com, 1999, mtv.com, 1999, and mtvnews.com, 1999.

9. Biographical information and discography for The Notorious B.I.G. compiled from listings entitled "The Notorious B.I.G." on rollingstone.com, 1999, mtv.com, 1999, and mtvnews.com, 1999.

10. "Marilyn Manson," rollingstone.com, November 12, 1999.

11. Biographical information and discography for Marilyn Manson compiled from listings entitled "Marilyn Manson" on rollingstone.com, 1999, mtv.com, 1999, and mtvnews.com, 1999.

12. Marilyn Manson—Dead to the World: The Tour America Didn't Want You To See (Interscope Records, 1998).

13. M. L. Elrick, "Eminem's Dirty Secrets," salon.com, July 25, 2000.

14. Eric Boehlert, "Eminem Steals the Show," salon.com, February 22, 2001.

15. Eric Boehlert, "Invisible Man," salon.com, June 7, 2000.

16. Ibid.

17. Ibid.

18. Alex Abramovich, "A Season In Hell," feedmag.com, 2001.

19. For an example, see Elrick, "Eminem's Dirty Secret."

20. Ruben Navarrete Jr., "Eminem's Bad Rap," worldnetdaily.com, February 28, 2001.

21. Jackson Katz and Sut Jhally, "Missing the Mark," *Boston Globe*, May 2, 1999, p. E1.

22. Edward LaFrance, *Men, Media, and Masculinity* (Dubuque, Iowa: Kendall/Hunt, 1995), p. 75.

4. YOUTHFUL HATRED: ARE WE TOUGH ENOUGH?

1. Name changed.

2. Jody M. Roy, *Rhetorical Campaigns of the Nineteenth-Century Catholics and Anti-Catholics in America* (Lewiston, N.Y.: The Edwin Mellen Press, 2000), p. 56.

3. United Way of Greater Los Angeles, "Statistics," www.unitedwayla.org, 2000.

4. Crystal Balbach and Jenni Mayer, "Statistics on Teen Violence," http://tri-path.colosys.net, 1999.

5. Phelan Wyrick, United States Department of Justice/Office of Juvenile Justice and Delinquency Prevention Research and Program Development Division, personal correspondence, February 15, 2000.

6. Dr. Dre, *Dr. Dre 2001* (Aftermath/Interscope Records, 1999).

7. Biographical information and discography for Snoop Dogg compiled from listings entitled "Snoop Dogg" on rollingstone.com, 2001, mtv.com, 2001, and mtvnews.com, 2001.

8. "Archive: Bone Thugs-N-Harmony," mtvnews.com, 2001.

9. Snoop was allegedly a member of the Crips gang of Los Angeles.

10. Justice Policy Institute, "Child Deaths in America in Context, 1997–1998," www.cjcj.org, 1999.

11. Associated Press, "Students Open Fire in School," trnonline.com, April 21, 1999.

12. *Dateline* (NBC: December 13, 1999).

13. I have decided not to list this young woman's formal Web address because I do not want to encourage her by publicizing direct contact information.

14. Scott Kalvert, *The Basketball Diaries* (1995).

15. Rammstein, "Du Hast," *Sehnsucht* (Slash Records, 1998).

16. Quentin Tarantino, *Reservoir Dogs* (1992).

17. Ellen A. Wartella, "The Context of Television Violence," *The Carroll C. Arnold Distinguished Lecture, Speech Communication Association Annual Convention* (Boston: Allyn and Bacon, 1996), pp. 5–6.

18. *Dateline*.

19. Sissela Bok, *Mayhem: Violence as Public Entertainment* (Reading, Mass.: Perseus Books, 1998), pp. 15–24.

20. Justice Policy Institute.

21. Ibid.

5. GLAMORIZED HATRED: OUR OBSESSION
WITH SERIAL KILLERS

1. Historical data about the Manson family and their crime spree compiled from The Crime Library, "Charles Manson, the Manson Family," http://va.crimelibrary.com, 2000; Vincent Bugliosi, *Helter Skelter* (New York: Mass Market Paperback/Bantam Doubleday Dell Publishing Group, 1995).

2. Crime Library, "Charles Manson, the Manson Family."

3. Bugliosi, *Helter Skelter*.

4. Jonathan Demme, *Silence of the Lambs* (1991).

5. Oliver Stone, *Natural Born Killers* (1994).

6. Alfred Hitchcock, *Psycho* (1960).

7. Biographical information about Edward Gein as well as historical accounts of his crimes compiled from Crime Library, "Eddie Gein," www.crimelibrary.com, 2000; Harold Schechter, *Deviant: The Shocking True Story of Ed Gein, the Original "Psycho"* (New York: Pocket Books, 1989).

8. Schechter, *Deviant*, p.36.

9. Biographical information about Jeffrey Dahmer, as well as historical accounts of his crimes, compiled from Crime Library, "Jeffrey Dahmer," www.crimelibrary.com, 2000; Lionel Dahmer, *A Father's Story* (New York: Morrow, 1994); Don Davis, *The Milwaukee Murders* (New York: St. Martin's Press, 1991); Anne E. Schwartz, *The Man Who Could Not Kill Enough* (New York: Birch Lane Press, 1992).

10. Kathleen Treanor, press conference, CNN *Live Coverage of McVeigh Execution* (June 11, 2001).

6. ORGANIZED HATRED: SUPREMACY MOVEMENTS

1. Some set the date at 1867, the year of the Klan's first "night ride."

2. Historical information about the nineteenth-century anti-Catholic movement was compiled from Jody M. Roy, *Rhetorical Campaigns of the Nineteenth-Century Catholics and Anti-Catholics in America* (Lewiston, N.Y.: The Edwin Mellen Press, 2000).

3. Brutus [Samuel F. B. Morse], *Foreign Conspiracy Against the Liberties of the United States: The Numbers of Brutus, Originally Published in the New York Observer* (New York: Leavitt, Lord, and Co., 1835; reprint, New York: Arno Press, 1977).

4. Maria Monk, *Awful Disclosures of the Hotel Dieu Nunnery at Montreal* (London: n.p., 1836).

5. Historical information about the Ku Klux Klan compiled from Ku Klux Klan, www.danger.com/kkk, 2000; Bill Stanton, *Klanwatch: Bringing the Ku Klux Klan to Justice* (New York: Mentor, 1991).

6. Thomas Dixon Jr., *The Clansman* (New York: Grosset and Dunlap, 1905)

7. D. W. Griffith, *Birth of a Nation* (1915).

8. Biographical data about George Lincoln Rockwell, as well as information about The National Alliance, compiled from National Socialist White People's Party, www.stormfront.org, 2001; The Nizkor Project, "The National Socialist White People's Party," www.nizkor.org, 2001.

9. Southern Poverty Law Center, "Active Hate Groups in the United States in 2000," *Intelligence Report* 101 (Spring 2001): 33.

10. Historical information about the National Alliance gathered from National Alliance, www.natall.com, 2001.

11. Andrew Macdonald [William Pierce], *The Turner Diaries* (Hillsboro, W Va.: National Vanguard Books, 1980).

12. Patrick E. Cole, "McVeigh: Diaries Dearest," *Time* 49, no. 13 (1997): 26.

13. Historical information about Aryan Nations and Identity Theology, as well as biographical data about Richard Butler and Wesley Swift, compiled from Anti-Defamation League of B'nai B'rith, "Aryan Nations," www.adl.org, 2000; Anti-Defamation League of B'nai B'rith, "The 'Identity Churches': A Theology of Hate," ADL Facts 28 (1983): 1; Aryan Nations, www.nidlink.com/aryanvic, 2000; Aryan Nations, www.aryan-nations.org, 2001.

14. Sam Howe Verhouck, "New Future For Idaho Aryan Nations Compound," www.nytimes.com, March 7, 2001.

15. Information about the Metzgers, White Aryan Resistance, and Aryan Youth Movement compiled from Anti-Defamation League of B'nai B'rith,

"White Aryan Resistance," www.adl.org, 2000; White Aryan Resistance, www.resist.com, 2000.

16. "Klan TV," *The Oprah Winfrey Show* (WLS-TV, September 8, 1988).

17. Morris Dees and Steve Fiffer, *Hate on Trial: The Case Against America's Most Dangerous Neo-Nazi* (New York: Villard Books, 1993).

18. Information about the rise of skinhead movements in Europe and America gathered from Nick Knight, *Skinhead* (London: Omnibus Press, 1982); Jack Moore, *Skinheads Shaved for Battle: A Cultural History of American Skinheads* (Bowling Green, Ohio: Bowling Green State University Press, 1993); Jody M. Roy, "Fragments of Hitler in Contemporary Oi!: Skinhead Music and the Propensity for Violence in Hate Gangs," *Journal of the Wisconsin Communication Association* 30 (1999): 1–8.

19. Moore, *Skinheads Shaved for Battle*, p. 47.

20. Southern Poverty Law Center, p. 36.

21. Resistance Records, www.natall.com, 2001. Burdi has since renounced racism.

22. World Church of the Creator, www.wcotc.com, 2001.

23. National Alliance, www.natall.com, 2001.

24. Dees and Fiffer, *Hate on Trial*, p. 273.

25. For examples, see Aryan Nations' publicly accessible Web site, www.nidlink.com/aryanvic and White Aryan Resistance's publicly accessible Web site, www.resist.com.

26. Ibid.

27. Ibid.

28. Ibid.

29. Walter F. Parkes and Keith F. Critchlow, *The California Reich* (City Life Films, 1975).

30. Student requested not to be identified by name.

31. James Madison, *The Federalist*, Number Ten (1787) in R. Hofstadter, ed., *Great Issues in American History From the Revolution to the Civil War, 1765–1865* (New York: Vintage Books, 1958), pp.124–132.

32. Dees and Fiffer, *Hate on Trial*, p. 169.

CONCLUSION: FREEING OURSELVES FROM OUR OBSESSION
WITH HATRED AND VIOLENCE

1. Biographical information about Matthew Shepard, as well as accounts of the crime that took his life, compiled from "Funeral for Gay Hate-Crime Victim Brutally Murdered," www.geocities.com/westhollywood/stonewall, 1998; Hatecrime.org, "Matthew Shepard On-Line Resources," www.wiredstrategies.com/shepard, 2000; Tom Kenworthy, "McKinney Avoids Death Sentence," www.washingtonpost.com, November 5, 1999; The Matthew Shepard

Foundation, www.matthewshepard.org, 2001; "Matthew Shepard Time Line," www.advocate.com, 1999; "Religious Leaders, Activists Hold Vigils for Slain Gay Student," www.cnn.com, 1998; Brent Scarpo and Martin Bedogne, *Journey to a Hate Free Millennium* (Denver: New Light Media, 2000).

2. "Funeral For Gay Hate-Crime Victim" p. 1.

3. Ibid.

4. "Religious Leaders, Activists," p. 1.

5. George Lane, "Shepard's Mom: Hate is No Option," www.denverpost.com, November 2, 2000, p. 1.

6. Ibid.

7. Background information about New Light Media and *Journey to a Hate Free Millennium* can be found in "Media Guide," *Journey to a Hate Free Millennium* (Denver: New Light Media, 2000).

8. Ibid.

9. Matthew Shepard Foundation, "Mission Statement," www.matthewshepard.org, 2001.

INDEX